TERRIBLE OMENS

HAPPINESS IS THE OTHER WAY

Thinktorium
PO Box 901
Raleigh, NC 27602-0901
www.thintoriumbooks.com

ISBN-13: 978-1-937258-20-7
Library of Congress Control Number: 2018964795

Cover Design: M. Jay Allport
Certain elements of the cover design obtained with license from VectorStock.com.
This book was set primarily in Adobe Garamond Pro.
Song lyric credit: Mould, B. (2016). Voices in My Head (Bob Mould). On *Patch the Sky*. Durham, NC: Merge Records.

Terrible Omens: Happiness is the Other Way is a work of creative nonfiction. The names and identifying characteristics of the individuals involved have been changed in order to disguise their identities. Any resulting resemblance to persons living or dead is entirely coincidental and unintentional.

Printed in the U.S.A.

TERRIBLE OMENS

HAPPINESS IS THE OTHER WAY

ALANE GRAY

THINK TORIUM

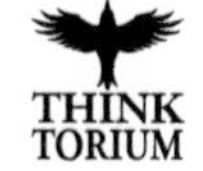

I decide to listen to the voices in my head
Strange hallucinations I avoid
The people and the places, the living and the dead
Can I find some truth within the noise?

—Bob Mould

Proem

What you are about to read is mostly true. The names have been changed to protect the innocent (as well as the guilty) but the stories, themselves, have been told exactly as I experienced them. Let's be very clear—this is my version of things. That's not anything nefarious; it's just the nature of the human experience. It's plagued by the confines of perspective. Sometimes I think it's our lack of omnipotence that makes life really interesting.

This whole thing started as a single journal entry. I called it my Reluctant Divorcé's Grimoire—which is kind of funny now that it's done. As it turns out, I was not really reluctant at all. Stupid, maybe, but definitely not reluctant. As for the grimoire part...that's a story for some other day. It all seemed to make sense in the beginning, but as the project really started to take shape, I realized that the real story is less about what came after and more about what happened in the moment. It's about all of the things that were happening right in front of my face that I couldn't process until much later.

Now that it's done, I'm still not sure what this book is, exactly. What came out of my head is what my arts school choreography instructor would probably have categorized as a "shameless self-masturbatory work." I got that feedback a lot back then. I wasn't exactly prepared for that kind of critique at 16, but I hold no grudges today. Looking back, he was right about it most of the time.

The process of writing this book was treacherous. To do it right, I had to delve into the depths of my experience and shine light on things that I have never told another soul. I had to take a long and honest look at myself, too, which might have been the hardest part of the whole thing. Luckily, for you, my story has been edited for time and boring content. There were so many things that happened and so many ridiculous details that there just wasn't room for them all, and after a point, it just became too much, anyway.

One of my biggest fears with this project was that the finished product would sound too much like exactly what it was—the journal entries of a situationally borderline mind—or worse—the hormone-fueled ravings of a marginally literate teenage girl that reads like: "I hate this. I am sad. He was mean. She's a bitch. This outfit makes me look fat…" and so on. I hope I've managed to avoid that, but I am sure that some of it's in there. For that, I am sorry. It probably couldn't be helped.

Nevertheless, here it is, my accounting of fifteen odd years during the prime of my adult life. Now that it's done, it's done.

Chapter 1

It was like something snapped. The last fiber of a fraying invisible rope let go. It was over. I had wanted it, denied it, dreamed about it, avoided it, screamed it, retracted it, wished for it, and it was finally here.

I didn't even have to say it. He said it. "I can't do this anymore." After all of the fighting and crying in the name of eternal love, that was it. He uttered those five words and changed everything.

In retrospect, I shouldn't have been surprised. It had been over for a long time. It was undeniable, like a dead animal in the wall of an old house. It had a stench. Friends would come over and try to be polite. They didn't want to embarrass us by pointing it out, but you could see it on their faces. They smelled it. They knew exactly what it was.

Our marriage started out the way many of them do. We were madly and passionately in love. We never wanted to be away from each other. We were making our future together—a marriage, a business, a family. We were going to have everything we thought we could possibly want. To be honest, it was kind of disgusting. It was that nauseating, romance novel kind of love.

We were certain it was meant to be, too. In the beginning, we even mused about how perfect it was and how lucky we were (and how sad everybody else must have been). The air around us smelled sweeter. The colors we saw in the sky were more intense. It was like the light of the world emanated from the space between us. We were special. We were chosen. Chosen for what, exactly, we didn't know, but it was something. We were certain of that. To sum it up, ours was the kind relationship that makes you puke if you look directly at it for too long.

Then one day, it changed. Our perfect relationship succumbed to its own truth. The shine wore off and revealed a big lump of nothing underneath. The intoxicating rush of romance waned and left me with an epic headache and the need to hurl anytime I thought about the choices I had made. We were two completely different people, from two totally different worlds, with two laundry lists of irreconcilable wants and needs. We were strangers when we met, and we were strangers when it ended. Our marriage became nothing more than a contract.

The reality of our incompatibility had always been there. I just wasn't able to see it through a fog of hormones mixed with copious amounts of affordable merlot. When we met, I was 26 and primed for commitment—still young enough to feel entitled to a fairy tale romance and definitely old enough to feel the pressures of social expectation and biological imperative. Any of my usual fail-safes that might have inspired me to run (as I usually did within the first 3 to 6 months of any given relationship) I ignored. I was feeling *The Feelings*. I had been waiting my whole life for those feelings. So, what was a little conflict? All of the best stories were about surviving through struggles, heartache, and tears. I mean, you don't win an Oscar for a role without conflict and oppression. Right? Passion is passion. I never expected it to be easy.

For 20 years before I met Darren, the man who would become my husband, I danced. I don't mean "Dolly-Dinkle's" once-a-year-recital-to-torture-your-parents kind of dance. I mean real dance—the performing arts boarding school, first professional gig at 9 years old, willing to walk around with bloody feet and a perma-bun kind of dance. It certainly wasn't easy. I loved dance more than anything else in the world. I was certain that romantic love would be the same. In a way, it was. In dance, I learned that pain was good most of the time. I learned that the show goes on regardless of how you feel about your partner that day—put on your makeup, smile, and dance into the wings. The audience doesn't get to see behind the curtain.

My marriage was much the same. The alarms were sounding, the red flags were waving, the costumes were shredded, and the footlights were busted, but the show went on.

Two years and thirty-three days elapsed between the day Darren and I met and the day we got married. It seemed like I should have had enough time to get clear on exactly what I was getting myself into, but it wasn't. I was too distracted by the rest of my life. We were in chiropractic college. That's where we met. (To clear up what that means, exactly—I was working toward a Doctorate in Chiropractic. Yes, that's a real thing. Yes, I am a real doctor. No, it's not the same thing as massage therapy. Yes, I still have student loans, and no, I did didn't go there because medical school was too hard for me...and yes, I have a chip on my shoulder about it.) Anyway, classes, tests, dissecting dead people, not to mention clinicals and national boards, consumed most of my energy. In fact, all of the pressure seemed to serve our relationship well. It gave us common goals, and it made us utterly oblivious to our overwhelming isolation. Our lives were driven by an external set of rules, demands, and deadlines. There was very little room for us to disagree and there was definitely no time to fight about it when we did.

To top it off, 30 was looming in the distance for me. I hadn't expected the idea of turning 30 to freak me out as much as it did. It was like a ghost lurking in the shadows—dark, oppressive, and unstoppable no matter how young I looked or how much moisturizer I used. The biological countdown clock to spinsterhood had started ticking loudly, and I succumbed to it. In the fairytales I read as a kid, I learned that every princess was owed a prince as long as she followed the rules and did everything she was supposed to do on time. If she missed her mark, she was destined to become a wart-faced hag who ate hapless children as a snack. I certainly didn't want that.

Obviously, I was supposed to get married. Life as a wart-faced hag was not for me. So, in the midst of the upheaval that I had chosen for myself, I did it to fulfill my destiny. Thanks to a preacher and the powers that be at the Allegheny County Courthouse, the contract was executed. The choice had been made, and there was no going back. A year and a half later, school was done, our board exams were passed, and we started off together, as husband and wife, toward the rest of our lives.

◆◆◆◆◆

In the aftermath of my divorce, I sometimes lose entire days to the grind of self-reflection. The events and the emotions swirl through my head as I struggle to make peace with the outcome. My mind clamors for an inkling of clarity that might let me rest and that might bring me a little peace.

Our marriage certainly wasn't all bad. There were times, especially in the beginning, that seemed like the fairytale I had been promised. We even joked that we would have a ten-year honeymoon because we were so happy and things were so perfect. Like I said, it was pretty disgusting there for a little while.

Needless to say, our honeymoon didn't make it for ten years. Real life hit us quickly, and we both suffered as a result. At the time, I was convinced that a good marriage demanded a little suffering to make it stronger, like suffering was a display of love, and my willingness to suffer was directly proportional to the amount of love I had to give. For love to be real and to last, I would have to fight for it. We fought so hard that our love should have been rock solid. It wasn't. Most of the time, it existed as a black hole in the murky nether region between passionate love-fucking and unbearable suffering.

It's curious…If I had known what the future had in store for us, would I have still said yes? If I had paid better attention in the beginning, would my decision have been the same?

I'm sad to say—probably so. There were too many hormones involved, not to mention my waning youth and general stupidity.

Okay, then…if I had known the future at any point, would I have stayed as long as I did? The answer to this question is also—probably so.

What I need to understand is why? Why did I stay as long as I did? Why was I unable, or worse—unwilling, to accept the inevitability of our marital decomposition as it was happening? Why didn't I do something about it? And, now that it's done, why am I so unwilling to move on.

Like I said before, my marriage kicked the bucket, but honestly, it was on life support from the beginning. I know for sure that it had completely flatlined by year nine. The alarm bells were sounding, the codes were being called. We ignored them. Eventually, we shut the entire warning system down. Those alarms can be so annoying, after all. When our marriage gasped its final breath, we were oblivious. We paid no to attention to it. Instead of respectfully covering it with a sheet and wheeling it off to the morgue, we ignored it and let it rot right under our noses.

That means a full postmortem is in order, no matter how ridiculous or painful it is.

Report of Autopsy

Case Type: Matrimonial

Reported Date of Death: September 12, 2012

Actual Date and Hour of Death: Indeterminate, refer to detailed report (attached)

Deceased: Exact date and time of death uncertain

Name, Age, Gender:

Darren Robert Danky, age 38, male

Alane Catherine Gray Danky (not hyphenated), Maiden Name-Gray, age 41, female

Cause of Death: Acute cardiac incompatibility with attendant intellectual rejection and genital ischemia. *Sluttus Vulgarus* exposure evident in male organs.

Upon further examination… I was 26 when I met Darren. He was 24. I turned 28 the day before I married him. I had never been particularly concerned with external pressures to bind myself to a man or to create a family before then. I was never bothered by maternal instincts until suddenly, one day, I was acutely aware of time. I was suddenly aware of my lack of legacy. Suddenly, I wanted to belong to something or someone in a way that had never been necessary for me before. As these imperatives started to worm their way through my psyche, Darren appeared, and that was all it took. Everything clicked into place like a thick set of beer goggles at last call, and that was it.

Our marriage wasn't my destiny. Our introduction wasn't cosmically ordained. There was nothing inherently supernatural about it. Darren was nothing special. He could have been almost anybody with half a brain, a full set of teeth, and working genitalia.

Sometimes Free Will has its drawbacks. I chose Darren all by myself. I chose him over all other potential breeding mates despite all of the things that should have scared me away.

That explains how it started. It's much harder to explain the 15 years that followed.

◆◆◆◆◆

Why did I stay in it as long as I did? Maybe I believed in his basic decency. Maybe I thought he had potential. Maybe I was just afraid of the unknown. Maybe it was a distorted sense of loyalty. Maybe it was the mountain of debt we had created. Maybe I thought I'd win a prize for suffering the longest? (Ah, the coveted "World's Longest Sufferer" award. What an honor.) Maybe I was just stubborn and unwilling to admit that I was wrong about one of the biggest life decisions I had ever made. (I do hate being wrong.) Maybe I felt pressured by an unseen patriarchal social construct. I was supposed to be educated, successful, married, and childbearing no matter what I actually wanted out my life.

Truthfully, it seems like it was a little bit of all of it. Ultimately, however, I believe it was the vow that really sealed it. I stayed because I took a vow.

I took *The Vow*.

I know that the whole "my word is my bond" thing is pretty melodramatic, but it is true for me. If I say the words, specifically those words, then I have taken *The Vow*. For me, it was a covenant with a power much bigger than one small human. It wasn't just because I took *The Vow* in a church "in front of God and everybody" as my grandmother used to say. It wasn't just because I had entered into a legally binding marital agreement or had been issued an official license or anything. It wasn't because I spent a bunch of money we didn't have on a party for Darren's friends and family to publicly celebrate it. Nope, it was simpler than that. I took *The Vow*. I made the big promise. I had never made that promise to anyone before. I had sworn to myself that when the day came that I made that promise, I was going to keep it. It was a one-shot deal. One and done. No backsies.

But everything dies eventually—even marriages.

Sometimes, the end is a natural progression like going to sleep and just never waking up. Other times, you have to blow the whole thing up and salt the earth behind you to kill it. Sometimes that isn't even enough. The ghost of my marriage still haunts me. It screams in the back of my brain with a single wraithlike wail stuck in a repeating loop.

I tried just about everything to shut it up. I prayed. I meditated. I kept journals, of both the regular and the gratitude variety. I thought positive thoughts. I let a "life coach" show me my "authentic self" which was, according to her, "a sad, aging Barbie doll" who was hamstrung by "a distorted need for affirmation from men." (I "authentically" wanted to punch that tiny wrinkled bitch right in the face…but I digress.) I made vision boards. I even saw a "shaman" who said he cleansed my aura of "parasites," although he was unable to explain to me what they were, why they were there, or where they went once he was done. It was all useless except for the journals (the real ones, not the fake-happiness-until-you-make-it gratitude bullshit, of course.)

So, here's my story—my expanded autopsy of a rotting corpse of marriage.

Chapter 2

Let's go back to the beginning of the thing that was my marriage to Darren, the person I used to call my husband.

Over the course of his life, Darren Robert Danky had answered to several different names depending on the circumstance or the person he fancied himself to be at the time. Some he chose. Others were bestowed upon him out of fondness or humor. His favorite was his own last name. Most specifically, the first syllable of his last name. Since I was never comfortable with being the wife of "last name guy" or the wife of "last name first syllable guy," I always just called him Darren since that's the way he introduced himself to me from the start.

Darren and I met on our second day of orientation at Palmer College of Chiropractic in Davenport, Iowa. He introduced himself that day as "Darren," striking up an awkward conversation as we stood in line. He was an attractive guy. It was obvious that he worked out but wasn't one of the gym-rat mouth-breathers that I tried hard to avoid. His style was what I considered as mid-90's regulation frat boy—khaki cargo shorts, a pastel polo shirt, and Bass leather sandals with a large dollop of carefully considered hair gel on top. A dark tribal tattoo band around his ankle made him a wannabe rebel. By today's standard, it would be considered a pretty lame tattoo at best, but at the time, it was sort of edgy, especially for an otherwise clean-cut college guy. Where I came from, only girls had ankle tattoos, but for some reason, it didn't bother me. It created just enough visual contradiction to make him interesting.

As far as first impressions went, our first encounter was marginal. I wasn't looking for a relationship. I had more important things on my mind, namely, my first day of gross anatomy lab and the looming reality that I was going to be cutting up an actual dead person. He wasn't my type at all. I never had much patience for frat boys. I found them uninteresting and shallow. Darren must have sensed this—or maybe I said it to his face, knowing my general demeanor at the time—because he worked really hard to show me how deep he was. Wherever I was, he would be there, too.

He was persistent, to be sure. He would find me at lunch. He found me at the gym. He was in the anatomy lab every time I went in even though he had a completely different lab group that met at a different time. If we hadn't been in school, I would have thought he was a stalker. Sure enough, little by little, he wore me down. We seemed to be interested in the same things. He clearly cared about me. I don't know what it was specifically that changed my view of him. Maybe it was the stress, or maybe the embalming fluid fumes in the anatomy lab. Maybe it was just his relentless flattery. I don't know, exactly. I managed to hold him off for almost three months before I decided to officially go out with him for something more than coffee between classes or a protein bar at the gym. It took another month for us to officially start dating.

As it turned out, Darren really wasn't that shallow. He wasn't the same as the sensitive, artistic types I had dated before, but he was certainly more interesting than the arrogant upwardly mobiles that I had accidentally dated after undergrad. (It was a short-lived phase, and a bad one at that.) It wasn't that there was a great deal of depth to Darren nor did he have a wealth of profound life experience that molded his ambitions. It was more about his desire. He seemed to want to know things. He seemed to want to experience the world and people. He seemed passionate, motivated, and most of all, kind. I think it was my perception of his kindness (and maybe the fumes in the lab) that finally reeled me in.

I might also have been his love of food. I always liked guys who didn't mind if I ate. Darren didn't just not mind it, he encouraged it. He was oddly obsessed with eating though you would never know it to look at him. Early on, he decided that he was going to cook for me. To start, he had no real skill in the kitchen, but with his passion for food, a Jeff Smith cookbook and a few quick calls home to his mother, he started to figure it out. He would make himself at home in my tiny apartment kitchen and courted me in clouds of garlic and oregano with a splash a red wine every now and then for a little extra kick.

His kitchen efforts might have been born as much out of self-preservation as it was out of romance. I considered my refrigerator fully stocked with a head of lettuce, a half-empty bottle of mustard, cream cheese, and a bottle of OJ, with some frozen bagels and a pint of double fudge brownie in the freezer. I didn't know it was a problem. There was, after all, usually a box of cheese crackers in the cabinet and pizza delivery on speed dial if he got hungry. It's not that I couldn't cook, I just had other things on my mind.

Thanks to Darren, we had a full blown three-course meal at least once a week. Every time he came over, he instituted an obligatory stop at the local supermarket. He would descend on my apartment lugging bags of meat, cheese, tomatoes, and herbs. Every evening started with bread for testing the sauce and some red wine. I'm not sure if it was the tomato sauce or the wine, but whatever it was, it worked very well. My stomach was smitten.

With hindsight being as it is, those dinners seem a little suspect to me, now. Darren was too intent on embracing the Italian half of his heritage for starters. He liked to call himself "Eye-talian" which was kind of humorous when I was studying and only half-listening. It wasn't until I got to know his parents that I realized he wasn't really joking around. His passion for food was actually an uncontrollable obsession, and although I thought they were sweet in the beginning, his phone calls to his mother were actually signs of a latent Oedipal complex that I wouldn't figure out until much, much later.

Of course, there were warning signs. Some of them were right there in front of my face. For example, there was the supermarket bakery bread that he bought every week. It read:

"Italian Pain $3.99."

No, it didn't say *Pane Italiano*-it said "*Italian Pain.*" It was clearly a translational mistake keyed in by some lackadaisical midwestern grocery worker, but with the 20/20 hindsight, it was more like an oracle than a simple oversight. It was an omen stuck unceremoniously on a bag of fresh, crusty, deliciousness. Every week, a warning letter walked right into my kitchen carried in a grocery bag. We even joked about it at the time. I thought it was so amusing...

So, every week, I stuffed my face with *Italian Pain*. I ate it with the hubris of a D-list horror movie actress who laughs as a creepy old man ominously hisses, "You're all going to die," as she casually walks down the street. She's always the first bimbo to get laid and the first to get tossed into the wood chipper. Sometimes, there are consequences for such predictable and archetypal arrogance, and in the movies, the point is usually made with a lot of spurting blood.

Had I been able to watch my own movie, I would have known that a wood chipper was in my future. I would have known to run away screaming and to run as far and as fast as I could. Instead, I stood over a pot of simmering marinara blithely anointing my *Italian Pain* with it and washing it all down with a nice Chianti.

Chapter 3

We had only been dating about three months when Darren asked me to marry him. As far as proposals go, his was lackluster, at best. It wasn't a grand romantic gesture. It wasn't well thought out. I'm not sure that he thought about it at all before he popped the question. Honestly, it wasn't even a question. He just blurted out, "Marry me!" one night after a particularly athletic romp in the sack.

I was caught off-guard and weirdly flattered. It was the third time I had had been asked in my lifetime, but it was the first time I considered it a viable option. I loved him. The sex was good. It seemed like we wanted the same things based on the hours of talking we had done since we met. In that moment, there was no reason I could find to say no. Deep down, I was filled with reservations. Frankly, the notion of marriage to anyone scared the hell out of me, but fear and reservation had been my normal operational state for most of my life. Uncertainty was a familiar feeling, and every other uncertain choice I had made had worked out for me in one way or another. Making such a big decision without a high degree of uncertainty would have seemed abnormal.

So, five seconds after he asked, I said yes.

Three weeks later, Darren took me home for Christmas to meet his family. As we drove East on I-80 toward Pittsburgh, our excitement grew. Darren was practically beside himself with anticipation. He hadn't taken very many girls home, especially not over a major a holiday, and he had never taken anyone home as his fiancé. I was quite atwitter myself. I was visiting a new city. I was meeting Darren's family. My expectations were high. An engagement announcement to an Italian family from Pittsburgh at Christmas sounded like something out of a movie. I was certain that it would be wonderful and we would be greeted at the door with a grand hug, a kiss on both cheeks, and a giant plate of cannoli.

Well, sometimes the movies miss the mark a little.

When we arrived at their house, it was cold and overcast with a blanket of gray snow covering the scene. I remember thinking things seemed odd. The muted hue of the snow was different than the bright white snow in Iowa, and Darren said they lived in Pittsburgh but a city skyline was nowhere in sight and the sign we passed as we drove up the hill said: "Welcome to Verona."

The house seemed quaint and sentimental on the outside. It was small and had been built brick by brick by his grandfather's hands. It had white painted wrought iron rails, and Astroturf covered the cement slab breezeway that connected the house to the matching brick garage. The gutters were decorated with white icicle lights, and there was a festive quilt Santa Claus hanging on the door.

Darren tried the knob on the side door but it was locked, so he knocked…twice. When Darren's mother, Charlene, opened the door, she spat out an annoyed "hello" around the freshly lit cigarette she held between her lips. She looked at me sideways, turned her back and croaked, "The refrigerator's broken. Christmas is ruined. My life sucks," and walked back into the kitchen. So, it wasn't exactly how I had envisioned it. There were no hugs, no kisses, and definitely no cannolis. It was an inauspicious beginning, to say the least.

Despite the appliance that destroyed Christmas, I was determined to settle in as best I could. I wanted to experience all of it.

Darren had grown up here. This was the backdrop for his whole life up to this point. I wanted to know everything about it.

When I crossed the threshold, I entered a tiny smoke-filled cauldron of a living space. To maneuver through most of the rooms, everyone had to turn sideways except for the cat. There was one bathroom on the main level, and the only shower in the house was a spray nozzle over a drain in the cement floor of the basement which had been walled off with 70's era paneling for privacy. (Yes, I said a wood-paneled shower. At one time there had been a so-called Pittsburgh Potty—seriously, look it up—in the basement, too. By the time I showed up, it was just an open pipe in the floor.) Darren's childhood bedroom was only slightly bigger than the closet in my first college apartment and had become Charlene's computer and smoking room in his absence. Generally speaking, there was no privacy. Every breath was audible throughout the entire house, which was about to offer me complete emersion into the Danky family Christmas experience.

Darren's younger sister by two years, Krystal, stalked around the house like a feral cat, gazing intensely at me from around the corner and then darting off when I looked directly at her. It was hard to remember that she was in college. She was home for the holiday just as we were, and instead of bonding with her over embarrassing stories about her brother, I felt like I needed to lure her out into the open with a treat and let her chase after the light from my laser pointer.

I knew that this was not going to be the warm, joyous occasion I had anticipated. It was clear that I was an interloper whose presence in the house probably caused the refrigerator to break in the first place. At the end of that first night, Darren apologized profusely. He swore that it usually wasn't like this and that it would be better in the morning after everyone got some sleep. He was sure that once they heard our news and understood that this was the real thing, everything would be perfect.

The next night, it was on. It was finally time to make our big announcement. To make it special, he reserved a table for the two of us and his parents at Vitali's, an old-school, family-owned Italian restaurant with dark wood and mirrors on the wall and red vinyl covering all of the chairs. It was built precariously on the side of a hill overlooking the Allegheny River and the abandoned steel plants that lined its shores. According to the sign and the plastic-covered menu, it was a "viewtiful" place to dine. Thanks to the twinkling lights from across the river and the perfect amount of snowfall, that night, it was true.

The hostess seated us in front of the giant window wall that ran along the back of the dining room. From my vantage point, it looked like I could hurl myself over the edge if the evening didn't go well, but mostly I was hoping that the windows didn't open. I wasn't sure what Charlene might be capable of with the right motivation. The four of us sat in awkward silence after we finally got settled in our seats. Charlene and I jockeyed entirely too long for the seat next to Darren before he asked her if he could sit next to me. Charlene sat down across from me glowering like a jilted ex-girlfriend. I'd be lying if I said it wasn't strange.

At long last, our waiter appeared to take our orders. Darren and I ordered wine and Chicken Marsala. Charlene and Earl ordered pasta. Earl also ordered a beer despite Charlene's comments about how expensive the drinks would be.

As the waiter turned to walk away, Darren said confidently, "We have something we want to tell you."

"Oh, SHIT…" his mother belched out before the word "you" had fully left his mouth. Forks and spoons clattered on plates, and the restaurant went silent. Our waiter's stride stuttered as he walked away. If a needle could have scratched across a record, it would have. "Are you pregnant?" she spat at me with disgust. Every head in the room turned to look to at the show. "You're pregnant, aren't you?! I saw those books on the bed. Oh..." she groaned as though she had been gutted with a knife.

I was completely bewildered. I had no idea what was happening or what to do. The waiter turned back to catch a glimpse of the commotion before hurrying out of the room.

Darren cut in, "Ma, no. She's not pregnant. I asked her to marry me. She said yes."

"Oh, shit..." she bellowed out again. "I can't sit here and listen to this," she said as she heaved her ample backside upward and pushed away from the table in a graceless effort to stand. "I need a cigarette."

"Ma...Mom!" Darren said. She waddled out without looking back.

"That went well," I said.

"She'll be alright," Earl finally contributed. Those were the first words he had uttered in my presence all day.

"Dad! What the hell is her problem?" Darren asked with frustration.

His father sighed with resignation as he stood, "We'll be back," he said as though he had dealt with this kind of thing before and followed her out of the room.

Holy fuck, I thought to myself as I considered how hard it would be to lob my chair through the window and escape. Darren sat there in silence like nothing had happened. It was weird.

Gradually, as we sat there alone, the rest of the room returned to normal conversation. The waiter delivered me a second glass of wine with a sympathetic glance over Darren's head. He must have read my mind, or maybe another kindhearted diner sent it as a charitable donation to my cause. Maybe he knew I was thinking about making a break for it and thought I needed another glassful of motivation. Another minute later, he set our salads out on the half-abandoned table.

Finally, Darren spoke, "Don't worry about it," he said before downing the remains of his wine in a single, large gulp. How on Earth he thought I was not going to worry about all of this was beyond me, but since Charlene and Earl were most likely by the front door and there was a sheer cliff face on the other side of the window, I didn't have a lot of options. All I could do was wait.

Eventually, they returned together. Earl sat first. Charlene flopped into her chair, sniffling loudly as she sat to draw more attention to the table, and more importantly, to the unattended tear streaks in her makeup. "I have been told that I have to apologize," she announced as she stared pointedly out the window. There was a very long pause, "…but I am not going to."

"Damn it," Earl groaned.

Darren and I said nothing.

"*You* are trying to trap my son. *You* are a gold digger, and *you* are trying to take advantage of us," she snorted defiantly. The room went silent again.

"A gold digger?" I said with contempt.

"Ma! She's no gold digger!" Darren said loudly. "I don't have any money and neither do you. We are getting the same degree. We will both be doctors. What the hell are you talking about?"

"Your father and I have money! You don't know what we have, *AND*…I saw those books on the bed, the one with the *FETUS* on it! Nobody reads books like that unless they are pregnant!" Earl shoved a large fork full of pasta into his mouth and stared at the table as he chewed.

It was starting to make sense, now…at least sort of. I had left my textbooks on the bed earlier that day. Why she hadn't asked me about it directly, I couldn't figure out. Why she saw that specific book cover was curious since I had left that one in my bag. Why she was in the room at all was even a little disconcerting.

"Um, do you know what a doctor is?" I said sharply. "I…actually, *we* are studying embryology!" Darren grabbed my knee hard under the table. "What the…" I started.

"Ma" he interrupted, "she's not pregnant, and she's not taking advantage of our family!"

There was another tense pause. "Well, what did you expect me to think, with books like that? And you brought her home! What did you expect me to think?!" She started blubbering loudly like she was crying, but there were no tears.

"Maybe, that I'm smart and he wants to marry me?" I said under my breath. Darren gripped my knee harder.

"I didn't ask you!" she spat.

"Alright," Earl said through another very large mouthful of pasta, "that's enough. Everybody, say you're sorry and let's eat."

"Ma, I'm sorry," Darren said obediently.

"Really?!" I snorted in disbelief.

"I guess I'm sorry," Charlene said to Darren, "You're just my son, and I wasn't prepared."

"Thanks, ma," he replied.

"Seriously?!" It was like walking into a store full of stuffed animals and getting hit in the face with a frying pan. I just didn't see it coming. "He had skipped coming home for Thanksgiving to be with me, and he told you both that he had good news to share when we got here. What do you mean you were unprepared?" I said insistently.

By now, Charlene was aggressively eating her pasta as she gazed out the window.

"Seriously?" I said again as I scanned the table for some kind of response. "You can't just…"

"We can talk about it later," Darren said flatly. He let go of my knee, picked up his fork… and that was it.

I don't really remember what happened later that night. It was all a blur. I know I forced myself to eat everything on my plate and dessert. (Yes, I finally got a cannoli.) I know that I didn't get a third glass of wine because Charlene said "no" for me when the waiter asked if I wanted another. I know that I didn't try to hurl myself through the wall of windows and down to the Allegheny River below, mostly because I have an unreasonable fear of falling. (I really hate sitting next to the edge of high places. It's not the height that's the problem so much. It's the falling, even though I have never actually fallen from a height of more than about 3 or 4 feet. I thought that I had mentioned this to Darren by this point, but maybe not.) I know we drove back to the house, and I know I went to bed. It was definitely not the wedding announcement event that I had envisioned in my mind, but at least I finally got to eat that cannoli. Surprisingly, it was just as delicious as I had hoped, but there wasn't enough sugar and ricotta cheese in all of Pittsburgh to make that night easy to swallow.

The next day was Christmas Eve. Everyone spent it in a low-grade state of emotional inflammation as Darren and Krystal (a.k.a. Wall-Cat) bickered about what church we would go to for the Christmas Eve service and when we would open presents. If I hadn't known better, I would have thought they were a couple of kids. They argued and stormed around the house yelling about Jesus's birthday party and Santa. It crescendoed with Wall-Cat hiding in her room crying and Darren's mother shouting out the final word on the matter. In the end, we would be going to Wall-Cat's favorite church for the Christmas Eve service and presents would be off limits until Christmas morning as Wall-Cat demanded.

Darren looked dejected after losing both battles, and his sister emerged from her room with a smug look of superiority on her face. Through the wall, I heard Charlene consoling her by telling her not to worry; they were not going to change everything because "*somebody*" (meaning me, most likely) wanted to take over.

What the whole mess had to do with me, I had no idea. I didn't care about church or presents. I was just hoping that I wouldn't burst into flames when I walked through the chapel doors. I hadn't set foot inside a church for over a decade. It's not like I was afraid of going church. I had been to church before. I had grown up with Southern Baptists on one side of my family and Appalachian Pentecostals on the other. I knew church and church knew me, and up until then, we had both decided to just steer clear of each other. Darren hadn't given me any warning, either. He hadn't mentioned one word about a mandatory Christmas Eve church service before that morning, so I was a bit shocked when he was so adamant about where we should go.

Nevertheless, that night we went to Christmas Eve service at Harmony Presbyterian Church. Happily, I did not spontaneously combust when I walked through the door, although I was entirely overdressed. (No one told me I could wear sweatpants to a church service.) Behind the typical Protestant church alter, there was a 3-piece garage band, where the choir should have been, complete with an electric guitar, a synthesizer, and a drum kit with a large projection screen hanging over their heads. The lyrics for all of the music (yes, even the Christmas carols) blinked on the screen as the congregation sang along. I guess the old church hymnal orchestrations didn't allow for enough epic guitar solos, so they had to go a different direction. The whole contemporary Christian service thing was never an option for my family. We were more in the Hell

Fire and Brimstone church camp, so I'm sure that one or both of my dead grandmothers were rolling over in their urns if they were watching this play out from the other side.

As for Bible content, it was what could be classified as "church-lite." There was a whole lot of baby Jesus talk, but in a shiny, cellophane-wrapped, easily digestible format that might appeal to the Only-on-Christmas (and maybe Easter if they needed something) Christian set. It wasn't great, but it wasn't terrible. I survived it. Darren eventually stopped complaining about it, and Charlene took every opportunity to introduce me as her future daughter-in-law which was a total shock to me in light of the crying and yelling from the night before. On the upside, it made Wall-Cat grimace every time a new introduction was made. It wasn't long before she slunk away to sulk alone in the car.

Christmas morning arrived without much fanfare which was a surprise after all of the hubbub from the days leading up to it. I had very low expectations at this point and was braced for it to be a slow day in Hell. Once the second pot of coffee was made, and Wall-Cat forced Charlene out of bed, the five of us gathered in the living room to open presents. Wall-Cat had taken the liberty of arranging five towers of wrapped packages, one tower for each of us, in a circle around the room. Darren's sister sat on the floor across from me in her pajamas with cartoon kittens on them and emitted a gleeful "yay!" and clapped her hands together excitedly as she looked around at each of us seated behind our designated gift tower. Honestly, it really was hard to remember that she was in college.

Surprisingly, Charlene had included a pile of packages for me. I thought it was a sweet gesture considering the tone of the last two days. I wasn't sure she even wanted me in her house, so I was surprised she had made an effort to include me. Mostly, I was grateful.

I thought I could just fade into the background and offer a polite "thank you" here and there while I let them enjoy their Christmas as a family. Just as I was ready to relax behind a flurry of wrapping paper, Wall-Cat yelled, "Me first! Me first!"

Darren grimaced and said, "Let's all just open our gifts at the same time."

"No!" Wall-Cat whined insistently. "We open gifts one at a time! Mom!"

"You can go first," Charlene said with authority and looking intently at me. "We're not going to change everything just because you say so." As she spoke she lit her second cigarette of the morning.

I blinked back at her, trying to decide if looking away would read as smug or as a sign of weakness.

"Ma, come on," Darren said as she continued to glare at me through puffs of smoke.

"Open your packages, Krystal," she said gesturing to Wall-Cat without moving her eyes away from me and without blinking.

"Yay!" Wall-Cat said clapping her hands vigorously before starting in on her first package.

For the next 45 minutes, there we sat. Wall-Cat picked her way down through her tower of gifts. One at a time, she gingerly teased apart each piece of tape to preserve the wrapping paper, then, inspecting each gift thoroughly, added it to the unwrapped pile, and then repeated the whole process.

When she finished, she looked at me and announced, "You're next!" In that moment, I didn't know whether to be grateful for my tower of boxes or not. I was certainly not excited to be on the spot with no one to detract attention away. I was well aware that every breath, every word, and every facial expression would be up for critique, and I was certainly not prepared for the responses that were bound to come from behind the wall of smoke across the room.

Seeing no other options, I ripped into the first package.

...Bedazzled hairpins... "Thank you!" I said in a tone that I felt was joyful and sincere. Then, I was on to the next gift,

...Reindeer socks... "Thank you!" I said again. *This is going well*, I thought to myself.

...Christmas scented travel hand lotion... "Perfect!" I said. If it smelled like this Christmas, then it probably smelled like a wet ashtray, but it was the thought that was important.

On and on it went with only awkward silence from the rest of the room. Package after package of dollar store Christmas gifts. It was not lost on me that it was an attempt by Charlene to be nice and welcoming, but the oppressive silence and melodramatic chain smoking canceled all of the positive intentions right out. It was miserable.

With three packages left to go, Darren blurted out, "I can't wait anymore." He started in on his own tower of packages. The silence was gloriously broken. He and his dad started talking and laughing. Wall-Cat turned her attention to her pile of loot. Charlene's eyes narrowed as she glared at me for a minute more. I stared back, smiling as naturally as I could.

"Ma...Ma..." Darren said, "Ma, look at this!" Charlene blinked slowly and turned her attention to him.

The rest of the day passed slowly without any major blowups. For my part, I went out of my way to be helpful. I chopped, stirred, and cleaned whenever I could, spending much of the day in the kitchen attempting to bond with his mother and her cigarettes.

That slow day stretched into a slow week, and the dismal Pittsburgh sky didn't help things along, either. Darren and I did our best to get away from the house whenever we could. I met some of his college friends. He took me on a driving tour of his hometown so I could see where he grew up. He drove me into the city so I could try a sandwich (or rather, a "sammich") with french fries and coleslaw on it.

On New Year's Day, I flew to visit my family in North Carolina. Darren stayed in Pittsburgh with his. For the next week, we spoke on the phone and chatted online every day. When we went back to school, we moved in together.

I didn't see it for what it really was at the time, but that holiday turned out to be a super-sized sampler platter of what was coming. It was a not-so-subtle foreshadowing of the conflict, the accusations, and the very clear sense of repulsion that would one day come my way from Darren's mother. It should have been enough to put an end to the whole thing, but it wasn't. It was too late, and the more Charlene pushed, the closer we got.

Chapter 4

As a little girl, I never dreamed about my wedding day, but almost all of my friends did. Among the make-believe tea parties and impromptu recitals, intricate wedding ceremonies happened all the time. I am honored to say that I have personally witnessed the marriage of Ken and Barbie many, many times. Technically, I guess several of those would have been recommitment ceremonies, but Barbie also married GI Joe at least twice. The specifics around any separations or divorces were never revealed, but Barbie clearly had a thing for the tall, athletic, and plastic type.

When elementary wedding mania could no longer be satisfied by Bridezilla Barbie, we started marrying each other off instead. It was just as well. Ken and Barbie were obviously growing apart, and Joe was so focused on work that he had no room for a relationship.

Our weddings were elaborate events. We were elegantly clad in dusty old dresses and dance recital tiaras with the bride-du-jour directing the affair as adeptly as a professional wedding planner. Vows were uttered. Teddy the bear, the typical groom of choice, always seemed a bit wide-eyed and was most often at a loss for words. The bride, on the other hand, always seemed to know exactly what to say. She knew exactly what she wanted and what everyone else wanted, too, for that matter. Each bride had her wedding all planned out down to the tiniest detail—where to stand, what to say, and how to react. A missed cue usually led to an eruption of irritation and foot stamping, and it almost always meant starting over from the beginning. No matter what my friends were like in the rest of their lives, they were absolutely certain and absolutely in charge when their wedding day was at stake—except for me. It was obvious that I lacked this genetic coding. Whenever it was my turn to be the bride, my weddings were short, chaotic fiascos that were the source of extreme disappointment for my friends.

When the time came to marry Darren, nothing had really changed in that department. I was in over my head. Complicating things even further, we decided (in our infinite wisdom) to get married before we finished school. I don't remember why, exactly. We had already been living together for over a year, and it wasn't like "living in sin" was something that could be undone in the eyes of anyone who cared about that sort of thing. We should have waited. We should have taken our time. It would have been smarter to wait, but we were hell-bent on marriage.

In February, we set a date during our summer break in June to cap off the end of our second year. That's right, we gave ourselves a little over four months to make it all happen. Consequently, many of the details were decided by virtue of circumstance and availability starting with the location. A wedding in my hometown was not an option. My parents had left Florida behind the summer before and moved to North Carolina to be closer to my brother and his new family. To complicate things more, they had put almost everything they had into a brand-new retail shop. They had moved around a lot when they were younger, but this move was harder on them than any of us expected. Plus, small business ownership was something neither of them had ever done before. So, needless to say, my mother had no time to help me plan or manage much of anything. That left me with two options: a Pittsburgh wedding with stay-at-home Charlene as my wedding planner or doing it all by myself in Iowa. We could have tied the knot on the home plate of the Field of Dreams—a weirdly intriguing and entirely legitimate possibility since the actual movie location was less than two hours from the school and was available for events of almost any kind. It would have been a more even playing field (pun intended) as far as potential guest attendance was concerned, but I couldn't make myself do it. I had read *Children of the Corn*. I knew what happened to outsiders in corn fields. So, Pittsburgh, or rather, Verona it was—where few to none of my friends would be able or willing to attend.

It turned out that Charlene was thrilled to be so involved in our wedding. Her attitude toward me had settled down some since the beginning, although I wasn't sure why nor was I completely convinced she could be trusted. She assured the two of us that she was ready to help, and to prove it, she immediately started the process of my Italian indoctrination. If I wasn't Italian by blood, she was going to Italianize me through cooking, shopping, and a healthy dose of relentless badgering. That would make everything better.

It seemed like a nice gesture. It would have been easier if she had just bludgeoned me with a frozen sausage and dumped my lifeless body on a dirt road somewhere, but I digress…

Our prewedding mother-in-law honeymoon didn't last long. Right away, it was clear that Charlene and I were coming from very different places. In about two weeks, the difference of opinion turned to disagreements, then disagreements turned to conflict, and then conflict become outright psychological warfare. While I didn't have an exact plan and I was flexible on the details, I wasn't a soulless monster. I wasn't trying to hurt her feelings (as she claimed to Darren over the phone at least once a week.) There were traditions that were important to me. I wanted our wedding to be about us, and by "us" I meant Darren and me, not Darren, Charlene and me.

Take, for example, the all-important wedding dress. Charlene took me shopping for it once and only once. I tried on almost every dress in the store, while Charlene stood right there in the fitting room with me. She looked at me as I stood there in nothing but a thong between every sample. (Even the sales girl was uncomfortable.) I wanted classic lines, simple details, and a price tag of $300 or less. Charlene insisted on tulle, sequins and the need for a crane to put the thing on. I think if she could have lighted it with twinkle lights by remote control, it would have been perfect for her. (Notably, it would not have been the first time I was in such a dress. Like I said, I worked at a theme park.) Mostly, she was worried that I would choose something "tacky" if left to my own devices. Luckily for me, I was footing the bill for it, so she didn't hold much sway.

There was also the cookie table thing. To me, the cookie table (otherwise known as the poor bride's Venetian Hour) looked like a ridiculous exercise in gluttony. I thought the cake was enough. It was a standard, traditional thing. Little did I know that when marrying an Italian (or half-Italian as in this case) I was expected to send everyone out the door with enough cookies to feed their entire family with nothing but cookies for a week. They would leave insulted if I refused, and I would forever be remembered as the tacky, cookie-withholding, thong-wearing, non-Italian whore. I'll admit that I surrendered to this one. It was important not to be "tacky" and I had already pushed it with the dress. I wasn't interested in fighting over baked goods, and thanks to Charlene's very generous next-door neighbor, I didn't have to bake them.

There was also the bridesmaid situation. I couldn't afford to fly any of my friends in for the ceremony, and I couldn't bring myself to ask them to pay their own way. (I had been put in that position before and found it horrifically embarrassing to admit that I didn't have the cash or the vacation days to spare.) Instead, I asked my brother's wife to stand as my matron of honor. (I was entirely against the word "matron" since she was still young and hot despite just having had a baby, but she insisted on accuracy. There were rules, of course.) It was a convenient solution; she would be there anyway. Problem solved.

Except…unbeknownst to me, it was a requirement for the sister of the groom to be included in the wedding party. Charlene dropped that bomb over Easter break at the dining room table. I wasn't sure where this rule came from. I was certain that Jill would have told me about it when we cleared up the whole "matron" thing. Darren even had a spasm over this one. That meant picking another groomsman, which had been a complex and angst-inducing decision process already. The table erupted around me over my own wedding party. What else could I do but say yes? Wall-Cat was sitting right there looking as strange and awkward as ever. I couldn't say no without giving a good explanation, and I didn't have one. The threat of insufferable tackiness was closed in tighter. So, Wall-Cat was in, and that was that.

There were the wedding day hair appointments. (I'm getting a little ahead of myself, but this is worth a mention.) Charlene thought that I would prefer to spend the entire morning of my wedding with her and Wall-Cat at her salon with her stylist (and probably walking out with her hairdo) instead of with my mother and my family who drove for eight hours for the ceremony. She made my appointment without telling me and told me about it two days before the wedding. She cried when I said that my mother was handling my hair and makeup and asked me if I was sure that it would be good enough for a wedding. I told her that it would be fine. I considered going with no makeup and shaving my head just to prove a point. It would have looked great in the pictures.

The disagreements kept coming and going. Darren and I handled them together, which I took as another sign that our wedding was meant to be.

...and then there was the big one...

The mother of all the wedding planning problems actually happened before the hair appointment fiasco. It was...the invitation. (Insert ominous, tension-building music here.) We were still at school when we sent the invitations out. A few days later, our voicemail was full of excited messages, congratulating us on the happy news. Message after happy message played through until the last one. It started with a long silent lead-in marked only by jagged breathing on the other end of the line. Thanks to caller ID we knew it was Charlene and not a prank. The breathing continued on, and then there she said, "hello...call me." With so much anger and self-righteousness in it, I think it almost frightened the answering machine into self-imposed retirement, and that was it. (Honestly, that answering machine never worked quite the same after that day. It was weird.)

Darren and I paced the floor for hours trying to decide what the problem could be. It was always better to know beforehand. At least then there was a chance of keeping Charlene contained. By the end of the night, we were out of ideas and out of time. Darren had to make the call or run the risk of creating another problem entirely. The first 10 minutes he couldn't get in a word. Her raspy voice squawked through the receiver loud enough for me to hear every word. She was in a full-blown tirade. There was nothing anyone could say to stop it. She had been wronged. It was my fault. That was it.

She had received her invitation in the mail that day, and we had ordered them without consulting her. They were, of course, tacky, but that wasn't the real problem. The real problem was that her name was nowhere on it.

The invitation read as follows:

Dr. Louis W. and Marilyn M. Gray
cordially invite you
to the marriage of their daughter,
Alane Catherine Gray
to
Darren Robert Danky
at Olde Presbyterian Church
at 2:00pm
on the 19th of June, Nineteen hundred ninety-nine
Reception to follow at Vitali's Restaurant

It was old school traditional. Darren and I chose it that way, together, on purpose. My parents had barely been involved in any of it other than cutting checks when I ran out my own money. Darren was the one who suggested it after looking at books and books of invitation templates. He thought it would be the perfect way for them to feel included, and I agreed. To me, It was a sweet and romantic gesture. To Charlene, it was an evisceration. It was like she had forgotten that I had parents or was planning on switching me out with a replacement bride on the day of the wedding. (Of course, there would have to be the aforementioned crane involved somehow if Charlene had picked out her dress.)

Charlene screeched into the phone, "It's not like she has friends coming to your wedding. The guest list has my friends on it! What will they think? This is insulting. Disrespectful! So selfish! Tacky!" and she hung up.

We both sat there unable to move and sick to our stomachs. Darren's sweet, romantic gesture had blown up in his face. He called back to try to talk it over, but Charlene refused to come to the phone. Earl got stuck in the middle. He listened as Darren went through the whole thing, detailing all the ways that we had honored her wishes and all of the decisions that she had been allowed to make. Darren talked about my family and how frustrated my mother was that she couldn't be more of directly involved. Earl listened and said he was sure that Charlene would get over it, but that damage had been done. I needed "to make it right."

Making it right meant apologizing in a way that Charlene would find acceptable. I wasn't sure what that meant. Based on my first run-in with her, I wasn't sure there was enough time to make it happen before the wedding, and who knew what that would mean for the whole event. I didn't want to apologize. I didn't even want to see her, but I had to try. I had no choice.

It was then that I learned that apologizing to Charlene was like trying to reason with a rabid dog. In short, it was a total fiasco. She refused to talk to either of us on the phone. She would pick up the receiver and then just sit there on the line like she was waiting for some specific combination of words to free her from some magical verbal bondage. She could grunt and moan and smoke, but that was it. Nothing I said satisfied her. We were getting down to the wire. She was the primary contact for everything, and she had total control over the whole thing. I needed to pass my exams. I had no time for this insanity. All I could do was wait and see what she had done when we were able to get there.

Finals were over one week before the wedding. We drove back to Pittsburgh aware that there was very little time to work with whatever choices she had made. We walked in the door to their house and into a wall of cigarette smoke and painfully oppressive silence.

"Hi, Ma," Darren said as we lugged our bags through the door.

Charlene refused to make eye contact. She just sat at the kitchen table, puffing on a cigarette and staring off at nothing. "Ma, hello," he said louder. She kept puffing and staring. "Hello!" he bellowed as the two of us stood cramped just inside the kitchen door.

Earl came around the corner. "Hello!" he said cheerfully. "What are you doing standing there in the door? Charlene, are you going to say hello to your son?"

She turned her head slightly as she slowly blinked. "Hello," she said flatly before puffing again.

"Ok," Darren said and pushed his bag through the narrow kitchen. "Let's go," he said back at me. We each hugged Earl and headed to the back room.

We made our way back into the kitchen and sat down at the table. Charlene said flatly, "You should eat," as she heaved herself up out of her seat. "I've been cooking all day. I thought you were going to be here for dinner, but you weren't."

"I called you before we left," Darren said. "You know it's a ten-hour drive."

"Whatever," she shot back with disgust as she slammed her way around the tiny kitchen.

I was expecting things to be tense, but this was crazy. I had no idea what to do. I thanked her for the food. She said, "Don't bother. It's a thankless job. No need to be fake about it on my account."

I sat there quietly wishing I could feed a few bites of her food to Pepper the cat before I ate to be sure it was safe. The cat was in hiding. "Thanks for the food, anyway," I made myself say. I could barely swallow.

Darren kept talking at his mother. Charlene gave more disgusted responses followed by her trademark, "whatever." Earl had retreated to the TV room.

On a different day, the whole thing would have been almost

funny—a grown woman behaving like a petulant teenage girl and a grown man pretending that nothing was happening. It was the perfect formula sit-com in real life. On this day, it wasn't funny at all.

Eventually, Darren and I gave up and went to bed. We stayed awake for a long time watching the lights from the road streak across the ceiling and then fan around the room.

"Maybe this is a bad idea," I said.

"It'll be fine," Darren said. "Don't worry about it. Just go in and apologize to her in the morning and she'll be alright."

"Apologize to her? I've already apologized more than I should have for this. We decided on this together, and my parents are paying for it, anyway."

"Except for the bar," he said.

"What?"

"Except for the open bar. My parents are paying for the bar tab," he said. "Their names probably should have been on the invitation."

"What?!" I spat back at him in a whispered shout. "Are you serious, right now?"

"Yeah," he said, "you should have included them."

"I should have included them? We picked out the invitations together. We agreed on this together!"

"I was never okay with it," he said with a snarl.

"Yes, you were! It was practically your idea!" I whisper-shouted, "What the fuck?!"

"Just apologize," he whispered flatly.

"No!" I said in full voice.

"Whatever, you'll figure it out," he whispered and turned over on his side.

I couldn't let it go. I was sick with fear and uncertainty. It was that special kind of sickness that only happens right before you do something stupid. The room seemed to shrink as I went over and over it in my mind. I was marrying this person in one week, and for the first time since we met, I felt completely alone. This was such a petty thing. Darren had turned on me, and I was outnumbered. Was this how it was going to be from now on?

Then again, what was one more apology, really? It wasn't going to kill me. I could suck it up and take the high road. After all, Charlene had done a lot of work, and there were more important issues on the way. By the time I fell asleep, I had decided what to do. I felt like puking every time I pictured it, but I was determined to make this work.

The next morning, I was up before the rest of the house. Charlene walked into the kitchen as I was making a second pot of coffee.

"Hello," she said tersely as she squeezed by me. (If I haven't been adequately clear about it before now, the kitchen was exceedingly small.)

"Good morning," I replied. We moved around each other in awkward silence for what felt like an eternity. I think it was really about five minutes. She lit her morning cigarette and blew the smoke at me over the table. I sipped my coffee as I tried to quiet my inner emergency alert system that was screaming at me that this was total bullshit. I ignored it and dove right into a last-ditch apology. I kept telling myself that it wasn't about being right; it was about self-preservation. "I am sorry about the invitations," I said. "I didn't realize it would upset you. We...well, I guess I…no, I mean we…wanted something traditional. I assumed it was what you expected."

"Why would I expect that?" she spat out acerbically as she turned and leaned against the kitchen sink.

"Because it was just like your wedding invitation," I said calmly. "You showed it to me yourself."

Charlene wavered for a split second, and that was it. "You are so selfish. Selfish!" She carried on like I had said nothing. "How do you think that made me feel? And Darren's father…he was so insulted! He wanted more than anything to be on that invitation."

"Really? He told me he didn't care," I blurted out without thinking it through.

"That is because you are blind! He is too good of a man to tell you how hurt he is. You didn't think of us at all, and after everything I've done for you. I can't believe that you made my son treat us like this!" She sucked on her cigarette dramatically and posed in profile as she exhaled. "You have made this all about you and what you want. It's disgusting."

"Um, it's my wedding," I said, still not thinking it through.

"It's Darren's wedding, too, and his needs should be taken into consideration." She said puffing away on her cigarette and posing dramatically with every smoky exhalation.

"He helped me pick them out!" I said through my gritted teeth. I was seconds away from completely unraveling. I was getting married. I had just finished exams. I had orchestrated this whole wedding thing on a ridiculously low budget from 600 miles away. Yes, she had helped—but in the end, it had been on me, and I was sick of all of it. This was not the life I wanted, full of conflict and insanity. I didn't want to marry Charlene. The words "just forget the whole thing" were loaded and ready to blow.

Then, in a literal cloud of smoke, Darren walked in. "Ma, enough. The invitations were my idea. Her parents needed to feel included and this was the best way to do it. How many times did you call Marilyn to talk to her about all of this? None. How many hotel rooms and plane tickets and rental cars do you have to pay for? None. Out of the hundred guests that are coming to this thing, Alane has eight people coming. That's it. Eight. Of the other ninety-two, only twelve of them are my friends. The rest are either family or the people that you insisted we had to invite. So basically, her parents are throwing a party for a bunch of strangers. I think picking up the bar tab is the least you can do. So, enough!" He sat down next to me and grabbed my hand.

"And the rehearsal dinner…I am paying for the rehearsal dinner," Charlene shot back arrogantly.

"Okay, Ma. Fine. The rehearsal dinner, too!" Darren was getting angrier.

"See, she just doesn't appreciate me." Charlene waved her hand at me, sending ashes across the table.

"Enough!" Darren boomed. "We are NOT doing this today!"

"Well…" Charlene's attitude switched to full nonchalance in less than a second. She lit a fresh cigarette as she considered her next words. "I just want to be acknowledged. I did a lot of work on this."

"We know you did," I offered as calmly as I could.

She glared at me for a second and then smiled pointedly at Darren. "I know *you* know I did. We have to go shopping today. I'll be ready in an hour." And with that, she stood up and walked out.

The conflict was over. I didn't understand it, but it was done. Darren had saved everything. The moment. The day. Our wedding. When he took my hand, it felt like he took my side. I stayed fairly quiet for the rest of that day, stunned by how close I had come to calling it off. If he had walked in just a few seconds later, everything might have been different. He swept in and backed me up, just in time. I knew it had to be a sign. This was still meant to be.

◆◆◆◆◆

The day before the wedding, my parents arrived. The sight of them in the church sent a wave of relief through me. The reinforcements had arrived. It was actually kind of funny. When they walked into the church the entire room turned to look and went completely silent. You would have thought they were visitors from Mars, but I guess North Carolina might have seemed like Mars to a few of them. To be fair, my mother did have a way of commanding a room when she wanted to. She was tall and composed and always swept in with a smile and a flourish. She had never met a stranger in her life and was not easily deterred by a resistant demeanor.

When I made the introductions, Mom took Charlene's hands and pulled her in for a hug. I saw it all in slow motion. Mom's smile was calm and steady. Charlene was shocked and off balance (and maybe a little horrified). As they hugged, Mom said sweetly, "Thank you so much for working so hard." Her graceful drawl was markedly stronger than usual, "I'm so glad I am finally able to relieve you of the burden." Mom held the hug a bit longer than required, her smile never wavering. Thanks to my lifetime of training in Southern Tact, her intentions were perfectly clear to me, but I'm thinking everyone in the room could see exactly what was happening. Mom was sometimes like a mafia don in lipstick and kitten heels.

Charlene's face drained as she smiled painfully and grunted a few forced pleasantries. Stepping back, she said, "I need a cigarette," as her eyes darted around searching for a sympathetic face. Everyone else had retreated as far away as they could and refused to return her gaze.

After that, we all pressed forward. The rehearsal flew by under

Mom's steady, instructive hand. Memorials to dead grandparents were arranged despite all of the eye-rolling and derisive comments from across the aisle. The staging was tweaked. The music was re-arranged. We took it over from the top as many times as were required to get it right. It was exciting to watch Mom work, and I regretted that I hadn't done all of this with her from the start.

Immediately after came the obligatory rehearsal dinner. Instead of a small, intimate affair where our families could really connect and get to know each other, Charlene decided to have an outdoor barbeque at her tiny house to which she invited her immediate and extended family, all of her friends, and the neighbors.

A steady rain had started to fall on the drive from the church. The temperature dropped sharply at the same time. Still, Charlene managed to corral me and the five members of my family that weren't still traveling outside on the breezeway between the kitchen door and the garage at an old, splintered, wood picnic table. Her family and friends had been encouraged to congregate inside the house. It was awkward, to say the least, and really, what better way is there to welcome a Southerner than to feed them generic bottled barbecue sauce in the rain.

Occasionally a wayward Danky would venture out to the breezeway and make an effort, especially if Charlene needed to smoke. That morning she had decided that it was rude to smoke in the house. I think it backfired when she found herself in such close proximity to my parents.

To my family's credit, they held it together. Dad and I tried to divide and mingle, making the best of it with practiced and unwavering smiles. When Mom decided it was time for an invasion, she waltzed into the house, and in less than 10 minutes, she was telling tales and making new friends. Laughter poured out of the living room as she effervesced with excellent stories and seemingly endless interest in the others in the room.

Charlene shrank a little with every glowing remark she was forced to endure about me, my family, and (most especially) my mother. I think she had been expecting congratulations for her willingness to endure the backwards family of the bride. What she got was an unending stream of compliments on Darren's future in-laws and how lucky she was that he had found such a nice family. She could hardly contain her relief when we said our goodbyes for the evening.

Later that night, after my parents and I had finally worn ourselves out with conversation, I headed up to my hotel room. I closed the door behind me and realized that I was finally alone. It was the first time I had been alone in weeks. I flopped myself face down on the bed. I could hear the air whistle in and out of my nose as it was smooshed into the bed. (Usually, this would have totally grossed me out. Who knew what that ugly floral bed cover had seen before? In that moment, I didn't care.)

"What am I doing?" I said aloud into the mattress. "What the hell am I doing?!" I couldn't breathe. I couldn't move. It just felt wrong. I had held it together all day, and now that there was no Charlene to battle and no noise to drown out the doubt, it all started crashing in. This wasn't my home. These weren't my people. This wasn't what I wanted. Darren was a stranger. I was a fool. All of the terrible everything just kept rolling through my mind. I couldn't make it stop. I felt like this was all one giant mistake. I could feel a deluge of tears start to swell and my throat start to close. It was just about to unleash when I heard a knock at the door. It startled me enough to short circuit my tears and shake me out of my stupor.

I opened the door only a crack. This was a hotel, after all, and no one I knew was supposed to be out or about. Darren was standing there, smiling and looking a little too relaxed for a night like this. "I know I'm not supposed to be here, but I had to see you one last time before midnight," he said as he stepped through the door. "You look exhausted, so I won't stay." He sat down on the edge of the bed and grabbed my hands. "I just want to thank you for today," he went on looking intensely into my eyes. "I know it wasn't exactly what you wanted today to be like, but your family was so good. Everyone is saying how lucky I am."

It seemed like he was a little tipsy, but I couldn't be sure. Maybe he was just love-drunk. It seemed so sincere. It was like he sensed that I was having doubts. It was like we were connected and he knew just the right time to come and fix everything. I didn't have to a said a word. He pulled me into his arms and kissed my cheek. "I love you, and I can't wait to marry you tomorrow." Then he left.

It was another sign that this was meant to be. It had to be.

My doubts were there, but maybe I was overthinking it. He showed up right when I needed it. It had to be fate, and anyway, I was marrying Darren, not his mother. Once we were married, it would be different.

Clarity had finally arrived. After that, I even managed to get a little rest. The next morning, coffee was a requirement along with cold water and ice cubes to shrink my puffy face and the enormous bags under my eyes.

I spent the morning prepping with my family. We laughed and joked like we always did when we were under pressure. Mom was working diligently to make me presentable, covering blemishes, spraying my hair and ensuring that nothing stained my teeth. It was comfortable, familiar. My mother had been my entire entourage through my entire childhood of stage performances.

My father sat nearby, telling stories and sighing deeply. "You've never let us down," he said, "not once, in anything you've done."

He sighed again wistfully. "You were always so ambitious. You always seemed to know exactly what you wanted and exactly how to get it." He cleared his throat and exhaled again. "We were always so proud of you."

It was starting to feel more like a wake than a wedding. "You are talking in the past tense, Dad," I said, laughing a little as I said it.

"Well, I am. You always had to do things on your own terms," he went on. "I'm just reminiscing."

"Do you think I'm making a mistake?" I said, turning to face him.

Mom grabbed my head with both hands and turned my face back toward the mirror. "That's not at all what he is saying," she interjected as she sprayed hairspray at my head like she was hosing down a kitchen fire. "Here…have a sip." She handed me a bottle of red wine that they had opened with brunch.

"But what about my teeth?" I said.

"Just have a sip..." she said as she shoved bobby pins directly into my scalp. This was like a weird childhood dance recital flashback, but with wine.

"Can I have a glass?" I said, wincing with every scalp stab.

"Just drink it." I could see her giving a pursed-lipped smile toward my father.

"No, no, sweetheart. Everything's fine," Dad said. "Darren is a nice young man. You two seem very happy." He sighed yet again.

"Okay, everyone," my mother announced, "let's get it together. It's time to head down the road." The time for sighing and reminiscing was over, and there would definitely be no more wine, at least not until later. We piled into the cars and caravanned off to the church.

♦♦♦♦♦

The church where we got married (chosen without Wall-Cat's input) was a quaint, little relic from a time before cars and power lines. At first glance, it seemed out of place nestled among the dingy pizza shops and auto parts stores, but somehow its white painted boards gleamed ethereally no matter the time of day or the weather. Inside, the chapel was a visual feast of dark wood and stained glass with a domed wood slat ceiling lofting upward to form the base of the steeple. If you ignored the commercial grade carpet beneath your feet, it was like you had stepped backward in time about a hundred years or so.

It only took a few minutes for us to load in our little traveling show and take over most of the back of the church. With deft hands, my mother primped and fluffed every bow and every strand of hair in the room. Wall-Cat eventually skulked in during the final preparations. True to form she was skittish and antisocial, but in her own way, she made an effort to be involved, and to my surprise, she cleaned up very well.

When the reverend's assistant knocked, it was time. Everyone cleared out to take their assigned places except for my mother and me. When we were alone, she turned and looked me straight in the eye. "Your future will be exactly what it is supposed to be. My only wish for you is happiness. You are my best creation. I know that you are following your heart, but only you can know, deep down, if this is right. A little doubt is normal, but this is it. There is no going back after this. I love you, sweetie." Tears started welling up in my eyes. "Now, don't cry," she said. "That mascara is waterproof, but don't push it."

She held open the door to the back of the church. "It's time," she said as she ushered me out the door. The afternoon sunlight assaulted my eyes. I had to walk around the outside of the church to get to the chapel entrance. As I stepped out onto the steps, the nausea started. My ankles were wobbly, and I had to steady myself on the stair rail for a minute to regain my balance. I kept telling myself this was natural. Everybody feels like they are walking toward a guillotine right before they make this kind of commitment. Right?

I turned around for a last word of encouragement, but Mom was gone. She had disappeared inside, and I was on my own. Slowly, I descended the steps and started heading for my mark. My head was spinning as I tried to sort through all of the thoughts that were spiraling around in it.

Then it hit me…

I was surrounded by dead people. Not the fun, zombie/ghost/vampire variety of dead people—I mean actual dead people. Seriously. I was walking right through the middle of the church's graveyard. This was the one part I hadn't rehearsed the night before. If I had thought it through, I would have turned right instead of left and walked through the parking lot on the other side. Instead, there I was in my pristine white wedding dress and waterproof mascara, standing among the weathered headstones of at least a hundred long buried strangers.

A wave of panic washed over me. Was this an omen? Dead people shouldn't freak me out, I had cut several of them up over the last few years, and even if they suddenly popped up as zombies, I was prepared. I had seen all the movies and was generally good in a paranormally threatening situation. That obviously wasn't the problem. Still…a wave of terror was overtaking me. I couldn't breathe. I couldn't make myself take a step.

What the hell are you doing? Raged through my head over and over again. It was maddening. I wanted to scream.

Until it hit me…and the raging stopped as quickly as it started.

This was it. This was *The Vow. The Big One*. The thing that would link me to Darren until the day I die. Not even a divorce could eradicate the bond *The Vow* would create. We would forever be different. I would forever be different. Everything would change. In that moment, it sounded like insanity.

Until death do us part…

It's a pretty vague concept overall, and at the same time, it's undeniably specific. It could be five years or fifty—that part isn't guaranteed. Whatever the final year tally turns out to be doesn't matter. The only part that's really certain is the termination clause. Death—that's it. It's the only way out. Otherwise, it's going to be this one person until the end.

What the hell are you doing? sliced through my head again. I was about to voluntarily shackle myself to another person until I die. What the fuck? Was that supposed to be comforting or something?

The beginning of the rest of my life was feeling like the end. I wanted to stay right where I was. The headstones weren't going to judge me. I could fling myself melodramatically over one of them and bawl my eyes out, and the headstones wouldn't care. I think any zombies that might stagger by would be sensitive to my insanity and cut a wide path around me. All of my crying might taint their dining experience.

But I couldn't stay there forever. I forced myself to move my feet. If I never went inside the church, someone would eventually come looking for me. There I would be, crying in a wedding dress from atop a dead Victorian's headstone, in the middle of a cemetery. If the photographer was on his game, we could freeze that moment forever on the first page of the wedding album—my blotchy face streaked with tears over the caption "Happy Beginnings." On another day, this mental image would have been hysterical. This was not another day.

I stopped and started several times until, eventually, I reached the front of the church. Inside the foyer, Dad was waiting. I looked at him hoping he would say something profound and encouraging. He looked at me only for a second and then turned toward the entryway. I took my mark by his side. He stiffly smoothed his lapel and cleared his throat. "I have my keys in my pocket. It's not too late." He offered me his arm.

I stared at him wide-eyed and slack-jawed for a moment. How did he know? Was he watching me? Was he joking? Was he serious? He was right, after all. We could just leave. I could leave and maybe this horrible sick feeling in my gut would go away. There was still time…

The ornate double doors opened in front of me and the first chords of the wedding march hit my ears like a tornado siren. That's when the performer in me took over. I didn't think; I just stepped forward right on cue. That's why we practiced this. There was an audience. The show had to go on. There was no room for hesitation or improvisation.

…Just follow the music and smile…

And, that's exactly what I did. I made it down the aisle. I listened to the reverend. Everyone in the audience cried except for me. (There's no crying on stage unless it's part of the act, of course.) Darren cried. Even Charlene cried, but I think that was out of sadness more than joy. *The Vow* was uttered. We kissed…and it was done.

…Until death do us part.

Chapter 5

Once everything was all said and done, I felt silly for being so weird about it. I took *The Vow* in a church, but it wasn't the end of the world. It had been a pretty good show as it was happening. Everyone laughed a little and cried a little, and the whole thing ended before anyone got too bored or restless. As far as Saturday afternoon matinees go, it wasn't bad.

On the upside, it was official—Darren and I could claim community property, maybe get a tax break, and if I got knocked up, I wouldn't have to explain myself to anybody. On the spiritual side, we had God's blessing, according to the Reverend. In fact, God was supposedly in on the whole deal from the start. That's how two people, from two totally different worlds, could find each other. When I played the ceremony over in my head, the reverend's words became a comfort and an inspiration. Thanks to the Reverend's magic spell, I was now part of a powerful unified force that was capable of more than I was on my own—kind of like the Wonder Twins without the fist bumping.

Other than that, nothing else really changed. We had a little over a year left to go in school. Married or not, we went to class, took exams, studied for the boards, and racked up more student loan debt. In fact, if I hadn't been there at the wedding, I would have doubted that it happened at all.

Of course, those easy days had a time limit. Graduation was coming and, sooner or later, we would have to actually go to work.

Which brought us to our first, big, married, life-altering decision that we would have to make together—where do we go from here?

As I've mentioned once or twice, I was from Florida. Before the wedding, I always just expected we would go there. Florida is, after all, the Mecca for chiropractic practices. Pre-wedding Option 2 was North Carolina. My parents had retired to Charlotte. I had gone away to arts school in Winston-Salem when I was younger. In that moment in Iowa, it seemed like (after Florida, of course) NC was the place to be.

After the wedding, all of that changed. This Florida girl who hated the cold (which, in my world, meant anything below 65 degrees Fahrenheit) and was absolutely unable to drive successfully in the snow at that point (that's a completely embarrassing story for another day) moved to Pittsburgh…and worse, it was mostly my idea.

As much as I loved Florida and as pretty as Charlotte was… on paper, Pittsburgh seemed perfect. Darren had roots there. He had a network of friends and a big family. Pittsburgh offered us someplace familiar (at least to him) to start. In Charlotte, I knew all of five people. In Florida, most of the people I knew had moved on. It seemed like no matter where I went, I would be starting from scratch.

To make Pittsburgh even more enticing, Darren had a job offer. His friend Steve, who had been practicing on his own for several years, offered him a contract before we had even started our last term. Darren could graduate and walk right into an established office. There were several other opportunities in the area for me, too. It was the logical choice. It seemed perfect to me.

Darren, however, was not in the same place with it. He had all kinds of wild ideas about where we should go and what we should do that he never mentioned before the wedding. One day he woke up and announced that we should move out west and set up shop in Arizona or New Mexico. He had never been there. He didn't know a single person who had gone there on vacation, let alone opened a business, but for some reason, he was convinced that it was a brilliant and completely reasonable idea.

After weeks of researching cities and demographics and running the numbers and after I was finally coming around to the idea, he changed his mind. That night he took me to dinner at a small Italian restaurant, which was weird. He usually refused to eat Midwestern Italian food. We ate pasta while Bocelli was piped in through the speakers in the ceiling. The next thing I knew, he was talking about work visas and practicing in Italy.

It's important to understand that Darren knew nothing about living in Italy. He had never been there. He didn't speak the language. The closest thing to Italian he could muster was "lasagna" in a painful, mock Italian accent. (To be fair, he also knew several Italian slurs for female body parts and ethnic minority groups, but I refused to count those.) He was only half Italian, to boot. His great-grandparents had emigrated from Italy on a boat, and somehow, this meant that we could successfully practice there without starving to death or killing a patient.

He carried on the Italy sales pitch for weeks, but no matter how hard he tried, I was not convinced. It was far too risky for me. I couldn't understand why we were even talking about it. The more he lobbied, the sicker I felt about the whole thing, and the more I dug in my heels. After more than a month, it didn't matter to me if it was Italy or Arizona; we weren't going. I wasn't about to move to either of those places with no money, no connections, no help, and potentially no ability to ask for directions let alone successfully communicate with a patient. Our profession was hard enough. Why make it exponentially harder?

Darren was relentless. "What's the big deal?" he would say every time I brought up the cons part of the pros and cons list. His best argument was that people from other countries come here and open up businesses all the time. "What's the difference?" he would say with mounting frustration.

Every time he asked, I spat out lists of reasons as quickly as I could; every time he would circle back around to, "I don't see what the big deal is," in a disgruntled tone.

"Those people are coming here, not staying there!" I would say in return. It wasn't the most insightful argument in the world, and I wasn't really sure who *those people* were specifically, but it was the only thing I had left after all of my reasonable arguments failed. It was mystifying…at a month before graduation, we were still talking about this.

As my last resort, I dug deep and went straight for the gut. "You know…your great-grandparents came here sick, and hungry, and chasing the American Dream. Do you really want to let them down?" I went on, invoking images of Ellis Island and his cold, starving great grandfather being forced to change his surname by a soulless, overworked clerk, giving up the only thing he had left other than the clothes on his back. (I think I might have even welled up a little bit.)

Darren just blinked at me, and then off he went to buy a new copy of "Learn Italian Now!"

Merda… I thought to myself.

I kept hoping it would wear off. He was a capable guy, but not much of a studier. I expected that the need to learn a whole new language in order to feed himself might keep his Italian inferno from burning too brightly. It didn't.

Mio Dio…

Darren talked about these plans so much that his friends

thought he was serious, and worse, they thought that it was my idea. I started getting panicked phone calls from Pennsylvania. Steve called every other day to convince me that Pittsburgh was a great place to live. His fraternity brothers called to talk me out of leaving the country like they were talking me down off of a ledge. His mother even called me to ask me what my problem was.

Figlio di puttana...

After a long Sunday afternoon on the phone, Charlene finally accepted that this was not my doing. Then she made an offer that she thought he wouldn't refuse. It was weird, and it felt a little icky, but it worked. It was also the first time she and I had agreed on anything. There's nothing like a little subversive manipulation to bring two people together.

She offered to help us if we moved to Pittsburgh instead of moving to Italy. Charlene's promise of support made me feel like moving to Pittsburgh was the best and the safest choice we could make (even though I found the idea of living there was more than a little distasteful). I thought that it would lessen my load if Darren didn't have to work so hard to assimilate. He had struggled to get along with a lot of the people we met in school. I figured that I could get along and make it work out no matter where we went. I was a social chameleon, and if nothing else, I could play a part if I had to. So, if we started somewhere that Darren had connections and felt at home, it would be easier for him and by extension easier for me. Add on top of that free food and a roof over our head while we were getting settled, and it seemed like the right thing to do. I was not going to let us fail. I was determined to make us a success no matter what, even if I had to do it all by myself.

With Charlene's promise of support behind me and with the certainty that moving there would be the best and safest choice we could make, I made my final push...and I won... but I really don't know how or why. That change away from, then back to Pittsburgh again would always mystify me. Pittsburgh, it would be.

Vittoria!...

The day after graduation we headed off toward our future. With all of our belongings loaded up in a U-Haul moving van, we drove with his family, like a caravan of cranky gypsies, to Pittsburgh.

Hour after hour, we drove on I-80 with nothing to look at but farms, fields, and the back of the moving van in front of me. I had made that drive many times before, especially before the wedding, but this time it felt different. Despite the visual monotony, the overwhelming exhaustion, and Charlene sitting in the passenger seat next to me, things felt pretty good. The sun was shining. The air was cool and crisp. I felt like nothing was going to stop us from moving forward toward a happy, prosperous future. It was our time. Darren was finally focused. All of our hard work was getting ready to start paying off. My excitement grew as we drove. With every mile, it intensified like shuffling stocking feet over a carpeted floor. The charge was building, and I couldn't wait for it to release.

We arrived at our new home (otherwise known as Darren's parents' house) that night in the dark. That's right, I was 29 years old, married, and a doctor, and I was moving in with my mother-in-law. It wasn't at all what I had imagined I would be doing after graduation when I started school. Big picture-wise, it wasn't at all what I wanted, either, but I had lobbied hard for this. I had even conspired with Charlene to make this happen. Whether it was the right thing to do or not, I wasn't sure—but it was a means to an end.

As I stood there in the driveway in the dark staring at their tiny beige brick house, I realized that I had never stayed there for more than a week or possibly two. A mere twelve hours earlier, we had been in our own rented townhouse, with our own stuff and our own way of doing things. It had been just the two of us. Now it was the two of us and his parents—four full-grown adults—all living together in a matchbox.

I had no idea how this was going to work. My relationship with Charlene was shaky, at best. What would happen once we were locked in together with no firm end date in sight? I don't want to sound like a snob or anything, but their house was not what I was used to. It was fine for two people. It might have been fine for two people with a couple of small children, but for four adults, it was a challenge.

It had 950 square feet of living space with 3 bedrooms crammed into it, 1 bathroom, and no central air. There were plenty of amenities like the basement that also served as a storage facility, liquor cabinet, laundry room (and spider sanctuary), the creepy basement shower, and the pool.

The pool was a real showpiece. It was surrounded by a 3-foot margin of concrete and a 6-foot rotting wooden fence with rusted locks. Since it was Pennsylvania, it was usable for about 3 months out of the year and was really only warm enough (based on Florida standards) for about four weeks of the year between the hours of 11 a.m. and 4 p.m.

All things considered, it wasn't the best of circumstances, but it was all we had other than a moving truck full of stuff and a boatload of student loan debt. We needed help, and I certainly wasn't going to turn my nose up at it just because things might be a little uncomfortable. So, we moved into Wall-Cat's old bedroom, with her high school musical flyers on the wall, her "Lion King" cartoon bedsheets, and the bedroom furniture set that Charlene and Earl bought right after they got married.

For her part, Charlene did her best to make us comfortable. She was so happy that we were there that she would come into our bedroom at least once a day to move our things off the top of the dresser and put them in the floor where Sausage the cat could chew on them in his spare time. She loved that furniture and couldn't stand to see anything on it for fear of something marring the top of it. Charlene also promised she would only smoke in her computer room (formerly known as Darren's old bedroom) and turn on the circa 1974 smoke-eater whenever she was in there. Her favorite pastime was smoking and playing computer solitaire. When she was in there, it was like the back room of an off-track betting site, but at least she was making an effort.

The first month was rough. Darren and I were interviewing for jobs as we waited for the state to issue our licenses. Darren turned down Steve's job offer even though that was one of the primary reasons we moved there. He thought he could do better. I thought a job offer right out of school was a gift. He wasn't convinced, and Steve was uninterested in transferring his to me.

By the end of the second month, things took a sharp downward turn. The job market for newbie chiropractors was thin and things, in general, just weren't going our way. I thought that maybe the overwhelming aroma of cigarette smoke and kitty litter on my clothes might have been a detriment. Of course, no one could possibly know for sure. Charlene suggested that maybe I was too slow to get hired in a place like Pittsburgh, being that I was from the South and all. It was hard for me to tell exactly what she was saying through all of that fast-talking Pittsburghese. Maybe I misunderstood.

As the days dragged on, the four of us remained there, squeezed together in that stinky little smokebox. It was almost winter by the calendar's tally, but the gray skies and dingy snow made it look like winter had already been there for a while. I hadn't seen the sun in weeks. I had no place to go and no money to spend. No one was interviewing that close to Christmas, and I had missed my chance at any of the seasonal retail jobs—thanks to my own arrogance and my assumption that Darren would end up taking that job with Steve. That meant that there was no permanent escape coming my way until February, at the earliest. It was probably going to be more like March or April if I let myself think about it realistically.

Between the stress and the smoke and the lack of sunshine, I was starting to lose my grip. Actually, I was straight up unraveling. Darren didn't want to hear it and told me so in exactly those words on more than one occasion. Charlene would just ask, "What's wrong with her?" like I wasn't in the room anytime I seemed to even hint at unhappiness. I didn't want to call home and upset my parents.

Mom's fledgling store was headlong into the Christmas shopping crush, and they really needed to stay focused. I was on my own with it. I had no choice but to work things out for myself. That's when I started my journal. Actually, it was just some blank pages at the back of one of Darren's old lab notebooks. It was nothing special. I had to handle my shit somehow, and journaling was the only thing I knew to do.

I had kept a journal off and on since I was a kid. My mom gave me my first one when I was 6, so I would have a place to keep my private thoughts. It even had a lock and key on it to keep it away from my older brother's prying eyes. From there, journals became a regular part of my life. Over the years, I had kept fancy ones and plain ones. I had kept a special one when I traveled through France for the first time, and I had kept several throughout chiropractic college. It was a place for me to keep track of what happened and how I felt about things. When things were bad, it was a way to get all of the mental bile out of my system without puking it up at the dinner table or on an unsuspecting stranger in line at the grocery store.

This particular journal, the one I kept at the back of that old lab notebook, was a half-mad stream of consciousness mash-up of every unspoken judgment, every off-color witty zinger, and every silent complaint that had crossed my mind since the day we moved in. That unremarkable little notebook was a trash can for all of my inappropriate anger, rage, sadness, fear, and frustration. It existed so that I wouldn't say whatever I thought when I thought it, thereby making a horrible situation that much worse. In a way, it was my gift to the Dankys for all of their generosity—a gift that they didn't even know they wanted.

That journal became my escape. It was the only thing that was all mine. The front was filled with lab experiments and chemical reactions scrawled carelessly across its pages in Darren's nearly illegible handwriting. I asked him if I could have it before I started using it.

"Do what you want with it," he said. "I'm just going to throw it out."

In my mind, throwing it out would have been a waste of perfectly good paper. It wasn't like I had money to buy anything else. From that moment on, it was mine. I even signed my name at the bottom of the front cover.

After that, I started writing. That notebook instantly became my solace in an otherwise miserable circumstance. I wrote about everything—every critical jab that Charlene lobbed my way, every comment on my habits, or my clothes, or my accent. Charlene had something to say about everything I did, from the way I washed the dishes after dinner to the amount of toilet paper I used. (I was never really certain how she knew exactly how much I was using, but it really was a thing.) That notebook absorbed every last ounce of emotion I had about every insult she made. I filled up page after page, trying to get it all out. It wasn't pretty, but it was all mine, and it worked. I felt better. There was no real open conflict to speak of because it was all tucked away in my journal.

Chapter 6

As Christmas approached, even Darren was having trouble keeping it together. He needed a break; I needed some sunshine. So, he scrounged together some gas money and told his parents that he was taking me to Charlotte as a Christmas present. This, of course, sent Charlene into spasms of passive-aggressive rage and depression, but that was no different than any other day. Earl looked kind of relieved. Wall-Cat, who was home for the holidays, clapped her hands and actually said, "Yay!" when she heard the news.

Darren's whole plan was devised and executed in less than a day. As we were packing, Darren was insistent that we shouldn't take too much. He wanted his mother to know that we weren't gone for good. He was afraid she would feel abandoned. So, I packed as lightly as I could in the middle of December and left everything else. I shoved what was left in the dresser drawers. I even left my notebook behind at the bottom of the bottom drawer with a haphazard wad of my underwear and t-shirts stuffed in on top. The only thing left to do was to head south.

As always, the drive to Charlotte was invigorating. We drove over the West Virginia mountains and across the mildly terrifying bridge that spans the New River Gorge. The drive was always scenic. This time, however, was a little different. As we crossed the state line into North Carolina, it felt almost like a mystical experience. The sun looked brighter. The colors were more intense. I am sure that it was all in my head, but my head was pretty consistent on the matter. Once we crossed that line, it was like a choir of angels was singing just for me. I felt like we were home even though I wasn't.

This was our fourth Christmas together, and the first Christmas we spent with my family. For the most part, it was gloriously unremarkable. We traded Wall-Cat's old room from my parents' spare bedroom. There was a lot of eating and drinking and celebrating—maybe even a little too much of all of it some of the time. There was also my three-year-old nephew, the only grandchild in the family so far. He held almost everyone's attention most of the time. There was not much more to it than that. It was nice.

Christmas and the week after flew by quickly. The night before New Year's Eve we all went over to my brother's house for dinner after which we packed into the living room to watch a movie.

Just as the movie started, Darren got a call and stepped outside. The rest of us kept watching and talking while Mom tried to explain a brutal gladiator movie in terms that a 3-year-old was willing to accept. My nephew took it in stride and only cried a little when the horses died. We kept telling him that they were only going to sleep, but that was a tough sell when the blood started spurting all over the screen. Like I said, maybe there was too much merriment.

Thirty minutes went by. Darren still wasn't back. I wasn't sure what it meant, but the longer he was gone, the tighter my stomach twisted. Too much time had passed for Darren to still be on the phone with a friend. If it had been an emergency, he would have come inside to get me. Even so, this was weird. Something big must have had happened. I could feel it. My first thought was that it was a job offer, which would have been excellent news, but my gut was telling me that it was something else. I had to go and find out what it was.

As the movie played on, I stepped out the front door. Darren was hunched over on the porch step with his phone to his ear. I sat down next to him.

He flinched away, cutting his eyes to the side to glare at me. "Go back inside," he said with a growl.

"It's ok," I said back without moving, "I'll watch the movie with you again later. How are your parents?"

"Go back inside!" he growled, again. "I'll deal with you later!"

"Deal with me later?" I said incredulously. "What's that supposed to mean?"

Darren refused to answer. He was holding the phone away from his ear. I heard Charlene's voice bleating away at the other end of the line. "Is that her? Is that her? What is she…"

Darren moved the phone to his ear and said, "Give me a minute." He then glared straight at me and said, "Go the fuck inside!"

We sat there staring at each other, his face full of a rage that I had never seen before. I couldn't make myself move. No one had ever barked an order at me like that, at least not anyone that wasn't my own flesh and blood, and certainly not anyone that had ever shared my bed.

I was confused, with a rapidly escalating undercurrent of anger. Every fiber of my being was screaming at me to fight back, but I didn't. I just sat there.

"GO!" he yelled as he stood up and stormed off down the driveway.

I sat on the step staring at his back as he skulked away in the dark. It probably looked like an act of defiance, but it wasn't. I was completely staggered and unable to move on command.

Darren kept his back to me as he carried on with his mother. I finally pulled myself up and went inside the house.

"Everything alright?" my bother said as I sat down on the stairs.

The rest of the room was still fixated on the screen.

I shrugged.

"What happened?" he said furrowing his brow.

"It's fine," I said. "He's just on the phone with his mom."

"Oh," he said with a sarcastic flourish, "No wonder. I guess he'll be out there for a while…Momma's Boy!" He was chuckling out loud at his own remark as Darren walked through the front door. "There's Momma's Boy!" he announced to the room as he stood up and clapped Darren hard on the back. Darren's eyes narrowed. "Oh, sorry man. Just joking around," my brother said flippantly as he stepped away.

Darren shifted his glare to me. My brother made an awkward face behind Darren's back from across the room and then laughed as he stepped into the kitchen.

I looked at Darren with a big smile and said, "Everything okay?"

Darren refused to respond.

We were still sitting in the living room with my entire family. I babbled on with polite conversation in a desperate attempt to keep whatever this was from becoming the center of attention. It seemed like keeping up appearances would be the right way to go for the moment. Darren would not be moved. He sat there like a giant vortex sucking all of the fun right out of the room. It only took about five minutes for everyone to notice which, of course, meant they had to try to talk him out of it. He refused to answer anyone with more than a grunt or a shrug of his shoulders. Within fifteen minutes, the TV was off, and everyone had said their good nights.

The car ride to my parents' house was long and tense. We had driven ourselves that night, so the additional embarrassment from Darren's bizarre and inexplicable human vortex was temporarily avoided.

When I couldn't stand it any longer, I broke the silence. "What was that all about?"

"Like you don't know," he replied in a low and angry voice.

"Actually, I don't know," I said. "What happened?"

"You know," he spat out again.

"No, I really don't know, and if you won't tell me, then there is nothing I can do about it."

"There is nothing you can do about it anyway."

"Darren, what the fuck? You killed the night, and everyone left feeling really uncomfortable. What is the problem?" I said with growing frustration.

"Why would you hurt my parents like that?" he yelled.

"What did I do to your parents? I haven't even talked to them." I replied. I was fighting hard to remain calm.

"I can't believe you would do something like this. Why did you do it?" he yelled again.

"I didn't do anything! What is going on?" I said a little louder.

We went on like this for a good ten minutes or more. Back and forth it went. *"How could you do this?" "Do what?" "You know what you did." "No, I don't. Why won't you tell me?"* It went on so long and so loudly that we were almost at the exit to my parents' house. There was no way we could go on like this in front of them. This was a problem.

Without discussing it, he drove past our turn off and sped down the highway, taking a random exit onto a dark two-lane road with no streetlights and only an occasional numbered road marker.

Eventually, Darren pulled off the road and parked. I had no idea where we were, but it was as good a place as any to hash this out before we went back.

He broke the silence this time, "Why did you leave that stuff for my mom to read?"

"I don't know what you are talking about," I replied. "I didn't leave anything for your mom. I just left our stuff there."

"She said you did," he said. "She said you left your notebook for her with all of that horrible stuff written in it."

My stomach felt like it dropped to the floor of the car, ripping the rest of my insides out with it. "I didn't leave that for her!" I insisted. My throat tightened as I spoke, "It was at the bottom of my drawer with a bunch of my clothes on top of it. Did she go through my stuff? Why did she go through my stuff?"

"Don't you mean our stuff?" he said accusingly. "So, you really did write that about them?"

"I wrote about them in my journal. What stuff is she talking about, and why was she going through my drawers?"

"You mean our drawers," he corrected dismissively. "She said you left it for her to read. That was such a bitch move, Alane. I can't believe you'd do that to me or to my parents. They're letting you live in their house for free, and this is how you repay them?"

"Wow, you certainly *have* been talking to your mother, haven't you," I said under my breath.

"What did you just say?" he shot back.

"I said I didn't leave that for your mother. I have been doing everything I can to help your mother and to stay out of the way while she constantly criticizes me and what I do and what I say and where I'm from… I'm a grown woman. I lived on my own for a long time before we got together. Excuse me if I am having a little trouble moving in with my husband's mommy!" I was hyperventilating. "I wrote it all down—in what I thought was my journal—instead of blurting it out to you or to them."

"You should never have done that," he said.

"What, keep a journal?"

"Yes. You were writing all of this behind my back and then

lying straight to my face," he sat back in his seat arrogantly like he had just been vindicated.

"No. I was working through my shit on my own and doing my best to treat you and your parents with respect."

"You are a liar!" he yelled. "You know that I hate liars."

"I never lied to you!" I yelled back.

"Yes, you did!" he screamed so loudly that the reverberation inside the car made my ears ring.

"How, Darren? How did I lie to you?" I was trying not to scream at him, too, but I don't think it worked.

"You smiled and pretended like everything is fine and then you went and wrote a bunch of lies in *my* notebook and then you turned around and lied to my mother's face." Darren's face was bright red, and sweat was flinging off of his forehead every time he moved.

"You are insane! I told you that I was having trouble adjusting. I told you that I needed someone to talk to and as for *your notebook*, a.k.a. *MY JOURNAL*, you studied psychology. You know that it's a valid technique. Therefore…I did nothing wrong!"

"You lied," he sneered, "I am your husband. You should have talked to me about it rather leaving it for my mother to read. That's so passive aggressive, Alane—emphasis on aggressive!"

"For fuck sake, Darren, I didn't leave it for her to read! Don't you care that your mom was rummaging through our stuff? Why aren't you upset about that?"

"It's her house, she has a right to go through anything that's under her roof," he shot back.

"Well, nobody told me that. If I had known that, I never would have agreed to move in there."

"You should have known," He boomed.

"I should have known what? That at 30 years old I would have no right to privacy just because I married you and your mommy? That's absurd."

"It's not absurd! That's how good people are raised," he spat back instantly.

"Are you saying that I am not a good person?" the shrillness was building in my voice.

"Maybe," he shrugged.

"Really?" I replied even louder.

"I said, maybe," he said sneering his lip as he spoke.

"Oh, my God! This can't be happening!" I screamed at my reflection in the car window.

"Well, it is and it's because you left that for my mother, and what's worse is that she read it to my dad and he's really hurt."

Great, now he was bringing his dad into it. I tried to regain my composure and drop things back to a more reasonable decibel level, "I am sorry he is hurt, but she never should have been in my stuff to begin with."

Darren moved his face directly in front of mine and yelled, "You—left—it—out!" one word at a time for emphasis.

I pulled my head back to get away from him and bumped my head hard on the window. "Oh, my God, Darren! No—I—did—not!" I yelled back as hot tears ran down my face. "It was in the back of the chemistry notebook I asked you about, in the bottom of a drawer with a bunch of my underwear on top of it! How is that leaving it out?"

For a second, I saw his certainty waiver. Then he added arrogantly, "She likes to keep a clean house."

"That's no excuse!" I said with exasperation, "Oh, my God! This is insane." My eyes were on fire. I couldn't catch my breath.

"Stop crying!" he ordered.

"I won't!" I yelled back at him. "Don't tell me what to do!"

"I will! You hurt my parents, and you will do what I tell you to do!" he yelled back.

"What?!" I pleaded, "Are you kidding me? What the fuck, Darren! They hurt me! Actually, they hurt us! Why aren't you on my side with this? She went through my private stuff! She went through my underwear!... That's so gross!"

"I am done talking about this, "he said as he sat back.

"Well, I am not! I…"

"Save it...I don't want to hear it," he interrupted as he threw the car into reverse.

We rode in painful silence for the next twenty minutes as we made our way back to the house. When we arrived, Darren got out of the car and slammed the door before I could even get my seatbelt off.

By the time I got inside, Darren was nowhere to be seen. Thankfully, my parents were in their room, so I didn't have to explain his attitude or the tear streaks on my face. I went back to our room and found him in bed with the light out and his back to the door. I stood there in the dark for a while, unable to decide what to do.

I really wanted to talk this out. It seemed simple enough to me. Charlene invaded my privacy. It was unfortunate that happened. My words certainly were hurtful (believe me, I held nothing back), but she should never have gone through my things. At the very least, she could have warned me that anything I brought in the house would be subject to periodic search and seizure. A heads-up would have been nice. I thought I was staying with my new family. I didn't know I had moved into a police state.

When I walked into the dark bedroom, Darren was still awake. I could tell by his jagged breathing. I whispered at him, "Can we talk?" and got nothing but silence in response.

The heat was building in my eyes, but I was not going to let him know that I was crying again. It wasn't because he told me to stop, but because I hated crying, especially in an argument. It felt like weakness. The whole ordeal had caught me off balance, and I had reacted out of pure emotion. I lost control. I had never experienced anything quite like that before. Darren and I were not strangers to conflict. We had fights, but even in our most contentious moments there had been a sense of togetherness running underneath it all, like our marriage came first and disagreements were transient things that we might even laugh about later on.

This time, it was different. For the first time in 3 years, I felt a sense of disconnection from him, like the invisible cord between us that held us so tightly together had gone slack. Plus, the thought that someone had helped themselves to my writing, my ugliest thoughts, and darkest anxieties, made me physically ill. Despite the unceremonious condition of that notebook, those were hallowed pages. It was the only place I had that was completely mine. I was being vilified for the contents of my own brain. It felt like I had been gutted and my intestines had been ripped out.

In the background, I heard the master bedroom door open. My stomach clenched again, and the dark room started to spin a little. My parents were still awake. I didn't want them to know about any of this. I grabbed some fresh clothes, hurried into the bathroom, and turned on the shower. When the hot water hit my face, my stomach let go and so did the tears. I cried and puked and cried. I cried and puked so hard that I couldn't stand up straight.

I stayed there, doubled over in the shower and hoping that the water would drown out my sobs, until the hot water was gone. I didn't want the shower to end. I didn't want to go into the bedroom. I didn't want to smile and put on a show for my parents. I wanted to stay there until I disintegrated and washed away in little bits down the drain, but the cold water was more than I could take.

When I got out of the shower and finished up as slowly as I could. The face I saw in the mirror was puffy and splotched and distorted. It didn't even look like my face, at least not like the face I had known for the twenty-nine and a half years that came before this moment. That me would never have been in this situation. She would have flipped them all the bird and hitchhiked her way to anywhere to get away from bullshit like this. I wished that me was there in the mirror, but she wasn't. She was gone. All that was left was the pathetic me inside my exhausted body and the splotchy freak show that was staring back at me across the sink.

Looking back at it now, the choices seem so simple and clear. I should have marched right out into the living room and told my mother everything. I should have let her in. I should have let her help me. That was the only rational choice there was to make...but I didn't make it. I knew that once I opened that door, there would be no going back. Once my family learned what had happened, they would take my side—and they would never trust Charlene or Darren or anyone named Danky ever again. (It sounds like I'm being melodramatic, but I'm not. They loved Darren because he loved me, but once they changed their minds, that would be that. It would be a reaction born out of parental love and the instinct to protect me, but it would get ugly, they would take it too far, and sooner or later, I would have to turn around and defend Darren to them.)

When I went back to our room, Darren was asleep. I could tell by the low, metered, snores that rumbled from his side of the bed. I crawled gently into bed and spent the rest of the night staring at the ceiling. I think I slept at some point, but it didn't feel like it. The next morning, things weren't much different than the night before. Darren was angry and refused to look at me. He refused to talk to anyone. He ignored my parents, meeting their attempts at polite conversation with uncomfortably pointed silence. My gut still felt ripped open, and I looked like I had been punched in the face. There was no amount of make-up in the world that could hide it.

I spent the morning making excuses for my appearance and Darren's odd behavior. I don't know what my parents really thought, but they were satisfied enough that they didn't push us. When I told them we had to leave, they didn't ask any questions. We packed up our bags and left before noon.

Chapter 7

The car ride north was torture. With every mile, I felt worse. I felt trapped all over again. I knew that working through this was what I was supposed to do. We were married, not just screwing around or dating like a couple of kids. Even if I wanted to, I couldn't just quit. Everything was all bound together, now—bank accounts, car titles, all of our worldly possessions…and then, of course, there was *The Vow*…that hadn't gone away either. I tried talking about what had happened, but Darren wasn't willing. I tried to get him to talk about something…anything, but he wasn't interested in that either.

As we drove in silence, I watched the outside world fly by the window… all of the other places I could have been other than in that car. There was a light coating of snow blanketing everything we passed, even the ground inside the tree stands that lined the highway.

The snow and the dismal color of the sky magnified the dread that was overriding everything else. As I looked out at the tree-covered hills, I tried to imagine what it might have been like to live out there before the power grid or before indoor plumbing. I wondered how cold it would have been walking down those hills in the snow before high-tech outerwear or thermal socks. My life was so much easier than it would have been then, but at that moment, I would gladly have walked those hills naked with my hair on fire if it meant I did not have to be in this car, on this road, and headed toward this nightmare. At least I would have had my burning tresses to keep me warm for a little while.

Somewhere in West Virginia, I must have fallen asleep, because I was suddenly out of the car and standing alone in the snow, on one of the gentle hillsides I had seen through the window. Darren wasn't with me. There were no cars and no roads. There was just silence insulating the hills and the trees and the sparkling snow. It was beautiful.

The cold was oddly comforting. I closed my eyes and inhaled deeply forcing the clean, cold air into my lungs. I opened my eyes to watch my breath hit the air as I exhaled. For the first time in 24 hours, I felt peaceful.

Far away on the next hill, I saw a pale woman in a crimson medieval-era gown and leading a large white horse walking in my direction between the trees. Her image was shocking against the whiteness of the snow. Her wraithlike glide was slow and measured. I thought I knew her, but I couldn't remember how. Maybe I had read too many fantasy novels. Wherever she came from, it didn't matter to me. She was ominous and comforting all at the same time. I wasn't afraid. I was just rapt by her image.

She looked at me intensely as she came closer, gliding easily around the obstacles in her path as if the physical world was an afterthought. "Come with me," she said as she walked. She was still a good distance away from me, but I heard her voice like she was speaking right into my ear. "Come with me," she said again, as her eyes stared directly into mine. She walked in silence until she and her horse stood only a few feet in front of me. "We're waiting for you," she said as if it was something I should have already known.

"Who are you?" I said to her. She held her gaze and said nothing. Even the horse appeared to be looking right at me. "Please," I said, "tell me who you are."

"Your pain called me here," she said. "You already know what to do, but first, you must remember. Then, you will find your answers." The horse lowered his head, but she was motionless.

"Please, I don't understand." I felt drawn to her. I wanted to go to her, but I couldn't make my dream legs move.

"We will wait for you." She guided the horse around and started to glide away.

As she drifted out of sight, my brain snapped back into the car. We were entering the tunnel that led into Downtown Pittsburgh. We were almost there. The tension in the car was still there, but the images from my dream held my attention. I have always been an intense dreamer, but this felt like something else. It felt real. I felt somehow changed, but I couldn't pinpoint why or how. I could still see the woman clearly in my mind. She had seemed so familiar. I even felt like I knew the horse, which made absolutely no sense at all. I had only ever been around one horse, and that was when I was very young, and I only knew that because there was a picture to prove it. Still, the image of the woman and her horse made my chest vibrate. Whether it was some kind of psychic phenomenon or a dissociative fugue, I didn't really care. I wanted more of it.

There was no more time to indulge myself in warm, fuzzy feelings or the snow woman and her horse. The end of the tunnel opened up on the downtown skyline which meant that there were only about thirty minutes left between this hideous car ride and the exponentially greater hideousness that was waiting for me at the house. I wasn't entirely sure what was waiting for me, but I knew it wasn't good.

As we drove up the last hill before the house, Darren finally spoke. "You need to apologize. I don't know if that will be enough, but it's what you have to do." His words hit my ears like a buzz saw.

I didn't want to apologize. "You have to," he said again with more command in his voice. "You have to make this right."

I wanted to yell "What the fuck, Darren?!" but I held back and placidly said, "I will," instead.

After a few more minutes of silence, his tone softened, "you didn't do anything wrong, but thank you for fixing this."

I was stunned. This sudden switch knocked me off balance. Why couldn't he have said that earlier? Was this a trick? Or did he finally get it? Was he on my side, after all? If so, it would make the idea of going belly up in front of Charlene a tiny bit more tolerable.

A moment later we pulled into the driveway.

There was a coating of snow on the ground there, too. It wasn't the pretty white snow that had been on the hills out in the country, and it definitely wasn't the glistening perfection that coated the landscape of my dream. It was Pittsburgh snow, so it was covered by a film of grime that turned everything the color of cigarette ash or diesel exhaust.

We went into the house together, hauling our luggage in with us. As usual, there was an awkward moment at the door as we tried to manage our bags, remove our shoes, and close the door as quickly as possible. The lights were out, and only Sausage the cat came in to sniff at our bags before running away to hide.

"Ma!" Darren called out into the dark. "Ma!" he said louder. "Dad!" The overwhelming smell of cigarette smoke and dusty baseboard radiator heat filled the air. We had been away just long enough for me to lose my tolerance for it.

"Ma!" Darren called, again. We walked toward the back of the house, following the smoke trail that was hanging in the air. The low sound of a TV was coming from his parents' bedroom. Darren rounded the corner following the sound. I stayed back to let him enter alone.

"Ma," Darren said calmly as he entered.

Charlene said nothing and kept looking at the TV on top of the tall dresser by the door.

"Ma," he said firmly, "why won't you answer me?"

We all held our positions for what seemed like an eternity.

"Ma!" Darren said forcefully. "Hello…Ma!"

Charlene sighed before dragging on her cigarette. She exhaled a large puff of smoke through her mouth and her nose at the same time. At the end of it, she said "Hello" curtly as she held her gaze at the TV.

"Whatcha doin'?" he asked.

Charlene didn't answer.

"Where's Dad?" he asked, next.

She sucked pointedly on her cigarette and continued to say nothing.

There was an eternity of silence. I thought I was going to crawl out of my skin. As we stood there, Sausage wandered between us into the room. Halfway between the door and the bed, he stopped and scrunched his body into half its normal size before growling and running at full speed back out the way he came. I guess even the cat could sense what happening. He was the only one smart enough to leave.

"Ma, Alane has something she wants to say to you." Darren stepped to the side and waved me into the room.

I look at him like he was leading me to my execution. This was not at all how I wanted this to go. I wanted to talk it through and work up an organic moment of apology for the both of us. I didn't expect to throw myself on her sword the minute I walked through the door.

Darren squinted his eyes at me and waved again.

I stepped into the room and willed myself to look at Charlene's face in the inconsistent light of the TV. Before we left, she told me to start calling her "Ma," but that seemed wrong in this particular moment. Calling her "Charlene" seemed wrong, too, so I skipped that part and got straight to it. "I'm sorry you found my journal," I said quietly, "I had no intention of sharing any of that with you."

"Ha," she uttered sarcastically as she stared at the TV.

"I'm sorry that what I wrote hurt you," I said next followed by another long, uncomfortable silence. Darren looked at me like I should continue, but I had already apologized as much as I was willing to apologize, and I certainly wasn't about to grovel.

"Ma," Darren said calmly, "see, I told you she was sorry."

Charlene sat up quickly with an ease of movement that I had never witnessed from her before. I guess self-righteous indignation beats fibromyalgia. "She left that for me on purpose!" she exploded. Instant tears poured from her eyes. "She's not sorry! She's sick! She's sick!" She went on, pointing at me forcefully and flinging the ashes on the end of her cigarette into the air like confetti.

"I never intended for you to find my journal," I said, trying hard to remain calm.

"Journal? Journal?" Charlene said melodramatically, "That was no journal! That was no journal!"

"It was my journal," I said with less restraint. "You should never have read it."

"She's sick!" she spat out again before collapsing backward onto her pillows. "She left it for me to find!" She lit a new cigarette.

Darren motioned me out of the room and into our bedroom at the other end of the short hall. He closed the door quietly and turned to look at me. "Why did you do it?"

"What?!" I was stunned. I thought he understood what had happened. He had said so in the car.

"I said, why did you do it?" he said over-enunciating each word of the question as if English was suddenly my second language.

"I thought you said I didn't do anything wrong!" I enunciated back at him.

"That was before! Now, I understand what you did," he shouted in a whisper. "You left that shit out for my mother to find! It's right there!" He pointed to the bed behind me where Charlene had staged the notebook.

"That's not where I left it," I said louder and with a bit of a growl. "Do you want to see where it was? Do you?" I snatched the book off the bed and spun around on my heels to face the chest behind me.

"I don't care where it was, Alane."

"I'll show you exactly where it was!" I insisted as I threw open the drawer and shoved the book to the bottom of the drawer. I didn't even bother to fully reset my clothes on top of it, and it was already completely obscured. "There," I said, "it was there! Can you see it?"

"My mother said you left it for her. Are you calling her a liar?" Darren said smugly. He refused to look at the drawer.

"No, I did not!" I insisted, "Can you see it?"

He ignored the question, again, "Why would you do that to them, Alane?"

"I didn't do anything to them! I was trying *not* to do anything to them!" I shouted in full voice.

"Why are you lying? You know how I feel about liars."

"I am not lying!" I shouted back. I was about to lose it, entirely.

"Yes, she is!" Charlene yelled from down the hall before breaking into an over the top fit of sobbing. "She's trying to hurt me, Darren. Don't let her hurt me anymore…" she wailed.

Darren reached in the drawer and pulled out the notebook.

He opened it and found his chemistry notes. He flipped through page after page of notes followed by five or six blank pages before he found it. It was all there—my stressed out scrawling penmanship that comprised my makeshift journal mixed in with notes I had taken on interviews and job postings. Darren was hesitating. I could see that his certainty was shaken based on the evidence in front of him.

"Why, Alane…why did you do this?" Darren asked after the sound of his mother's wailing started up again down the hall.

I was mortified. I wasn't used to being intellectually violated like this. Never before had my private conversations with myself been invaded like that—ever—and never had they been used against me. I knew marriage would mean that some things would be different and that I would have to consider other people more often than before, but this fiasco was too much. I no idea what to do. No one was listening to reason. No one was even talking; there was only crying, yelling, and accusations. All I wanted to do was run, but I couldn't. Even if I mustered the strength to leave, Darren was blocking the door, and the only windows in the room were too high up off the ground below for me to jump safely. I was completely trapped.

"I didn't do this," I replied, trying hard to regain a more reasonable tone.

"You did! It's right here in your handwriting!" little droplets of spit flew out of Darren's mouth and hit me in the face.

"No! I mean I didn't leave it out for your mother to find," I said as I wiped my face. "It was my private stuff...why did she go through my things?"

"Didn't you at least think that *I* would read it?" he yelled and spat, sending several little projectile droplets straight into my eye.

I blinked and wiped at my eye as I tried to get words to come out of my mouth. The argument was starting to wear me down, and the surprise eyeball spit bath was making it hard for me to stay focused. "No! I asked you! You said you didn't want that stupid notebook anymore. You were going to throw it away!"

"So, you were just going to keep lying to me," he said accusingly. "You were going to smile and pretend to be nice to their faces while you were thinking nasty things all along."

"Yes," I replied, "yes, I was."

"So, you admit to being a liar!" he yelled.

"Where I come from, we call it tact!" I said shouted.

Darren threw up his hand and rolled his eyes, "Jesus Christ, that again!"

"Yes," I volleyed back, "that again! I had to work some things through for myself. It's not like I could talk to you about it. You wouldn't have listened even if I had."

"You are a liar!" he yelled at the top of his voice.

I heard Charlene wail "Liar!" in the background like a one-woman Greek chorus.

"And there you have it…" I said with exasperation.

"What the fuck, Alane?" Darren shot back.

…and the chorus wailed out "Liar! Liar! Liarrrrrrr!"

"It's not like I could talk to my parents about it," I said. "I don't have any friends left, and you think counseling is bullshit, so what was I supposed to do?...and I am not a liar!"

"We are married, you are supposed to tell me everything and for fuck's sake, who keeps a journal?" Darren said getting louder as he said it.

"Lots of people," I said defiantly.

"No, they don't!" he barked. Another chorus of "Liar!" rang out from down the hall. "When did you start keeping a journal?"

"When I was six!"

"Bullshit!" he shouted.

The chorus continued on in the background with wails of "Liar!" and a "Bullshit" added in for a little extra flair. Charlene had told me in the past that she was personally offended by the use of foul language. I guess she was willing to offend her own delicate sensibilities for such a special circumstance.

"You are a fucking liar!" Darren went on. "I can't believe I married such a fucking liar...What hateful things did you write about me?"

"What...when I was six?" I said sarcastically.

"Damn it, Alane!" he replied. "Not when you were six! In your other journals? What lies have you written about me in them?"

"None!" I spat back.

"Bullshit!" he yelled.

"No Bullshit! I haven't written a single lie about you in any journal I have ever had! Not even that one!" I yelled back.

"There were others?" he asked incredulously.

"Yes! Of course! You saw me writing in them. My mom gives me a new blank one almost every year at Christmas. Christ, she gave you a blank one just last year!"

Darren hesitated. I could see that he was remembering.

"She talked shit about you, too," Charlene shouted from her bedroom...

...and Darren was once again impervious to rational thought. "Great...just great..." he said at me as he held the notebook up in front of my face. Then he turned toward the door and grabbed the knob.

"Can I have my journal, please?" I said as steadily as I could.

"You mean *my chemistry notebook*?" He turned back around sharply holding the notebook up between us, again. "No, you can't have *my chemistry notebook*. I want to read what you wrote about me in my chemistry notebook for myself."

"Darren!" I shouted as he turned and stormed out of the room, slamming the door behind him.

I stood there dumbstruck. I heard Darren slam the kitchen door. His mother did the same not long after. I could hear them going back and forth out on the porch, but what they were saying, exactly, was drowned out by the high-pitched ringing and the pounding of my pulse in both of my ears. I couldn't catch my breath, and my guts were wound into an ever-tightening knot. I just stood there hyperventilating and staring at the hollow plywood door that separated me from the rest of the house.

The room started spinning. I guess I had been hyperventilating through that whole fiasco without realizing it. I sat straight down on the floor. It seemed safer to sit by choice than to faint and risk cracking my skull on any of Charlene's precious furniture. It would have been one more thing added to the list of my egregious offenses, I was sure.

My brain tried to sort through what had just happened. The whole thing had gone totally sideways. Darren had said that he believed me. I trusted him, and I apologized for my part in it. I honestly thought she was going to apologize, too. I thought that we were going to cry and hug it out and get on with the rest of our lives.

Holy shit was I wrong.

I had been making it work in that house for months. I had cooked and cleaned and shopped as Charlene instructed. I had listened to her commentaries about my clothes, my family, and the life I had lived before becoming her son's property. Charlene rarely came right out and said exactly what was on her mind, but she always got her point across, and always left herself a way out if Darren or Earl walked into the room. She delivered everything as a warped morality play about a mythical character she called *Somebody*. *Somebody* was usually attacking her directly in some way, and *Somebody* almost always met some terrible fate. *Somebody* was usually also to blame whenever anything in the house was out of place. Most of Charlene's stories about *Somebody* sounded remarkably (if not exactly) like something I had done. I was never really sure how *Somebody's* choice to wear a thong instead of regular underwear was able to offend an entire table full of people (when no one would have known it was there had Charlene not been talking freely about what she saw in my laundry) or why anyone would care what *Somebody* might choose to wear on her ass. But really, who am I to question the emotional power of a thong?

As the days passed, *Somebody* started coming up more and more often, and Charlene stopped talking to me directly about whatever it was that *Somebody* had done. Instead, she would pace through the house talking loudly into the air, "*Somebody* left a dirty towel on the floor. *Somebody* hasn't cleaned the litter box. *Somebody* needs to carry her weight…" I was never officially named as *Somebody*, but it wasn't hard to figure out. Darren apologized once or twice for the towels on the floor since they were his anyway. Charlene responded to him with a cheerful, "That's okay, I didn't know it was yours."

Earl, on the other hand, had been nice enough. He was quiet and usually kept to himself. He would laugh at Charlene's shotgun approach to household management and then leave the room before she had a chance to really get into it. For his contribution to my general experience in the house, he would time my showers and count the number of times I used the toilet throughout the day, but for the most part, he kept to himself.

I never really expected living in their house to be fun. I also expected to work hard and pull my weight. What I didn't expect was full-fledged indentured servitude. It's not like I wasn't trying. Darren and I talked about it. Sometimes he commiserated. Occasionally, like with the towels on the floor, he would speak up on my behalf. Most of the time, however, he just said, "don't worry about it," or "that's not what she means," or he would shrug and change the subject.

...and that was her opinion of me before the notebook. What was to come afterward had no chance of being any better. I stayed there on the floor for a long time, clutching my stomach and rocking back and forth as I stared at the matted green carpet. Hot tears welled up in my eyes. I didn't want to cry. I didn't want Darren to see me like this. I didn't want to give Charlene the satisfaction. I never intended for anyone to read any of that. I never really expected to read it again, myself. I was alone in a strange place with relative strangers 10 feet away from me almost all of the time. I just needed some place to put my frustration. I just needed to rearrange the shit in my head. It wasn't a diabolical plot to harm anyone.

I don't know how long I sat there. I kept rocking back and forth with my forearms jammed into my gut hoping that something would tell me what to do next. I sat there in the floor until the light through the tiny windows faded from dreary Pittsburgh gray to darkness.

Not long after, Darren and Charlene came back in the house. Their voices were low, and their tone seemed calm—maybe too calm. Charlene started clanging pots and pans in the kitchen which meant that Earl would be home soon.

I heard the clank of the storm door not long after. Earl muttered a forced "Happy New Year!" as he unloaded his things into the corner and took off his shoes.

I heard Darren reply with, "Hey, Dad," in a low voice.

The kitchen went quiet. They must have been staring at each other, or maybe they had secret hand signals for special occasions that I didn't know about. Whatever it was, it was nerve wracking.

Earl finally broke the silence with forced, "Happy New Year," followed by a very prickly, "…Dear!"

Charlene let out a flat, dismissive, "hello." From there, I could only hear Charlene slamming around as she set the table.

Not long after, Darren opened the door to our room. "What are you doing?" he asked impatiently as if I had been keeping them waiting.

I just sat there, staring at the carpet. The scent of fried meat and cigarette smoke wafted in from the hallway. My knotted stomach started to flop over.

"What are you doing?" he said, again. "Dinner's ready and Dad's home. Come on."

Did he really think I was going to go out there to sit next to the three of them at their cramped kitchen dinette? Did he really think I could look at any of them, let alone eat, after what just happened? I scanned through my options in my head. The window escape route was still no good, but it was starting to look better. Maybe I would only break one of my legs, instead of both, leaving me one good leg for hobbling away. The only other paths to freedom went straight through the kitchen, and I didn't think I could make it through all three of them or the wall of Charlene's cigarette smoke. It seemed that I was stuck, at least for the immediate future.

"Let's go," he said, again.

"I can't," I said quietly. My voice was hoarse and shaky from all the yelling and crying.

"You need to apologize to Dad," he insisted.

"No," I said.

"You will… let's go," he said firmly and walked out of the room.

I hated him in that moment. Who was he to tell me what I would or wouldn't do? I just wanted out, but all of my options were bad. If I tried to leave, I would be screwed. I had nowhere to go and no money for a hotel. If I stayed in the room, I'd be screwed. I'd still be cornered, and I would be at the mercy of the three of them. This was a nightmare that wasn't going away. I had no choice but to face it.

I pulled myself up off the floor and reluctantly stepped into the hall. Darren was standing there waiting for me. He said nothing as he turned to walk toward the kitchen. I wasn't ready to follow him. I darted into the bathroom and closed myself in. I leaned my weight on the sink and looked up at my reflection in the mirror. I was a bloated, splotchy mess, again—death warmed over, as my mother always said. The thought of my mother made me well up, again. What in the world would she think of me if she knew about any of this?

The longer I stared at myself, the worse I looked. I was on the cusp of full-on zombie, and honestly, it didn't seem like a bad option. I felt like I was going to die anyway. If I could have made myself a zombie just after I kicked it, it would have been perfect. The element of surprise would have been on my side. With zombie strength and no active pain receptors, I could have exacted a degree of justice on all of them as I staggered and chomped my way toward the door. At the very least, they might have backed off and let me leave. I would have, too, unless my insatiable need to eat their faces off was difficult to overcome. Zombies tend to be pretty single-minded.

"Dinner's ready!" Darren barked loudly through the door as he rapped on it, making it rattle on its hinges and sending a jolt of adrenaline through my heart. (I had just started wondering if George Romero had been thinking of his mother-in-law when he made *Night of the Living Dead*. It seemed unlikely, but this was the second time the thought had come up for me, and I hadn't been in the greater Pittsburgh area that long. It all somehow had to be related.)

I turned my back on my reflection and re-inventoried my lack of options. I wanted to run now more than ever. I didn't want to deal with this mess any more than I already had, but the bathroom window was even smaller and higher off the ground than the one in the bedroom. I was still trapped. "Okay, coming," I said. I tried to sound upbeat, but it came out more like a croak.

"Hurry up," he added.

I turned and took one last look at myself in the mirror. I wasn't going to run away. I had to just get on with it.

I walked the few steps from the bathroom to the kitchen and stepped into the fluorescent light. No one looked up. My mom's voice ran through my mind, "Head up…shoulders back…and onward." That was always her advice when things were bad. Following her instruction, I took my place at the cramped dinette next to Charlene.

"Hey there," Earl said halfheartedly through a mouthful of food. It was something, at least.

"Hey," I said quietly in return. "Happy New Year."

"Happy New Year to you, too," he said in an exhausted and weirdly sincere tone.

"YES!" Charlene blurted out sarcastically, "Happy New Year! It's such a nice time!" Little bits of buttered corn flew out of her mouth as she spoke.

My thoughts of zombie-ism resurfaced. Maybe Charlene's face would taste like corn, or maybe it would have a nice salted butter finish on my highly evolved zombie palate. It wasn't completely unreasonable to assume that a zombie could have flavor preferences.

"Dear!" Earl said without looking up from his food.

"What!" Charlene spat at him.

No one responded.

Then Charlene spat some more, "She's ruined everything! Look at what she has done to us!"

"I don't think she meant to hurt you. Did she apologize?" Earl asked turning toward Darren.

"Yes, she did," Darren said. They were carrying on like I wasn't even in the room.

"There," Earl said as he turned to Charlene, "that's great. She's apologized. That's what you wanted."

"It's not what I wanted!" Charlene spat out, this time without a spray of corn bits. She must not have had time to reload. I was going to need her to eat more if zombie-me was going to really enjoy eating her face. "She didn't mean it. She didn't mean it!"

"Did you mean it?" Earl asked.

Seeing this as my only chance for help, I calmly said, "Yes, I meant it." It really didn't matter that I had rescinded all issued apologies for the last 24 hours on the grounds of entrapment and forced emotional crapulence. I wasn't that stupid.

"See, Dear, she meant it," he said to Charlene while he motioned my direction and continued eating all at the same time. No matter how he really felt about it, I was getting the sense that he wanted this to end just as much as I did. I decided to keep quiet and let him run with it.

"No, she didn't!" Charlene cried. She pushed herself away from the table and reached for her cigarettes.

"Dear!" Earl said, again.

"She apologized, Dad," Darren chimed in.

Finally! I thought to myself.

"...but she could have said more," he added.

"What?!" I blurted out before I realized I was speaking.

"Well…you could have done better," he said without a look at me.

"Are you kidding me?" I felt myself flush and tremble.

"Well, you could have," Darren said dismissively.

"See…see!" Charlene squawked at Earl as she flailed her hand in front of my face.

"This is unbelievable," I said aloud. The filter between my mouth and brain had completely eroded away.

"She is evil!" Charlene said. "Even Krystal thinks so! She said that I shouldn't have let her back in the house."

"Well…" Earl started.

"Even Krystal thinks so?" Darren looked at his mother. "Why does she know about this?"

"Because I told her about it," Charlene said, adding, "She was really upset when she read it."

"She read it, too?" I cried in disbelief. "How many people know about this?"

"I needed help, so I told everybody who needed to know."

"Who needed to know, Ma?" Darren insisted.

"I made a copy for each of us. I sent one to Krystal and one to your grandfather. Betty and Paula thought it was horrible, too. That's exactly what they said about it. Horrible, just horrible."

"You made copies?" my anger was building.

"Ma!" Darren shouted.

"I did. I'm not going to tell you where they are, either. Either of you. If I die, Krystal knows where they are and will give them to our attorney."

"Do you have an attorney?" Darren directed at Earl.

"No," he said flatly.

"Well, we will. She's not getting anything of mine when I die!"

Charlene said, pointing at me with her cigarette sending ashes flying all over the table and my lap. The three of them then burst into a flurry of hand flailing and corn spitting in Pittsburghese, most of which I couldn't understand, but it wasn't hard to get the gist.

All of this was really getting zombie-me worked up. I kept imagining what it would be like to eat human flesh and if brains are considered a staple of zombie cuisine or if some zombie palates are more refined than others. Would only the most discriminating zombies be able to appreciate an aged Nobel Laureate's gray matter or is one brain just as tasty as another? Would I find the zombie lifestyle fulfilling or would it just become a daily grind like everything else? And would I be able to only eat Charlene's face off and spare Earl's? Maybe there could be such a thing as transient zombie-ism…or maybe just zombitarianism…or maybe ovo-lacto-zombitarianism…all the flesh and brain-eating fun of zombitarianism with some eggs and cheese so you can still enjoy yourself at a party without eating the host.

Another flurry of Pittsburghese cut right through my thoughts, and I remembered what my mind was trying to avoid.

"I don't want anything of yours," I yelled. I turned to Charlene and looked her right in the eye. "I told you earlier today that I did not leave that for you to find. And furthermore, I never thought you would have the gall to rifle through my underwear while I was gone."

"This is my house and I can look at anything I want in my house!" Charlene sniped back at me.

"Well, I wish you had told me that before!" I shot back. "I am almost 30 years old, and I lived on my own for a long time before I ever even met your son. My own parents don't go through my things when I go to visit them."

"Well, maybe they should," she said.

"No, they shouldn't. You are absurd." I blasted. "Look, I am sorry that what I wrote hurt you, but you invaded my privacy! And frankly, it was none of your business!"

"What sort of person writes like that?" she cut over me at Earl like I wasn't speaking. "A liar! That's what!"

"I am not a liar!" I said with building fury.

"You said nice things to my face and then wrote all those evil words in that notebook. That's lying!" she screamed.

"That's tact!" I boomed back. The room went silent except for Charlene who was sucking air in an out of her nostrils like a charging bull. I saw my opening and continued, "I was taught to use a journal to work through my emotions rather than just blurting out what I think all the time."

"What idiot taught you that bullshit?" she asked arrogantly.

"My mother!" I shot back. There was another long pause. I think Darren and Earl would have crawled under the table if there had been enough room.

"Well…" Charlene started with a snide laugh.

"Are you going to insult my mother, too? Are going to call her a liar?" I boomed.

Charlene smirked, "The apple doesn't fall far…"

"Alright, that's enough," Earl interjected. Little beads of sweat had formed between the gray stubble on his balding head "Charlene, she apologized. Just let it go." He spoke with a forcefulness that I had never heard from him before.

"I can't just let it go! She ruining Darren's life!" she cried melodramatically.

"Ma! She's not ruining my life," Darren insisted.

"I can't do this anymore," I said with unexpected calmness. It was awkward. "I am going to bed." I stood up and started to leave the room.

"Good night," Earl said equally awkwardly.

I headed back to the bedroom and burst into tears as soon my foot touched the matted green carpet. This was insane. Charlene made copies. She made copies and distributed them to the neighbors and to Wall-Cat. For all I knew she had copied them to a thumb drive and shoved it down Sausage the cat's throat for safe keeping.

I could hear the three of them continuing on with the argument in the kitchen. From a distance, it sounded like Darren was trying to argue in my favor, but I couldn't be sure. He had already turned on me more than once. There was no way I could trust him at that moment, even if he was trying to back me up.

I stood in the middle of the room with the lights off listening to the insanity cloud of Pittsburghese that was building just a few short feet away. Through the split in the curtain covering the tiny windows, I could see fireworks going off in the distance. Wherever that was, people were celebrating the New Year. When I was a kid, Mom told me that whatever I was doing on New Year's Eve was what I would be doing the most throughout the year to come. This New Year's Eve had been a nightmare. I crawled into bed, turned my back to the door, and tried to sleep. I didn't know if I could take a whole year of this.

Chapter 8

Sometime before dawn, I woke up. Darren was asleep next to me. He was sprawled on his back with his mouth slack and open, snoring. The stench of stale beer wafted into the air with every exhalation.

...lovely...

The look of him turned my stomach. He looked like a sweaty, naked, asshole, frat boy sleeping off a kegger. He had been drunk before. In fact, he had been asshole drunk before, but this was the first time I saw him exactly this way...and I hated it. I hated everything about him. All the stupid, childish things that I had ignored because he was just having a good time or just letting off some steam had resurfaced and congealed into the smelly blob lying next to me.

I had never felt anything like this before about anybody. I hated him. I hated him, and I hated his mother. Even though Earl had tried to calm things down, I hated him, too. I was angry. I was hurt. I was alone. I was trapped.

The night before, I could hear their conversation clearly enough. It wasn't as much of a conversation as it was just Charlene blathering on about all the ways I had ruined their family and their holiday. I heard her scream that I was the devil and that I was evil and that Darren should divorce me. They just let her go on. Occasionally Earl would say, "Dear," in varying degrees of emphasis and emotions, but mostly he just remained quiet.

It was unbearable. I couldn't believe this was happening. I knew that what I had written was awful. That was the whole reason I wrote it down. I needed those feelings to pass. I knew that they were irrational. I handled them the best way I could short of talking to a shrink. We had no money for that, anyway. We didn't even have enough money for a blank notebook.

Darren hadn't even tried to stay neutral, he had just told me what I wanted to hear to get me to do what he wanted and then he turned on me. He called me a liar. He said I was a liar for not telling his mother to fuck off and leave me alone. He said I was a liar for not telling his mother that I didn't like the food she cooked for us for free. He said I was a liar for not shouting about how offended I was when she said everyone from the South was "stupid" and that she didn't want her grandchildren to "talk funny." He said that I should only talk to him about my feelings—that nobody keeps a journal, and if I do, then I am just hiding things from him. He said that when we got married, we became one—not two separate people—one person—and I shouldn't keep thinking only about myself.

It was a punch right in the gut. No one told me that a vow of marriage meant giving up myself and my basic civil rights entirely. Darren had said he loved my independence and self-reliance. I thought he married me because he loved and respected me. No matter how we started, in that moment, I couldn't trust him.

I wanted out. I wanted to run as far away as I could, no matter the consequences. I wasn't welcome there anymore. Charlene obviously didn't want me there. She called me the Devil, for God's sake. It wasn't as if she was unclear about her feelings. Every fiber of my being wanted out. It was like the Universe was whispering intently in my ear, telling me over and over again to go.

I ran a mental inventory of my personal possessions, where they were, and how much I thought I could shove into my car before anyone woke up. My bags were still packed. I was still dressed. I hadn't even been in that house for a full 24 hours yet. I had a window of opportunity; I should take it. I could do it. This was it.

As the first gray light of the day started to creep into the room, I made my move. Cautiously, I picked my way over Darren's sprawling body. The bed squeaked and bounced with the slightest movement, causing him to stir and sputter slightly before slipping back into his rhythmic snore. Once my feet were on the floor, I froze. All of the practical things I thought I would need and all of the things that Charlene could destroy went firing through my head… my certificates…my licenses…that damned green notebook…my old my photos and videos…gifts from my dead grandparents…irreplaceable keepsakes…the tangible remains of my entire life story were held hostage in that house. I knew I had to liberate what I could in the little time I had left.

Maneuvering quietly in that tiny room was a challenge. No matter how careful I tried to be, everything made a noise. I squatted down and opened the plastic file box that housed all of our critical documents. Usually, I kept things like that perfectly organized, but this time it was a mess. I couldn't be sure if I had let it get that bad or if Charlene had rifled through it while we were gone. Either way, it was a mess. I started panicking. I couldn't breathe. I couldn't make sense of what I was looking at. *Fuck it,* I thought, *just take the whole thing.* As I reached for the lid, I lost my balance and rocked backward hard against the dresser.

"What are you doing?" Darren said as he sat straight up like a corpse with rigor mortis.

"Holy shit!" I whispered hard. My heart jumped up into my throat. Darren stared at me with wide, unblinking eyes. I hadn't thought this part through at all. "Uhh…just going through some things. I didn't want to wake your parents."

"Happy New Year," he said.

"Um, yeah…Happy New Year," I said in return.

…that was weird…

I was hoping that he was just talking in his sleep.

"I'm sorry about last night," he said stiffly and still without blinking.

…also weird…

I looked at him without saying anything in return, hoping that he would collapse backward and start snoring.

"Really…I'm sorry," he said as he blinked and swung his legs off the side of the bed.

Shit, I thought. We both sat there in silence for what felt like forever. I felt like I should say something, but nothing seemed right. Finally, I pushed out, "why?" in a low voice. It was the only thing that came to mind that didn't involve a string of profanity in one way or another.

Darren flung himself on the floor in a burst of movement. He crawled toward me on his hands and knees and positioned his face right in front of mine. His eyes were wide and intense. "I'm… sorry…" he said slowly. His eyes darted back and forth from my right eye to my left eye.

"Why?" I said again with more defiance.

"You know why."

"No, I don't. Tell me why."

"Because we're married," he said.

I waited for more words to follow. That couldn't really be all he had to say about it. When it was clear he was waiting for me to speak next, I said, "That's it?" It was really more of a statement than a question.

"That's everything," he answered right away. "We're married, and we should be together on these things." Now I was sure he was awake. He couldn't be that intentionally vague in his sleep. It had to be a trick.

"So," I started cautiously, "you get that you should have backed me up in there last night?"

"We're married, so yes." His face was still inches from mine. His eyes were still darting back and forth.

"So…do you think this was my fault or not?" I really wanted him out of my face.

"It was your fault, but Ma should have let it go," he replied instantly, puffing more stale beer breath up my nostrils.

"In the car, you said it wasn't my fault."

He considered this for a second. "You should never have written that down," he said insistently.

"I can't go through this again." I crawled backward up the front of the dresser to get away from his face.

Darren sat back unsteadily. "Just admit that you shouldn't have done it," he said with exasperation.

I recoiled. "I'll admit that I should never have pushed for us to move here. I'll admit that I should never have left it here. But I will never admit that I shouldn't have done it."

"I want to put this to bed," he said, ignoring what I just said.

"So do I," I insisted. It was an honest response even if my idea of putting it to bed looked really different from his.

"Ok, then," he said like we had reached an agreement, "I told Ma that she needs to apologize to you and that you would apologize to her and that we would end it."

"I apologized yesterday," I pushed back, "and where is my notebook?"

"Ma's keeping it," Darren said like it was obvious.

"It's not hers to keep," I insisted.

"Don't worry about it," he said dismissively.

"I'm already worried about it," I said, "I've been worried about it."

He stood up and grabbed his pants off the floor. "It was my notebook anyway. I told her she can have it," he said flippantly. "I need breakfast," he said and left the room.

This was insane. I wanted to leave, but the window for fleeing in the dark of night had closed. If I went now, there would be a scene and fight. If I left now, he could shut off the credit cards before I made it to the first gas station. He could have even disabled my phone if he wanted to. He had insisted that everything be in his name or both names at the very least. I hadn't thought a thing about it before that moment. I was so tired. I didn't even know if I could drive. I should have driven away in the dark, consequences be damned. At 2:00 a.m. I was so certain. Now, I wasn't.

Needless to say, I stayed. The rest of that day was a strange combination of angry silence and uncomfortable small talk. Charlene hardly came out of her room all day. When she did, she would sigh and fling her lump of a body into her chair in the kitchen where she would pass the time by smoking and sighing. From time to time she would accept a New Year's Day phone call which gave her a chance to tell the story to even more people and then ask them over and over again if they could believe it. Each time, the story got a little longer and little more dramatic. By night, it sounded like I had plastered large font copies of everything all over the walls and then danced naked around a bonfire in the middle of the living room floor. On the up side, the more she talked and the more the story changed, the angrier Darren got. Even Earl couldn't take it anymore. He stopped giving her the phone, but thanks to caller ID, she just called them back.

The days that followed were mostly the same. Darren and I tried to stay away from the house as much as we could. Inside the house, I kept to myself and tried to stay out of sight. Charlene's story mutated every time she rehashed it, making it harder and harder for Darren and Earl to agree with her. As the week went on, her version of things barely resembled the actual events, which left Darren no choice but to defend me, which, of course, prompted Charlene to pull out the notebook and start reading it aloud as a diversion, which sent Earl skulking into whatever room was farthest away from all of it, which, of course, resulted in a round of crying and wailing from inside a fresh wall of cigarette smoke. Oh, yes, and don't forget the mandatory family dinner at the kitchen table every single night.

To be blunt, the whole thing was one big shit show.

This went on for two whole weeks before Charlene broke it for good. All it took was one final phone call with Wall-Cat to send her into a full on, eyes rolling into the back of her head, pea soup spewing, life-altering rant during which she pronounced to Darren, "She's the Devil! She's the Devil!" and topped it off with, "Divorce that bitch!"

I wasn't in the room for that one, but I heard all of it just the same. She was a tad loud when she was crazy.

From down the hall, I heard Darren's breathing getting harder before he burst out loud enough to shake the walls, "Enough! That's enough! I can't take it anymore."

Charlene barely hesitated for half a second before screaming at the top of her lungs, "It's never gonna be enough! Why are you letting her do this to me! That devil bitch is ruining our family!"

"Ma! Right now, you're the one ruining our family! She's done everything you've asked. You've treated her like shit, and she's still here trying to make you happy for me! I can't take it anymore! This shit is over!"

"It's only over when I say it's over!" Charlene said as she started up again. "You're living in my house!"

"Dear!" Earl interjected sternly.

Charlene shrieked, "If you don't divorce her, then you're a liar, just like she is!"

"Dear!" Earl interjected again.

Darren instantly became eerily calm, "That's great, Ma."

Charlene must have expected that the word "liar" thrown directly at Darren instead of me would have been enough to buckle him at the knees. She must have thought he would end things with me right there. I know that's what I thought was coming next. I had already started packing my bags. Instead, after a long wordless pause, Darren stormed down the hall to our room and slammed the door behind him.

"Pack everything," he said, "We're leaving in the morning."

I was frozen in place.

"Can we stay with your parents?" he asked.

"I'm sure. How are we going to move everything?" It had taken a U-Haul and two cars to get everything out of Iowa.

"We will take what we can and come back for the rest once we find our own place," he said with a certainty that I hadn't heard from him for quite a while.

"Are you sure?" I asked. This whole thing had been a wild and gut-wrenching ride. If he left with me, things with his mother would never be the same.

Without hesitation he said, "I'm sure…do you love me?

"Yes…do you still love me?"

"Yes." He dropped his gaze to the floor. "Can you forgive me?"

"Yes."

"Then, I'm sorry," he said as he looked up at me. "I thought the journal was bad, but you stayed, and you took everything she threw at you. You did that for me. Nobody deserves this shit. I can't stay here anymore."

"You don't want a divorce?" I asked. No hint of sarcasm or defiance was left in me.

"No, I don't want a divorce!" he shot back with panic. "I love you. You are my wife. My fucked up mother doesn't get to ruin that."

"I love you, too," was all I could say.

Charlene might never know how close she was to getting her wish. Only a few seconds before, I was ready to walk out the door and never look back. She just had to keep pushing, and it blew up in her face. Despite all of the doubt and hatred that had been going through my head for the last two weeks, in that moment, he chose me. I knew that he loved me, and the rest of it didn't matter.

Charlene had driven Darren back to me. Thanks to her, he remembered that he loved me. Thanks to her, he said that he was sorry. She gave me my husband back, and thanks to her, we left.

Our marriage was mortally wounded on that awful day in Verona. It's where it should have ended. It's hard to admit that Charlene was right, at least about the divorce part. That New Year's Eve, alone, should have been enough to send me screaming into the night. It should have ended it for me. For God's sake, she called me a bitch and the Devil. (Opinions are mixed on my "bitch" status, and I assume that if I really am the Devil, someone would have told me by now or there would have been a blood sacrifice on one of my birthdays or something.) I should have let Charlene win the fight, so I could celebrate winning the war as I drove southward on my own toward a better future…

…but I didn't.

I thought it was love that saved our marriage that day. It wasn't. It was only my ego and my childish belief that love can overcome all obstacles.

Chapter 9

I've always been weirdly aware of my own mortality. As a little girl, I was unreasonably worried about what happens when you die, even though death, itself, was more of an abstract concept rather than a tangible experience. At least once a year, I was forced to endure the stories about Jesus and the Crucifixion, but despite all of the torture, things seemed to turn out okay in the end. In fact, based on my brief time in Sunday school, it always seemed to me that I should be looking forward to death, even if the descriptions of heaven sounded pretty dull. Walking around on streets of gold and singing praises over and over and over again for eternity sounded more like nicely decorated punishment to me. Still, I found the whole Christian outlook on death and the afterlife to be pretty confusing. If everybody was saved and going to heaven, then why were we all procrastinating and hanging out here, and if heaven is so great, why does everybody cry so much when someone dies? It always seemed to me like a party would be more appropriate than a funeral. My Sunday school teacher told me that it was a thoroughly inappropriate thing to say and that my family must be Irish. I didn't know what that meant, but I thought maybe it would be nice to be Irish. My mom didn't make me go back after that and told my grandparents that she was leaving my religious future up to me.

Even without church and without being baptized, I never really feared death. What I feared was dying. That was the sticking point for me. Pain didn't excite me at all, and every story in every history class I ever took ended up with lots and lots of people dying brutal, horrifying deaths. There were wars where people were tortured and blown apart, racial and cultural genocide where people were tortured and torn apart, ancient religious rituals where people were tortured and cut apart—everything seemed to end with torture and coming apart, somehow. Even the seemingly good stuff like doctors courageously treating the sick often ended with suffering and painful dismemberment. As they say, sometimes the cure is worse than the disease. I don't know who "they" are, but that had to come from somewhere.

When I was a kid, I saw ghosts and spirits all the time. It wasn't like what you see in the movies or on TV. They weren't my invisible friends. I never talked to the strange lady in the hall like she was a perfectly normal person just hanging around outside my room. I might not have known exactly what they were at the time, but I knew they were not flesh and blood. I knew that they were something else, and I knew that other people had no idea they were there.

Sometimes they scared the hell out of me, especially the shadowy ones that lingered in doorways and around corners. I could see them peering around corners and watching me from down the hall while I ate dinner every night. There were only a few times that they ever got any closer than that, but those times were memorable since they were usually punctuated by the shaking of my bed or the rattling of a ceramic bunny on my dresser. My mother told me I had a vivid imagination, but I saw her checking every now and then, as she walked a little faster through the dimmer parts of the house.

Most of the time, though, my ghosts were just hanging around, like translucent people, watching me. They were still frightening, but I got used to them—eventually. They were just a part of the world, like mosquitos in the summertime. They're always around to annoy you, but you know they must have some greater purpose in the grand scheme of the universe.

Sometimes they would try to talk to me. When they did, I usually freaked out which meant that whatever deep insight they had for me was completely lost in the shower of terrified shrieking that I sprayed at them. I have tried to settle down about it over the years, but I just can't seem to relax about it. As normal as these things are for me, it's still most likely a dead person talking at me. That's fucked up, even if it is normal.

Darren saw one of my ghost people when we were first together. I thought it would be the end of our involvement, but it wasn't. Instead, he seemed to love it. He even named it. He called it the Blue Guy. It wasn't a particularly creative name, but it got his point across and confirmed that he did, indeed see the same, ephemeral, blue creature hanging out in the corner of my apartment bedroom. Darren thought his presence meant that we were destined to be together. On my end, the validation was nice to have for once, and the whole romantic destiny thing seemed like a really sweet idea. At the time, it didn't seem weird that Darren was all atwitter about the possibility of a supernatural romantic plot twist, but now, it really does. I should have been the one who was fawning over fantasies. After all, I was biologically the girl in the relationship.

Darren never saw any of the others that I know about. He heard several of them over the years. Those, of course, were some of the more terrifying ones that I can remember. I would know that someone was there, lurking around in the basement or outside the window. He would be dubious until some sort of repetitive thwacking or unidentifiable dragging sounds would start.

The most frightening ghost moment had happened when we

were still in school. We were in bed one night when I told him there was someone running around the outside of our house. He got out of bed to look outside and said, "You're imagining things. There is nothing out there."

"I can see it," I insisted, "it's running in circles around the house. I think it wants in. I'm really afraid."

Darren said, "Don't worry about it. It's fine." The romance of the supernatural had apparently waned for him.

"It's not fine," I replied. "It wants to come inside." The terror was building inside me as the human-sized thing stopped running long enough to stare directly at me through the window over Darren's shoulder.

"You're being ridiculous. Go to sleep," he said as he got back in bed and turned over.

I couldn't lie down. I couldn't relax. I couldn't see the thing anymore because he ran from the window as soon as Darren started to move, but I could feel that he was there. I could feel that he was getting closer.

"He's coming to the door," I whispered loudly. As I spoke, the motion detector garage light clicked on as it did when something had walked by it. The doorbell let out a loud electric buzz.

Darren shot upright, and the buzzing stopped. "Holy shit!" he shouted as he threw is arms around me. We were both shaking. "What the fuck! What the fuck was that?"

"I told you," I whispered, "I told you there's something out there."

"Shhhh!" Darren hissed. "It has to be a coincidence." The garage light turned off as it was supposed to when there was no movement to keep it activated.

"Whatever it was, it's gone by now. Right?" he whispered so quietly it was difficult to understand him.

"Maybe," I whispered back, "why don't you go check it out?"

The doorbell let out another long buzz followed by two shorter buzzes, like whatever was out there was irritated that we hadn't answered the door.

We both let out a little whimper.

"We have to look," I whispered. "What if it's one of our neighbors? What if it's an emergency?"

"Fine," Darren whispered back, "you're right. Let's go together." We got out of bed and crept slowly toward the backdoor. The kitchen window looked straight out onto the backdoor steps and the short sidewalk between the house and the garage. There was nothing, not a human, not a deer or a cat, not even trees reacting to a gust of wind could be seen out there in the moonlight. It was dark and still. It was a beautiful night. Nights in Iowa were that way most of the time—beautiful and eerily quiet.

Darren grabbed the heavy flashlight we kept in the kitchen and slowly opened the door. There was nothing there that either one of us could see. Darren slow-stepped out on the steps. "I'm going to check around," he said as he stepped cautiously down to the sidewalk.

"Great," I said back, "I'm going to stay here. Let me know if you find anything." I knew that he wouldn't find anything. Whatever had been out there wasn't out there anymore. I couldn't feel it or see it. I just hoped that we hadn't let it in when we opened the door.

"There's nothing out there," Darren said when he came back inside. "That was really weird."

"Agreed."

"What do you think it was?" he asked as he stepped up on one of our kitchen chairs to disconnect the doorbell.

"I have no idea," I said somewhat absently as I checked all of the other rooms for lurkers. "That was weird, even for me." There was nothing to be found.

We took ourselves back to bed and tried to sleep, but it didn't come easily. I never figured out what that strange dark thing was or why it was there, circling our house and asking to come in. It never came back and nothing like that night ever happened again, although the doorbell did buzz faintly twice more that night even after it had been disconnected.

As far as I know, Darren never forgot the events of that night, though he would try to minimize the story if I ever shared it with any of our friends. He never admitted to hearing or seeing very much after that night. Every now and then we would talk about the things that were around, but he seemed more and more detached from it. Ultimately, he started saying it was all a manifestation of my own fears rather than real things. He said I was just being paranoid. He even said, more than once, that they were all in my head and that he really didn't want to hear about it anymore. I don't know if he couldn't deal with it and shut it off, or if he never really saw the Blue Guy in the beginning and just lied to me because he wanted to get laid. Either way, I was alone with my ghosts again.

Chapter 10

Darren and I were vomited out into the chiropractic world during a time of great transition. Chiropractic, as a profession, was in the midst of an identity crisis. (Honestly, I'm not sure that it has ever not had an identity crisis, but that is a story for another day, entirely.)

Chiropractic jobs were hard to come by, at the time, and they were even harder to keep. Personally, I never lost any of them. I just couldn't abide staying at some of them. Most of the time, the money wasn't nearly enough to be worth the hours I had to work or the devastating toll the job took on my dignity. Sometimes, the billing practices were sketchy. Other times, I was asked to do things that were in direct opposition to everything I had been taught or to the basic standards of ethical behavior that any idiot could figure out even without a six digit education. I'm not saying that all chiropractors are shysters—not at all—but just like haircuts and cups of coffee, there are good ones and bad ones, and you never really know what you've got until you try it.

The other options at the time were to open a new practice from scratch or to buy a practice from another doctor who was either getting out of the game for some reason or who had expanded too much and needed to trim the proverbial overhead fat to survive. Both of these options were risky and expensive and either way we went, it was going to be a long and challenging journey toward stability.

Over the next eighteen months, Darren and I moved five times, starting with the move into my parents' spare bedroom right after we fled Verona. I was desperate to settle down and get to work. I wanted stability. I wanted security. I wanted to work hard and reap the benefits of our efforts. Most of all, I wanted to do all of it together with Darren. It was the two of us against the world. We were strong. We were together, and that was it.

Darren was less focused. As we were starting out in Charlotte, he thought he wanted to start from scratch, then he wanted to buy, and then he just wanted a job where he could earn some money. No matter what the offer was on the table, he was never satisfied with it. All the while, he was on the phone with Earl almost every other day, and every time he was about to make a decision, he got a phone call from Verona that would end up derailing the whole thing. That's how the wandering started. I wanted him to be happy. He had given up so much for me. I knew this because he told me every time he got off the phone with his dad. It might have been guilt, or maybe it was just what I thought was the path of least resistance. Either way, I let him choose where we looked for jobs and practices. I thought that if we could just get him settled, I would make it work for me, too.

So, Darren led the way to the future. He bounced us around the Mid Atlantic seaboard on the hunt for the perfect job or the perfect practice to buy for over a year, and I dutifully followed. Add that in with the general dearth of viable opportunities and all that's left is a Chevy Blazer with over 100,000 miles on it, massive credit card debt, and two six-figure student loans along with the loans we had each taken from our respective parents.

I thought we were going to settle down when Darren took a job in a gym outside of Philadelphia. He was supposed to work on a contract for a while and then buy the place outright for himself over time. It wasn't my first choice. It wasn't even my fifth or sixth choice, but it was the best chance I had at the time. Darren's ego was fragile, and I didn't think he could stand much resistance to his latest big idea, so we packed everything up and moved. It was Darren's first real job. Three weeks later, I started my own job in a tiny office close to our apartment. Ten days after that, 9/11 happened. I can't say that 9/11 directly changed things for us, but it definitely set a tone.

It took six months for Darren to quit his contract. He said it wasn't good enough and he was wasting his time. He wasn't entirely wrong about it. It was a terrible office, but at least it was a job. I thought that was worth something. He quit anyway and spent the next month watching TV and playing Snood on our desk top. (We were too broke for a Playstation.)

That's was when he applied for a job in Minnesota. That's right, I said Minnesota, because…why not Minnesota, right? He went after that job in Minnesota with vigor. He even got interviews lined up for me. We took personality tests. We flew out for our interviews. We sat through the sales pitch for their practice management system and how they were going to conquer chiropractic the way McDonald's had conquered fast food. We Applied for—and paid for—our shiny new Minnesota State Licenses. We shopped for apartments and put down deposits…and then Darren called it all off. (No offense to Minnesota, but I was really relieved. I was several grand deeper in the hole for that little adventure, but definitely relieved. It's cold up there.)

That meant it was back to TV and Snood for Darren while he waited for his next big idea. It was back to work for me. Luckily, I hadn't quit my job. It wasn't enough to cover all of our bills, but it was better than nothing.

…and then Darren found his "dream job"…

…and it was back in Pittsburgh…

In all of the towns, in all of the possible places we could have gone, the only job for him (according to him) was back there. It wasn't a discussion. It was a decision and a unilateral one at that. Darren went home to his parents' house, made a tentative peace with Charlene, got the job, and told me to come and join him because it was more expensive for me to keep working at my job than it was for me to quit. Sadly, he wasn't wrong.

But stepping one foot into Charlene's house was a terrible idea, and the idea of moving in was even worse. It was a pivotal moment, and I knew it as it was happening. If I chose to go with him, I was honoring my wedding vows. I was choosing our life over Charlene's insanity. If I chose to leave, I could start over again before I lost any more time, but it would be even more of a struggle. We had already taken the long way around to nowhere. While all of our friends from school had been building their careers and securing their futures, we were driving around in circles like a couple of idiots and digging ourselves a massive debt hole. With those thoughts banging around in my skull, it really seemed like I didn't have any other viable options. It didn't matter how much PCSD (to be clear, that's Post *Charlene* Stress Disorder) I had every time I heard Darren say "yinz" or mention the Steelers or any time I saw spiral bound college ruled paper. It didn't matter that Charlene kept that green notebook (a.k.a. my personal journal) as leverage and had an unknown number of copies hidden in multiple places that only she (and probably Wall-Cat) knew. It didn't matter that she kept the threat of the notebook alive in every way she could think of so that I never knew when, if, or how it would come up in any given situation. Despite all of that and as insane as it was, I went back to Verona. I circled right back around to where the whole mess started and moved back into Charlene's house. I chose my marriage. I chose Darren.

...Ugh...

On the up side, we were better at the physical moving part this time. We had moved so many times that we had it down to a fairly efficient system. This time we loaded everything directly into the basement through the cellar door rather than bringing it into the main part of the house. We thought maybe Charlene would feel less like my undies were her undies that way and that we might all get along with less turmoil.

The outside door to the cellar seemed smaller and inside the cellar seemed danker than I remembered. The overwhelming sense of shame and inadequacy I felt in returning to this vortex of despair was exacerbated by Charlene who had perched herself at the corner stair railing like a gargoyle troll and heckled us as we lugged our things off the truck.

"Daaa-rren," she squawked, "don't scratch up my floor." She flicked cigarette ash over the stair rail like she was punctuating a sentence.

I kept my head down and kept moving, trying hard to remember that I had chosen this path of my own freewill. It was up to me to make the best of it, and after all, it was her house.

The concrete floor of the basement was weathered and pitted. It hadn't been sealed or patched in at least two decades. As we tromped in and out over the floor, I occupied my mind by tracing every pit and crack. I also thought it might be useful in the event of a surprise post-load-in inspection. Line after line, chunk after missing chunk, I traced them all as we hefted and lugged our entire material lives inside.

After the last box had been moved in and the truck was on its way back to the rental lot, I sat down at the foot of the stairs that lead up to the kitchen. The metal staircase gave a familiar squeak as it shuttered under my weight. I closed my eyes and took in a long deep breath. The moldy basement smell was the same. The muffled TV sounds through the floor above my head were the same. I stood up and opened my eyes. The boxes and the furniture shoved in the center basement room looked exactly the same. It was all exactly the fucking same. This was really happening. It was a nightmare come to life.

A wave of nausea flooded through my gut as I thought back to the last time I was here—the anger, the crying, the notebook, the hurt, the privacy invasion, and the torment. Panic flooded in next. My mind started cataloging all of the things in all of the boxes and where everything that was mine might be. This was a powder keg, and the last time, it blew up in my face. Once again, my whole life was in her house with no foreseeable end date in sight. I was angry and tired and completely freaking out. Why did I let this happen? Why did Darren even suggest this? The more I thought about it, the more furious and terrified I became. As I scanned over the piles of our belongings, my eyes glazed over. My legs started to tremble. The floor beneath me started to vibrate. As I looked around the room, I saw all of the boxes and furniture start to shake and crash together. It was like an earthquake was happening right in front of my eyes. The concrete floor between my feet split apart into a wide crack. The crack spread across the entire basement floor, and everything we owned started to tumble, box by box, into the divide. I felt my feet being pulled apart and my legs starting to give way. My first thought was, *Shit, I'm going to get blamed for this*, followed by a second thought of, *Hallelujah!* With that, I relaxed into it and let go. I felt a rush of cool air, and everything went dark…

"What are you doing?" Darren said walking in through the outer door. He turned the lights back on at the switch. "Sorry I turned the lights off, I didn't know you were still down here."

I blinked rapidly, trying to regain my composure.

"Seriously, are you alright?" he said. "What the hell are you doing?"

"Nothing…no," I said, "I mean yes, I'm fine." I was fine and also overwhelmingly disappointed that I hadn't actually been swallowed up and taken out by a freak sinkhole.

"Ok, dinner's ready. Ma made sausage rolls for dinner." He walked past me and headed up the squeaky stairs. "Hey, is that a new crack in the floor? Put a box over it or something, ma's gonna lose it if she sees it and then I'll never hear the end of it."

"It was there before, I noticed it when we started today," I said as I continued to stare at the small crack where the sinkhole had started.

"Well, put a box over it anyway," he said as he stomped up the rest of the stairs. "No need to tempt fate." He turned the lights off as he walked past the switch. The darkness returned but it wasn't the same. "Oh, sorry," he said as he flipped the light switch again and closed the cellar door behind him.

For a second…I was free.

It had been so vivid. I really felt like it was all over. For one tiny second, the lights were permanently out. It was downright peaceful. There was no Charlene…no Darren…no Chiropractic. It was just me, floating in an endless void, surrounded by all of the silly things that I had collected over my life. It was quiet, and it was painless. It wasn't at all like I had imagined dying would be.

A second later…I was back. Darren was there…I was still in the basement…Charlene was already the topic of conversation.

Another second later…I was really disappointed that I was back.

I knew this had to be a terrible omen of something. Maybe this is what a real nervous breakdown was like, or maybe I was having a stroke. I wanted to remember everything about that moment so I could go back and analyze it later with a clearer head. It would have made an amazing journal entry, but as you can imagine, that certainly wasn't an option. Darren had demanded that I never keep one again.

Charlene's voice sliced through the floor. She wanted to know what I was doing in the cellar. That was my cue. If I waited any longer, it would only make things worse. I plodded up the stairs, leaving the crack Darren had pointed out uncovered. I don't think it was an intentional act of defiance. It could have merely been an oversight due to the shock. It certainly wasn't due to my excitement over sausage rolls. Nevertheless, up the stairs I went.

◆◆◆◆◆

Every day that followed, I returned to the basement and sat on the squeaky bottom step. I would scan the piles of our stuff while I pondered the likelihood of a spontaneous sinkhole appearing in Western Pennsylvania and traced the outline of the actual crack in the floor. By the second day, there was an old rug tossed crookedly over it. I was never sure who put it there. I only knew that every day I would straighten the rug out and every evening the rug would be crooked again. It seemed to me like a loose rug haphazardly situated at the bottom of the stairs was more off putting than a 20-year-old crack in the cement, but every day I would smooth and straighten the rug when I covered it back up before I walked away from it.

My sinkhole vision had seemed so real. I had never experienced anything like that before. I had experienced plenty of daydreams in my life, but they were just flights of fancy for a temporarily restless mind. I had never had a daydream or a day-mare where my perception of reality slipped so far that there was no obvious difference between reality and non-reality. It was only for a moment, but that moment was more than long enough. It left an indelible mark inside me—a crack in my head to match the one on the floor.

Day after day I revisited the cellar crack, and the sinkhole never returned. Eventually, I decided that the whole thing was just a transient reaction to an acute stressor. I didn't want to die. I wasn't suicidal. I didn't want to repeat what had happened before and my stress was a product of my doubts about returning to this place and repeating the past. I had chosen my marriage over my own comfort, and I just didn't want to be there. All I could hope was that the sacrifice would pay off in the end.

At the same time as all of that nonsense, I was looking for my own job. The sooner I went back to work, the sooner we could rent our own place and the sooner I could get a little distance from Charlene's vortex of despair. I went about my days making calls, sending resumes, and talking to anyone who would let me in the door. I tried my best to contribute to the housework, too. I cleaned the kitchen, did laundry, scooped litter boxes and vacuumed floors. I didn't really mind it that much. I would have done the same and more in my own space. It was Charlene that made it so unbearable. Whatever I did, it was never enough. She was almost always there, watching whatever I did—except for the mornings. She usually slept late, and I usually had a good 4 to 5 hours to myself each morning before she even thought about getting up.

The rest of my time was spent cleaning up the aftermath of our time in Philly. With every move, the account transfers and cancellation fees seemed to get worse and worse. The costs of life as wandering doctors were adding up fast.

As the days passed the tension kept magnifying. Darren was at work during the days. I was alone in the house with Charlene and the constant threat of the notebook. I couldn't stand it. It was like psychological warfare. She had turned my words into a weapon that could destroy everything I was trying to build with Darren. For a while, I tried searching for it, but it was pointless. The copies I found were too easy. They were practically sitting out in the open. I knew that they were a trap so Charlene would know that I was looking for it and that I was snooping through her things. I gave up the search after I found the first five copies. She was fucking with me. I realized that even if I found the original, it would never be enough. It was impossible to know how many copies there were—paper copies, digital file copies, transcription onto a series of stone tables that she chiseled on every night and then buried somewhere in the backyard—maybe even in the tomato garden. It was impossible to know, and it didn't really matter anymore, anyway. The worst of the damage had already been done.

While my sinkhole never came back, my sleeping dreams started changing to bizarre nightmares. In my dreams, I would be in the middle of a random scene when, suddenly, I would just start swallowing things—as an example, my keys. One minute I would be holding my keys in my hand, and the next, I would pop them squarely in my mouth and swallow them down. I could feel them traveling through my esophagus and cutting off my airway. The panic would kick in. I would try to grab the keys before they were too far gone, but it was always too late. I couldn't stop it. I would look down at my body and see the keys gouging through my stomach and intestines, eventually ripping me open as it zig-zagged through my guts and eventually turning my abdomen into bloody spaghetti. I would always wake up shaky and sweaty, and thankfully, all in one piece, but each time after I calmed myself down, a wave of melancholy and disappointment would hit me. It seemed a little odd that I was disappointed to be un-eviscerated from within, but it's honestly what I felt. Darren knew that it was happening. I woke up screaming most of the time, and he had a hard time sleeping through it. As instructed, I told Darren all about it instead of writing any of it down. Journaling was officially off limits, of course. He would laugh and tell me I was weird. He also asked me not to wake him up during the night because he really needed to sleep.

Night after night, the horrible dreams kept coming, and they always seemed to be the result of either my questionable choices or improbable natural disasters. I swallowed dimes and quarters. I swallowed things like rusted nails and bottle caps and pens (and pins for that matter) depending on what was around in that particular dream. Sometimes my teeth would crumble, and I would feel the shards scrape through my body. I fell off shaking buildings, crumbling cliffs and tumbled down unreasonably long flights of stairs. I always hit the bottom, and I always just stayed there. The sinkhole showed up again a few times, but it was never like the first one. Instead of a peaceful void, I'd get sucked down into a deep hole with whatever was nearby at the time piled in on top. I never tried to get out, though. I just stayed there, buried and suffocating in my sinkhole, until I eventually woke up sweaty, scared and inevitably disappointed.

As time passed, my nightmares morphed back into day-mares again. They were usually less violent but definitely just as absurd.

For example, one day I was washing the dishes at Charlene's sink. Rain was gently hitting the roof leading a mesmerizing undercurrent to Charlene's repetitious heaving sighs.

When Charlene sighed, it usually meant that she had something on her mind. It was her version of a conversation starter. She would sit and smoke and sigh. She would wander the house and smoke and sigh. She would pointedly straighten the already straight magazines, light her cigarettes with vaudevillian hand flourishes, and then sigh some more. She would sigh and sigh, louder and louder, until I would break and ask her if she was okay. It seemed like she lived for those moments. She would launch into a litany of complaints ranging from our things in the basement, to where we parked the car at night, to the neighbors, to her fibromyalgia and her "dumb" doctors. Nothing was off limits. She was free to say whatever bile-filled hate-sputum her brain could hock up, because of course, I asked.

This time, I was determined not to react. I focused my attention on the feel of the dishes in my hands and the warmth of the water in the sink. I let the sound of the rain take over in my head. I relaxed into it. Soon the roof faded away, and I was outside—still at the sink in the kitchen—but gloriously outside. I could feel the raindrops falling on my head, and I tipped my head up to look at the sky. As I did, thoughts of my first-grade teacher flowed into my mind. She said that a turkey would die if you left it out in the rain. She said it would look up to see what was touching its head, and it would stay that way until the raindrops filled its little turkey nostrils and it drowned. Of course, I always thought it was a ridiculous story. It's important to note that Mrs. Topper was involuntarily institutionalized later on that same year, but in that moment, I remembered that story with absolute clarity and I wondered…

…If I just tipped my head back a little farther…I felt the raindrops filling my nose as I held my breath and tried to let it happen…

"What are you doing?!" Darren's mother squawked startling me out of the rain. I inhaled sharply and choked on my own saliva as I whipped my head up straight. I had been so far down in it that I had forgotten she was there. Now I was in a full-on, saliva-induced coughing fit, and I couldn't make it stop.

"Holy shit, what's wrong with you? Didn't ya hear me?" she

asked with disgust. "I have been having a terrible day, and you didn't even notice," she said angrily as she walked out of the room. I could hear her mumbling until she slammed her bedroom door.

I gripped the edge of the sink to steady myself while I tried to settle my breath. I was clearly losing control of myself. I didn't know exactly what it meant, but I was certain that something had to change and fast.

The next day change came all by itself. I got a job offer. It was a good one, too. It was exactly what I had wanted since the day we finished school. It was genuine hands-on chiropractic with functional rehab and decompression therapy in a clean, professional building. There was no color therapy, no muscle testing of patients with slices of bread held on their chests, and no mandatory morning and afternoon prayer circles. (It sounds crazy, I know, but it happens. It's kind of a chiropractic thing that's entirely too much to explain here, but rest assured… It's not just chiropractic. Traditional medicine has its share of wackadoodles and hardliners, too.) There was, however, an actual support staff and an insurance manager. It was perfect, and the job was mine. It was just the change I needed. I even made it through a whole day without envisioning my own stupid death.

When Darren got back that night, I was bubbling over with the details. "It's perfect! I can start as soon as I am ready. It's a 60/40 split, and he will include me on all of his advertising. He wants to get me up to speed on his technique so I can cover his patients when he is out of the office. The office has everything, and it's stable, and he's not much older than we are. Like I said, it is perfect!" I practically had to cover my mouth with my hand to give him a moment to respond.

"A 60/40 split? He wants 40 percent?" Darren said wrinkling up his forehead.

"Yes! Can you believe it?" I responded excitedly.

"That's a lot," he said flatly. "Is he married?"

"Yes," I said with a slightly less excited tone. "Why?"

"Did he say why he wanted to hire you?" his tone was shifting toward cynicism.

"He said he thought I was perfect for the job. He was impressed with my CV. He wants a female doctor to balance out his office. He liked my technique…" I listed off easily.

"I bet he did," Darren said with contempt.

"Excuse me?" I shot back incredulously.

Darren refused to look at me. "You can keep looking," he said as though it was the obvious final word on the matter.

My enthusiasm drained out into the ether leaving a black hole in the middle of my chest. "What?" I said, "Why?"

"Sounds to me like he wants to pimp you out and then get some for himself on the side. You can't take that job, sorry." He spoke as if that was the end of it. Charlene had been at the sink the entire time listening to the whole thing. She almost looked like she was struggling with it. I could see it on her face. She puffed up with pride as her son asserted himself and then recoiled as she realized that we wouldn't be moving out.

"So, you're telling me that I should turn down a perfectly good job offer because you're jealous?" I spat back. My composure was slipping away.

"I'm not jealous. You're just being intentionally dumb about it. I know exactly what that guy is thinking, and this argument is mute. You aren't taking that job." The arrogance was dripping off of him like sweat.

"Do you mean moot?" I said trying to control my attitude.

"It's mute, and yes, I mean it's mute. There's no point. You're not taking that job," he said pompously. Charlene beamed a little more as she pretended she wasn't listening.

"The word is *moot*," I said forcefully, "and my point is definitely not *moot*...nor is it mute for that matter!"

"I am not arguing about this," he said, "and the correct word is mute! God, why do you have to act like you're right all the time?"

"Because I'm right. Look it up!" I said defiantly. I was totally deflated.

"I will, and I can prove it!" Darren bellowed as he stormed out of the room.

I sat despondently at the kitchen table. Without thinking, I said, "Oh my God...can you believe this?"

Charlene paused her work at the counter, and I instantly wished I could take my words back. "Yes," she said confidently, "I am sure he has his reasons." She turned and leaned up against the kitchen counter. "You're married. You have to honor your husband." I thought I heard a hint of remorse buried somewhere in her words, but it was only for a second. She stared at me for a moment longer before turning back around to the face the sink.

The truth of her words hit me. She was right. We were married, and I would be dealing with his reaction to my choices either way. All of my excitement was gone. If I took the job, it would be a daily struggle with Darren for who knew how long which would make the situation unbearable. If I didn't, I would be passing up a fantastic opportunity, and those didn't come around every day. All of the hope drained out of me and my old friend, Disappointment, started seeping back in through the black hole in my chest. If there was a way for this to work out... well, I couldn't see it.

Darren came back into the room looking irritated and sat down at the table. I looked at him expectantly. "So?" I said.

"What," he replied flatly.

I waited. He said nothing.

"What did you find out?" I asked, "or is the point moot?" I glared at him.

"You're not taking that job," he said defiantly.

"Dinner's ready," his mother cut in before I could respond. "Darren, set the table."

He never talked about it with me again. I tried to postpone my decision hoping that I could find a way to take the job and keep Darren happy, but the job wouldn't wait. The doctor gave it to his second choice when I seemed indecisive. My day-mares came back the very next day. I envisioned death by stupidity any time I was around running water—in the shower, making coffee, watering the tomato garden, and of course, every time it rained. In retrospect, it would have made more sense to envision drowning myself in the pool or hurling myself off a bridge into the Allegheny River. I guess my brain was making an artistic statement about my own ineptitude. Maybe my brain knew that I really didn't want to die and was simply refusing to provide me with any legitimate options to consider…and at least my mind wasn't killing off anybody else…yet.

Chapter 11

One week later we moved. I found us a house to rent on the slopes of Pittsburgh's South Side. It took more than we had to do it, but I made it happen on a shoestring and my credit card.

The house was a tiny insul-brick row house built around 1906. The first floor had the kitchen and the main living space with a bathroom that was added in by our landlord when she bought the place. (Before that there was only a toilet behind the door to the basement and shower nozzle over a drain hole in the basement for bathing.) Upstairs, there was one main bedroom that I liked to call the loft, even though it wasn't one, with an additional cramped storage space that extended under the eaves. Outside, there was a small yard with a cherry tree and a line of pink peony bushes that ran along the cracked cement steps that lead to the alley in the back. The house wasn't much to look at, but to me, it dripped with nostalgia and felt like heaven. I had finally found a place that I could make into a home.

I loved almost everything about living there, at least in the summertime. There were shops, restaurants and a dance studio down in the flats that were walking distance away. There was a network of winding public stairs that made getting down the hill an adventure and going home a cardio workout. (I lovingly dubbed the 317 steps that led up to our street Buzz Kill Hill. That trek plus a giant glass of water before bed was quite the hangover prevention.)

After we moved, I found a job for myself. It wasn't ideal, but it was work, and Darren had no complaints about it, so it was a good start. I made a flat $35,000 per year and had to adjust my boss in his boxer shorts at least once a month. (To be crystal clear, I mean chiropractic adjustments only, but it was still completely creepy and thoroughly inappropriate.)

Not long after we got settled, Darren discovered his next true love—home brewing beer. The look on his face the first time he stepped through the door at the brewing supply store said it all. He had found a new religion. Like a new convert at a tent revival, he was ready to prostrate himself and start speaking in tongues, which tended to happen naturally if he drank enough, anyway, so it was a perfect match from the start.

The whole thing was my fault to begin with. It all started several weeks earlier when we had dinner with Darren's friend and Best Man, Chris, one of Darren's old college Frat-Pack members. Being the young, upwardly mobile, business stud that Chris considered himself to be, his pre-dinner entertainment included a tour of two bedroom rented apartment and his new wine cellar. The wine cellar amounted to a community basement where he had several bubbling buckets of fermenting grape juice sitting next to a washing machine. It wasn't a wine cellar, exactly, and how he managed to successfully complete anything in that dank, mold covered basement was beyond me, but it was intriguing and was definitely good fodder for small talk.

I think, maybe, I might have appeared a little more interested than was required for such a social situation. Pittsburgh was lonely, and I had been bored for a long time. I really enjoyed all of the wine, too. The conversation got away from me. The easy small talk about vinification turned into more talk throughout the evening and then more on the way home and then every day with Darren for over a week. At the time, I thought we needed a hobby, something that we could enjoy doing together. Little did I know, I wasn't just talking about a new hobby, I was creating a giant wormhole that would suck the entirety of our lives into it.

First, there was the single wine kit that we bought from the home brewers' supply store. It was mostly idiot proof and relatively inexpensive, and it set us up with just about everything we needed to make any sort of bathtub style alcoholic beverage we could think of aside from moonshine. The whole thing made enough wine to last me for a couple of years at the rate I drank, and in the end, we lost most of it thanks to inadequate corks and careless bottle sanitizing.

But that was only the experiment that got the whole thing started. Darren had his sights set on bigger and more intricate alcoholic endeavors. As soon as the fermenting bucket was empty, it was all about the beer. Our low budget weekend excursions to the Strip District for lunch and some produce turned into weekly pilgrimages to the brewing supply store with a mandatory two-hour session with his old, hippy, brew guru, Dave.

The supply store, itself, was an odd place. There were herbs, grains, bottles, and pots covering the shelves and racks of tools for every possible need in the realm of alcoholic alchemy. Brew Guru Dave owned the shop and was happy to answer questions and tell stories of his home-brewing escapades like an old fisherman spinning yarns of giant fish. Darren was mesmerized by Brew Guru Dave's brewing tales. I would stare out at the people walking by, wishing that I was somewhere else and that I had never shown interest in any of it, ever.

Right away, Darren dove into his studies. His eyes would glow whenever he picked up his book of beer recipes, aptly titled The Home Brewer's Bible. Gingerly, he would trace his fingers over its cover before flipping through the pages. He spent long hours in his kitchen laboratory boiling, stirring, straining and pouring—far more time and energy than he had ever put into chiropractic college. The house would be filled with the distinct aroma of hops and barley, and nearly every other weekend he spent several hundred dollars (that we didn't have to spare) on more supplies.

In the beginning, the process was actually somewhat exciting to witness. It was like watching a little bit of world history mixed with a little chemistry and some biology. Darren was even reanimating bags of dry brewer's yeast. It was only the replication of a simple single-celled organism, but I think his passion and his piecemeal laboratory would definitely have been Dr. Frankenstein approved.

I don't know if Darren was a particularly gifted home brewer. I know that in the beginning, he tried to work with great precision. He sanitized, scrubbed, measured, and took notes as he went along. He collected recipes and brewing manuals. It was his passion replete with snobbish self-righteousness and disdain for common beer and the uninitiated. After his first sip of his first pint of his first batch, he was never the same. He was drunk on his own beer brewing power, and then with time...he was just drunk.

Brewing can be a finicky process, especially for someone with a short attention span. It requires time, patience, and a controlled environment for it to work well. This was a challenge for Darren. Patience and attention to detail were not his strengths. He struggled when he had to wait, which frequently lead to brewing shortcuts and to the procurement of commercially bottled beers to mitigate his anticipation between batches of his own product, but as he put it, "they just aren't the same."

As the months passed, Darren became markedly less meticulous and even less willing to clean up the kitchen after he was done. He would cite the old notion that a messy desk was a sign of a brilliant mind. At first, I pointed out that it was the kitchen, not a desk. When that didn't work, I declared that, "he who maketh the mess, shall cleaneth the mess." It had no effect on him, either. Since I was she who wanted-eth a clean house, I could regularly be found cleaning partially dried puddles of beer off the floor and the walls and sometimes the ceiling.

Over time, Darren's homebrews started to morph. They got stronger and more powerful. He started brewing recklessly and with little regard for consistency or other people's opinions. Despite the mess and his cowboy-like approach to established brewing norms, I was on board with Darren's hobby for a while. It kept him occupied when we weren't working. It gave him something to focus on other than chiropractic and his mother, whom he still talked to at least once a day.

Unfortunately for me, however, Darren's glorious homebrew started making me sick. I don't just mean I had a little hangover or a fuzzy head the morning after. I mean I was full-on puking, shaking, headache-for-at-least-two-days kind of sick. I started drinking less and less, but my physical rejection of his brews kept getting worse and worse. After a time, I couldn't even be in the house when he was brewing on the stove. He kept telling me I was overreacting and then later that I was just getting old, but I knew there was something more to it.

Despite my body's obvious rejections, every weekend Darren would plead with me, "Come on, just have a drink with me. I don't want to drink alone." He always made it seem like I was the unreasonable one for not wanting to imbibe. "You used to be so much fun. I like drunk-you."

As offensive as this should have been, I let myself be lured in by it more often than I care to admit. Somehow, I failed to ask any probing follow up questions, like, what do you mean by drunk-me? Don't you like the rest of me? Or, wow, am I really that different after one beer, maybe I need medication? Or maybe, if drunk-you doesn't get along with sober-me, why am I putting up with drunk-you so much? These are just a few of the possible questions that a normal, rational, person might have asked. I didn't ask.

I always wondered why my drunk-pronoun state was so much more appealing than my regular-pronoun state. If his goal had been to kill me slowly or to embarrass me, it might have made more sense, but if not, the cost of it was awfully high for very little return. It wasn't like drunk-me had an insatiable craving for passionate sex romps in the living room or mind-expanding intellectual conversation. I can't imagine that the cranky, vomitus lump of a human that greeted him the next morning was his intended result, but he carried on, nonetheless. Maybe he was secretly hoping I would just vaporize and be gone. Whatever the motivation, he never stopped asking and seemed really excited when I complied.

No matter what choice I made, he kept going most of the time. As you might suppose, he found friends who shared his passion for anything in a pint glass and were more than willing to help him test his brews. There was a steady parade of friends, both old and new, who made their way through our door, lured by the promise of free beer and a good time. I could usually judge the quality of any visitor based on their response to his concoctions. A vigorous "man, this is great!" was a clear sign of a man-baby and was usually followed by a progression of verbal deterioration, glass breaking, and lighting something on fire.

Some were merely curious and appropriately dubious about what was in their glass. Those who had managed to internalize the time-honored maternal directives about what to do if there isn't anything nice to say would give an obligatory, "mmmm…" as they gently placed the glass back on the table. Slowly they would work their way through the pint, but an hour of polite sipping was usually enough to change even the most discriminating palate to a swill swigging plebeian.

A few were bold enough to offer tasting notes as Darren stood by waiting for praise. This was never good for me or for the remains of my weekend. A simple comment like, "I think the Cascade hopps are a little overwhelming. Fuggles might be better next time," about the hopp content of his precious homebrew usually meant days of nonstop griping about such audacity and inability to appreciate his artistic choices. I, personally, never thought that something that unavoidably ended up as urine or vomit qualified as art, but according to Darren, I did not possess his refined palate and was ill equipped to judge the masterpieces he had fermenting in a plastic bucket at the top of the basement stairs.

I did have to give him points for creativity from time to time, even when his choices were bad enough to wreck my weekend and wake the dead. One cold winter night, Darren was fretting over his latest concoction which had been sitting silently in its fermentation bucket since the night before.

It was a bad sign for the beer and meant that the entire batch was a probably wasted thanks to the frigid outside temperatures that were too much for our rickety little house to keep at bay. In the living room, the temperature held at 58 degrees with the heat on, regardless of the thermostat's setting. The kitchen stayed at 54, and the bathroom (which had no heat source in it at all) usually reached about 42 degrees during the day and had a permanent waterfall of ice on the inside of the window next to the toilet. The radiators clunked and gurgled away as hard as they could which made the 3-inch radius around the ancient metal coils the only tolerable spots in the house. Neither I nor the beer found it to be a workable temperature.

So, what's a savvy homebrewer to do when his brewer's yeast

and his wife fail to thrive in such an environment? The only logical thing, of course. Hand your wife the fermentation bucket blanket and put your fermentation bucket directly on the radiator.

...genius...

The blanket only helped me a little and did nothing for the chilblains that were forming on my toes. His fermentation bucket, on the other hand, sprang to life in less than an hour.

"I told you this would work," Darren said the next night as the bucket bubbled away atop the kitchen radiator.

It seemed like a terrible idea. "I was reading online about higher alcohols that can form if the fermentation temp is too high. I am not sure this is such a good idea," I said, trying to credit the unsourced ramblings of an internet blogger instead of those pesky chemistry classes I took in college.

"It might be a little off, but it's fine. It's better than losing the whole batch," he assured me.

To my recollection, "a little off" in biochemical parlance was rarely considered "fine," but Darren let his bubbling cauldron of Frankenstein yeast ferment on. Over and over, it thumped and spat, as it sat alone on the kitchen radiator. There was no escaping it. The thumping went on and on until it finally stopped one night just as we were getting in bed. Darren was overjoyed. "I'll transfer it tomorrow. I told you it's fine," he said and then drifted off to sleep.

The constant thumping had been my constant companion for days. When it stopped, I felt oddly alone. The silence kept me from sleeping, and once I finally fell asleep, I was restless and full of dreams. I dreamed that I was in the kitchen with a tiny, old man. He looked like a life-sized Italian gnome, which I don't think was ever a real thing, but it's the best description I could find for him. He was short, fat, and bald, in a white undershirt and navy workpants. I half expected him to give me his special recipe for Italian gravy or to tell me there was a body cemented into the front patio. Instead, he stood just there in the moonlit kitchen shaking his head back and forth in slow motion. Next, there was a loud boom. I flinched and dropped to the floor, and then he was gone. I was alone in the moonlight, and my dream moved on to something else.

The next morning, I headed downstairs like it was any other morning. My dreams were fading away, and I was anxious for some coffee and some news headlines.

As I reached the bottom of the stairs, a rancid smell hit my nose like a spike to the brain. As I stepped through the kitchen door, I saw the full extent of the carnage. Darren's beer bucket had built up so much pressure that it blew its lid and spewed its yeasty innards from floor to ceiling. Primordial ale was dripping from the walls, the cabinets, the sink, and the loops of the radiator like zombie guts down a chain link fence.

It seemed that the gnome, whoever he was, had tried to warn me. I wasn't sure which was more shocking, the mess or the warning from the other side. Maybe he was the previous owner trying to protect his property. Maybe it was future Darren, short and bald, reminiscing about his past with such vigor that he made it into my dream as a warning. Whatever it was, it wasn't a very good job. It got my attention, but it didn't change the outcome.

Darren came into the kitchen as I stood there. "Holy shit," he said groggily. "What a fucking mess."

"Yeah, no kidding. Sorry about your beer. Maybe it's just too cold in here to brew in the winter," I said hoping that the kitchen might go back to being just a kitchen and not a brewery for a while.

"They make thermal wraps for this kind of thing." Darren

tiptoed through the beer guts and headed down the stairs to the basement.

A moment later, he returned with the rest of his beer equipment and some old towels. He tossed the towels on the floor in front of him and scooted his feet to absorb the liquid on his direct path to the radiator. "See, no big deal," he said as prepped the transfer bucket. "Don't worry. It'll be fine."

Realizing that he was only cleaning what was in his way, I grabbed the remaining towels and started blotting up the rest. "Why bother transferring it? It's ruined. There's no way it will be safe to drink," I said with genuine concern.

"Jesus, Alane, you're so negative. It's fine," he replied. "If it's bad, I'll throw it out later. It's too expensive to waste."

"Really, I don't think this is a good idea," I pushed back, "That thing has been bubbling too much and sitting open for who knows how long." Now was not the time to tell him that a ghost gnome actually knew exactly how long it had been. I could only handle one crazy conversation at a time, especially before coffee.

"It's fine," he said again.

"It's not fine. Who knows what has been growing in there and who knows what kind of alcohol it will be. You could go blind!" I said melodramatically as he continued the transfer. I was only partly joking.

"God!" Darren spat out with exasperation, "You're ridiculous. It's an experiment. Either it works, or it doesn't. But I'm not throwing it out." He sealed the glass carboy and scooted on his towel to the sink with the empty, dripping plastic bucket. "Anyway, Dave said the lid blew off his fermenter and his dog stuck his face in it and it was one of the best batches he ever made."

"I don't know if I would trust Dave all that much. He was clearly in need of a sale that day. I'm not sure his guidance was exactly solid," I ranted. "Obviously, it didn't kill him, but I don't know..."

"It's fine," Darren said flatly as he finished cleaning the bucket and tossed the soiled towels down the cellar stairs. "I'll get the rest of this mess later. I could use some coffee."

The beer guts were still dripping in the loops of the radiator. The wall splatter was mostly dry. "This needs to be cleaned before it dries," I said.

"Ok, I'll get the coffee myself, I guess." Darren exhaled with mild irritation.

"Alright, I guess I'll just clean this up myself, then," I said as I stepped around the sticky pools of beer to get to the basement door.

"I said I'll do it," he said in a high-pitched dismissive tone. "Everything has to be your way! 'Throw that out! You'll go blind! Clean this up before it dries!' Ugh!'" he mocked. It wasn't even a good imitation. I could have given him credit or even laughed for a good one, but that was just bitchy.

"Oh, I'm so sorry that I thought you should clean up after yourself. It's not an unreasonable expectation," I said with an overwhelming tone of indignation. "It stinks…and it's a fucking mess!"

"I didn't make this mess. It's called an accident. It just happened. You're the one who's always bitching about wasted money. I did this for you. God, you are such a fucking control freak!" he barked back.

I was blown out. I spun around on my heels, stomped down the basement stairs, and stepped off the last step straight onto a sopping wet towel full of stinking beer guts. I snorted sharply in frustration. My socks were saturated. Suddenly, there was a dark flash to my left among the boxes in the storage room behind the stairs. I turned to get a better look at it, but there was nothing there. As angry as I was about the beer-splosion and Darren and my disgusting socks, I couldn't help myself. After last night's dream, I had to investigate. What else was the stupid gnome trying to warn me about? Maybe there was some wild creature nesting in our basement, or maybe the gnome wanted to gripe at me, too, since I didn't understand his warning.

The floor in that part of the cellar was covered in a layer of gritty dirt that seemed to regenerate itself no matter how many times I cleaned it. I would sweep and scrub to the point of exhaustion, only to turn around and see little drifts of filth forming in my wake. Eventually, I stopped cleaning it at all and stacked our storage boxes right on top of the drifts. It had been months since the last time I ventured back there, and it was a mess. I picked my way around the piles and peeked behind the old furniture and frames. I found nothing out of place. If it was a rat, I wasn't really sure I knew what to do about it, and there was certainly no way I was going to ask Darren for help. If it was the gnome, he really needed to talk to Darren directly. And, if it was some homeless dude who was squatting in our basement, that would be a whole other story altogether and would probably land us a spot in the A block on the evening news. It was too much to think about.

The hairs on the back of my neck spiked. I had to get out of that storage room, and I had to focus. I picked up the towels by the stairs and hurried into the small laundry room. The smell of the hops shot into my nostrils and made my eyes water as I dumped the towels into the washing machine. I closed the lid and leaned my forearms on the smooth ceramic top. Dizzy sickness washed over me as pain throbbed in the top of my head. The air behind me moved like someone was at my back. I spun around and saw the gnome. He was standing right behind me. He didn't move or speak. He just stood there, motionlessly gazing into my eyes. His form was as solid as mine. Normally I would have screamed bloody murder at something like this, but not this time. I felt peaceful as I looked at him, and he returned my gaze with this odd, placid expression on his face.

I reached my hands forward to touch him, which was completely stupid. If he had been real, like some kind of homeless basement squatter, it could have ended very badly, but without thinking it through at all, I did it. As my fingers got closer to him, the hairs on my arms stood on end. A warm buzz enveloped my fingers. A sense of connection washed over me. In that moment, I understood everything. Everything about what, I can't say. I just knew, for that moment, I was okay. Everything else might explode, but I was fine. A sharp pain pierced my stomach. I winced and bent forward clutching my gut. The throbbing in my head intensified, and I dropped to my knees in one awkward slump. The connection was broken; the supernatural Xanax had left the building.

The gnome was gone, and I was alone. I was cold and sweaty. I was shaking uncontrollably. A few moments later, my gut pain stopped abruptly, leaving a reverberating hole where the pain had been. It was better, but I wasn't normal, by any means.

"Hey, you coming up sometime soon?" Darren said from the top of the stairs. "We need breakfast."

I slowly got to my feet. "Yeah, be there in a minute," I said as I tried to put the pieces of the last few minutes together in my head. I had experienced visions and daydreams before. I had seen translucent figures floating by the ceiling in my room. I had watched shadows dart from behind doors and slip into corners at twilight. I'd had visitors at the foot of my bed in the last lucid moments before sleep, and of course, there were the night terrors. I'd had all of that since I was a kid. This time was different from any of that. He lived in a dream and in the world somehow. He looked solid and real, and he certainly wasn't something I would have knowingly wished into existence. He was something else. All I knew is that I wanted to talk to him. I wanted to feel like I felt with that feeling again. It felt like it meant something. It felt important.

There was no time to contemplate it any longer. I had to pull myself together, and I certainly wasn't going to talk to Darren about it. I would have sounded like a lunatic. I turned back to the washer, dumped in the soap, and started it. I grabbed the mop, the bucket, and the remaining towels and headed toward the stairs. Before I started up to the kitchen, I took one last look around at the dingy cellar and wondered what else might be lurking there. I wondered if I would ever see the gnome again, and then I headed up the stairs.

Against all rational thought, Darren saw his brew-pocolypse beer through to completion and started another batch as soon as he could under the premise that he needed a backup batch in case the brew-pocolypse batch wasn't drinkable. It's important to consider Darren's specific use of the word "drinkable." It was a detail that I didn't catch in the moment. As with all communication, a clear and accurate understanding of situational definitions is critical. For example, I was not aware that "drinkable," to Darren, only accounted for his ability to swallow it without throwing it back up. It in no way implied that it tasted good, and it certainly didn't mean that it was safe for human consumption.

Once it was bottled, Darren was unreasonably proud of that particular batch of beer. When the time came to test it, he made sure I was there. I didn't need to taste it to know that it was going to be terrible, but I didn't want to hurt his feelings. From the moment the lid cracked off the bottle, the smell of it was acrid and stinging. He poured the bottle's contents into a pint glass and waited anxiously for me to taste it.

One tiny little sip was enough. "It's very pungent," I said as I put the pint glass as far away from me on the table as I could.

Darren laughed. "The word is 'hoppy.'" He sipped again and swished it around in his mouth before swallowing. "I think this worked out ok," he said as he held the pint glass up to the light. He took a full swig and finished swallowing with a decisive, "ahh... that'll work."

"I can't do it," I said. "That is all you. That's a headache in a pint glass, as far as I am concerned."

"It's an IPA," he said dismissively. "This is what real microbrew people live for." He grinned and swigged a little more.

"You're an aficionado, now?" I said with only the slightest hint of snarkiness.

"No," he said flatly.

"A connoisseur?" I said with no change in tone.

"No," he said, again.

"A beer buff, then?" I asked with a giggle.

"Stop it!" he snapped. "Why do you have to ruin everything?"

"I didn't ruin anything," I said with a smile. "The beer was already ruined when you siphoned it up off the floor."

Darren ignored my last comment and whined at me like a child, "I can't believe you called me that!"

"Called you what?" I laughed.

"A buff...you called me a buff. Why would you say that?" he said angrily, "I'm no buff."

"What's wrong with calling you a buff? You're an expert, now, aren't you?" I replied incredulously.

"I am an expert, but I am certainly not a buff!" he yelled.

"What exactly do you think a buff is?" I asked.

"I am not gay!" he yelled, spraying a mist of beer-pocolypse spittle into the air.

"Since when does buff mean gay?" I yelled back.

"Everybody knows that, Alane!"

"I don't know that," I said flatly.

Darren gurgled a short "aagh" and stormed out of the room. "You make me crazy!" he said as he stomped up the stairs.

...Ah, definitions...the cause of—and the answer to—so many of life's little problems...

A few moments later, he stomped back down the stairs to the kitchen, poured another bottle of his toxic brew and stomped back up to the bedroom.

For twenty minutes, I sat at the kitchen table contemplating the deeper nuances of the word buff. I knew that I could buff the floor. I could buff my leather shoes. I had worn a colored face powder named buff back when I was slightly less pale and anemic looking. I had been told I looked really buff, once, when I was in particularly good shape in my twenties. I was usually in the buff when I took a shower. It seemed like buff might even work as a British euphemism for masturbation, but I didn't know any Brits that I could call to find out for sure. I had never, in my entire life, known the word buff to equal gay. Even if it did, with all the other possible meanings, how did he land there, and why on Earth did he care so much? Maybe it was a Pittsburgh thing.

The whole thing was ridiculous. As I sat there contemplating our conversation, it slowly started to sink into my brain that I was genuinely upset. In fact, the whole thing was upsetting. It was not just upsetting because it was stupid. It wasn't just upsetting because I thought he was smarter than that. It wasn't just upsetting because he insisted that I taste his disgusting, noxious homebrew. It was upsetting because I was offended. I was offended by his asinine, bigoted, small-minded attitude about a simple word that, to my knowledge at the time, wasn't a particularly randy euphemism for much of anything! Why did he care so much? And moreover, why did I?

Maybe that disgusting swill was an accidental truth serum. Maybe he had properly killed just enough brain cells to have finally lost the filter between his brain and his mouth. Maybe we were really going to get down into it. It seemed like something we needed to talk about.

Darren finished every bottle of that horrible batch of toxic, beer-pocolypse brew. I often wondered if he really liked it, or if he only drank it to prove that he could. I couldn't stand to be in the room when he poured it into a glass, and I got my very first official migraine a few days later. Other than that, things went on as usual, and we never talked about the word "buff" or Darren's latent homophobia again.

Chapter 12

It was sometimes hard for me to admit that I married a frat-boy. Generally speaking, they weren't my type. I always thought they were trying a little too hard and weren't trying hard enough, all at the same time. In the beginning, Darren seemed like a frat-boy unicorn. He was so genuine and sincere. I assumed his blue-collar roots kept him grounded and gave him a depth that was missing from the rest of them. If that was ever true and not just the product of a hormonally deranged late twenty-something mind, then it was definitely a case of transient unicornism. As he got older, his frat-boy tendencies never faded away; they got stronger. He was a frat-boy through and through.

Whenever Darren's Frat-Pack came to town, it was always a party, at least in Darren's mind. They had gone to school at Duquesne University in downtown Pittsburgh, a school that Darren liked to claim was almost Ivy League, making the frat boy thing even more impressive in his own mind. (Since everybody knows that "almost" only counts in horseshoes and hand grenades, it's easy to draw conclusions about the validity of his claim. It just made him look like an asshole.)

Ivy League or not, Duquesne was full of kids with money, which might have been the reason Darren had a gorilla-sized chip on his shoulder. Darren's family wasn't poor. They were just generationally blue collar, which put Darren on the next to last rung on the financial success ladder, only ranking above the kids of campus employees who got to go there for free. I never cared much about any of it. My family was educated, but not wealthy. (For the record, I am a state school girl.) My mind was set on making my own way in the world. I'm not sure how much it mattered to his frat brothers, either, but I know that it bothered Darren. He spent a lot of time trying to belong, and his college credit card told the tale in numbers. Bar tabs can really add up over time.

Out of school, it actually got worse. Darren was a doctor in private practice with a doctor wife. In his mind, we should have been rolling in money. Needless to say, we weren't, but whenever his "bro's" came to town, it was all I could do to keep him from blowing out our credit cards on beer and shots. He never picked up a fine dining habit or the high-end dinner party bug. His thing was the bar and late-night "sammiches" scene with a few live bands and some pool thrown in for extra entertainment.

From where I sat, it looked like his friends loved to relive their glory days with good old "Dank," and then go home to their functional adult lives, secure with the notion that Darren would be there, bellied up to the bar and waiting for them whenever they needed a diversion.

Not long after beer-pocolypse, the holidays rolled around again, which meant extra family time with Charlene and a little guilt from my parents down in Charlotte for not visiting very often. It also meant it was Frat-Pack season.

Our house on the South Side was perfectly located for easy access to everything an aging frat-boy on the prowl could want. Whenever someone sent up the Frat Signal, Darren could be right there in thirty minutes or less unless I was going, which slowed him down considerably.

One night, Darren's closest frat-friend, Rizz, sent up the signal. Rizz was a likable guy who had taken his time moving on from undergrad and the rigors of parentally funded unemployment. This time, though, Rizz had started his first semester at a Caribbean medical school and looked very much like he was finally getting his shit together. When he called, Darren wasted no time. His brother-in-arms needed his support, so he set out down the icy, snow covered steps toward Carson Street.

I stayed home and went to bed.

The doorbell woke me up. It wasn't a simple ring of the bell, but a repeating, "DING-DONG! DING-DONG! DING-DONG!" followed by a pause and then another round of, "DING-DONG! DING-DONG! DING-DONG!" I had been sound asleep, so it took me a minute to understand what I was hearing. It wasn't often that people came to the door and rang the bell, so it wasn't a sound that I was particularly used to hearing and especially not in the middle of the night. Once I got my wits about me, I panicked. Something had to be wrong. *Oh my God, it's the police!* I thought to myself as I ran to the window. There was nothing unusual outside that I could see—no people, no police, no strange cars. There was only the repeating DING-DONGING of the doorbell.

Then, a warbling cry emanated from the covered porch below. "Baaaaay-bee!" I heard, "Baaaaaaaay-beeeee!"…DING-DONG… DING-DONG…DING-DONG-DING-DONG… "BAY-BEEEE! Pleeeeeeeeeease!" There was another long pause and then "BAY-BEE!...BAY-BEE!" It was Darren for sure. I ran down the stairs as fast as I could. If he kept up this kind of racquet, the police might just show up after all.

When I opened the door, Darren was standing there wobbling back and forth like he had rocker bottoms for feet. "Bay-bee!... hee-hee…" he slurred and giggled. His feet rocked forward, and he stumbled head first into the house, landing with his gut over the arm of the living room sofa and planting his face squarely into the sofa cushions. He giggled "hee-hee!" into the upholstery.

I couldn't catch my breath. My heart was slamming in my chest. The doorbell had freaked me out, the uncertainty had panicked me, and the drunk Weeble Wobble asshole in front of me was really pissing me off. He had his key, but he couldn't work it. All he could do was stab at the doorbell and warble at the bedroom window. At least he hadn't driven. But if he was this bad, what in the hell must Rizz have looked like? I could only hope that he had the good sense to call a cab.

Darren got himself up from the couch with an awkward fling that launched him back toward the entryway. His shoulder ricocheted off the door, sending his other shoulder into the adjacent wall. He scuffed his feet around and over themselves as he tried to balance and take his jacket off at the same time. On another day and at another time, this might have been funny or at least mildly amusing. This night, however, it was anything but.

"Bay-bee," he slurred, "I'm so happy to see you." He was that weird drunk kind of happy that only happened when he was really inebriated. I wondered if he could feel even a tinge of self-pity and loathing…or pity and self-loathing…or had any hint of self-awareness at all, but I doubted it. He had reached full id mode, and it looked like the rest of the world could suck it.

I stood there silently watching him stagger and stumble around in the entryway. He braced himself against the walls and pulled each boot off with the toe of the other foot before pushing off the wall and letting the weight of his head lead his body over to the stairs. He continued up the stairs missing most of the steps as he clung to the rail and eventually making his way to the bed before he passed out.

As I stood in the door to the kitchen watching Darren stumbled up the stairs away from me, I realized the gnome was with me. He was standing in the moonlit kitchen a mere 3 feet away. Like before, I probably should have freaked out in some way at the sight of a fully formed gnome-man standing inside my house in the dark, but I wasn't. I was oddly happy to see him. He didn't wave or speak. He was watching and listening without expression or clear intent. As I started to reach out for him, he turned and walked into the darkness.

I switched on the kitchen light to make sure there was no one there. "Why bother showing up if you're just gonna leave?" I said out loud into the empty kitchen, "It's kinda rude!" I switched off the light as little tendrils of disappointment wrapped around my chest. I hated that feeling; it was too familiar.

The adrenaline was starting to wear off, and exhaustion was setting in behind it. Darren had passed out fully dressed, but at least he had landed in the right place. Drunken asshole or no drunken asshole, I couldn't leave him like that in good conscience, so I checked his breathing, stripped off his jeans, and rolled him on his side before I climbed onto my side of the bed. I was irritated, bordering on angry, but my exhaustion beat all of it. All I wanted was to sleep. The rest of it could wait.

Sleeping with a wildly drunk person is rarely easy. They tend to snore loudly and a lot. They sleep in impossible physical positions, often taking their half out of the middle of the bed and contorting their arms and legs into shapes that defy the limits of normal human physiology. It was always worse when cigarettes or shots were involved.

Darren had always liked to drink. Actually, we were both highly experienced social drinkers in our twenties. In fact, most of our early dates included a few drinks or a bottle of wine. By this point, however, my physical tolerance for it was waning. I was getting sicker and sicker on fewer and fewer drinks, to the point that sometimes just being in the same room with a full pint was nauseating. Every time I drank, it ended with a brain splitting migraine or a vomiting extravaganza. Darren's body seemed to go the other way. He was getting more drunk, more often and pounding down amounts of microbrewed beer that should have leveled him. It looked like a problem, but I figured it was just a phase.

I was also too nice to banish him to the couch when he's had too much. Our couch wasn't really a couch, at all. It was a loveseat that was only half as long as an average human in scrunchiest of scrunched sleeping positions. It would have been too cruel, but that meant there was little to no escape from the noise or anything that he might do while he was checked out. That particular night, Darren's drunken tango started off as it usually did. I aggressively jockeyed for a tiny sliver of the mattress with a firm ass-shove and some small knee and foot jabs, all while anchoring the outer edge of the blanket with my body weight to keep him from pulling it off of me entirely. At some point, after all of that, I settled in and drifted off to sleep.

At exactly 3:27 a.m., I woke up to an unusual sound that I couldn't quite place in my mind. When I opened my eyes, I was only inches away from the digital clock on my bedside table. My body was exposed and cold. At some point in my sleep, I had apparently succumbed to the tango. There was one tiny corner of the sheet still wrapped around my hands, and the rest of the covers were in a wad at the foot of Darren's side of the bed.

As the unusual sound continued, a warm, wet, sprinkling sensation hit my back, and full consciousness crashed into my brain. In one motion, I flipped over in the bed. Darren was on his feet by the bed with one hand in the air and his doughy, beer ravaged penis in the other as an arching stream of urine spouted from its tip, like a demon cherub on top of some perverse Venetian fountain.

"HEY!" I yelled as I launched myself backward out of the bed, "WHAT THE FUCK?!"

He kept going, letting out a gleeful, "hee, hee…"

"WAKE UP!" I yelled. "WAKE THE FUCK UP!"

"What?" he said as the stream ended and he forced out the last few drops.

"Wake the fuck up! Wake the fuck up! Oh, my God! Fucking fuck!" I screamed and ran down the stairs. My sleep-deprived mind was completely blown out. I ran all the way down into the basement and grabbed all the dry towels I could find and an entire roll of paper towels.

By the time I made it back up the stairs, Darren had stripped the rest of his clothes off and was blotting at the bed with his shirt. "Rizzy……Riiizzzzzzzzz…hee-hee," he muttered with drunken glee as he dabbed. "Hee-hee-heeee." He giggled and dabbed some more. "We're goin' dahn to Fat Nicky's for dah show," he said in full Pittsburghese.

"Whatever, go shower while I clean this up," I said without controlling my rage at all.

"Noooo," he said in a drunk whisper like there was someone else listening in, "what time is it?"

"I don't know, God Damn it! Go take a shower!" I said even more forcefully.

"Tha clock's righ dare…can't yinz read it?" He pointed at the clock on my bedside table, "wait...z'tha clock right?"

"Yup!" I barked. "It sure is!" The piss-splattered man-baby slurring at me in my bedroom had pushed me over the edge.

"Fucker…I gotta sleep," he said grabbing the towel from my hands and threw it on the bed. "I'm sposta be dahn'ner in an 'ahr an-a haff…" He grabbed the rest of the towels off the floor and smashed them on top. "Sorry, I'll hannal dis tamarrah." With that, he threw himself on top of the towel pile and went immediately to sleep.

I stood there an unreasonably long time, watching him sleep and contemplating the situation at hand. My doctor husband had just used our bed as a toilet and laughed about it. Actually, it was way worse than that. He used our bed as a toilet, sprayed me with urine, laughed about it, and then went back to sleep.

. . . just fucking great....

I was cold. I was angry. My back and my hands were covered in pee. (As a general rule, I never used the word "pee." I preferred "urine," or simply "the bathroom" as in "I need to use 'the bathroom'" which kept things a little more mysterious. I could even handle calling it "piss" or at the very worst "tinkle," but "pee" was where I drew the line. It was lower than lowbrow and totally trailer, but in that moment, "pee" was exactly right.) I was totally unraveling. This was not what my life was supposed to be. It was all just too much.

The smell of urine was getting stronger as the back of my shirt started to dry. I couldn't look at him anymore, so I left him there. I stripped off my clothes and showered until the hot water was gone. When it was done and I had dry, warm clothes on, I sat down at the kitchen table to consider my options. I was so tired, my bed was a giant urinal cake, and for the first time in my life, I felt genuinely old.

I stayed up for the rest of the early morning. I drank half my body weight in coffee and started planning my escape. This time, there was no guiding voice in my head, there was no red princess with a horse talking to me in a dream. The gnome wasn't even there to make me feel better. There was just the clicking of the radiator and the jagged sound of my breath there with me...and bottomless amounts of pent up rage.

I spent at least an hour just pacing the kitchen floor and trying to decide what to do. What I came up with wasn't much of a plan. It was more of a gut reaction than an actionable blueprint, but it was a start. I was going to leave. That's all there was to do. This was not the life I wanted. This wasn't even a life that I thought I should have wanted. No, this was something else, entirely. I had turned my back on almost everything and everyone I had known before Darren. I had turned my back on myself. I had cashed in everything I had been and everything I had ever hoped to be for a drunken, piss-fountain of a husband. I had been chasing some other girl's fairy tale.

This wasn't what I thought 32 would look like. I thought I'd have a family by now. I thought I'd have a stable career and the beginnings of a retirement plan. I felt like time was running out. I had to do something to change things. I had to get myself back on track. There was still time to reconfigure. I just needed to be strong. All I had to do was turn my back on the vow that I took before God and everybody and go my own way. It wasn't a big deal. All I had to do was leave. Yes, it would hurt. Yes, I would be the bad guy. But, once it was done, Darren could pee on whomever he wanted. Charlene would get her wish… and most importantly, I would be free.

It seemed impossible. I switched to English Breakfast Tea hoping that would help.

Against all reasonable physical odds, Darren got himself up in time to meet Rizzy at the bar by 5:00 a.m. As wrecked as he had been, I don't know how he did it. When he came down, we didn't speak. I don't even think he knew I was there. I just sat quietly and watched him stumble out the door.

The walk to Fat Nicky's was about a mile and was mostly downhill. It was easy in the summer when ice wasn't covering the sidewalk and the steep stairs that wound down Buzz Kill Hill. On a dark winter morning like this one, it was a different story. It was treacherous for anyone, and most especially for the inebriated. It's possible that Darren chose to follow the road instead of the stairs. That route would have been just as icy and treacherous with the added complications of the vagrants and speeding city buses. There was usually a dead body dumped near the mission street bridge every couple of months, but we had already met our corpse quota for that quarter, so at least that was working in his favor.

The metal screen door slammed behind him as he left. His boots crunched on the icy snow and faded into the dark as he made his way down the street.

He was gone. This was my chance.

The time for deep intellectual discourse with myself was over. There was nothing left to consider. There was nothing left to weigh out. I just had to act. It had to be now. Every cell in my body was telling me to move, but I just sat there.

I was hesitating…again.

Irrational fear was winning…again.

I went through the plan in my head…again.

All I needed was the bear minimum—passport, social security card, transcripts, licenses, anything that I thought I couldn't stand to lose, and whatever spare cash I could find. I just had to gather it all together, throw it in my car, and drive off into the sunset. No one would even miss me. In fact, it seemed like everyone involved would be a relieved that I was gone. Darren might be hurt for a little while, but it was nothing a couple of beers and a "sammich" couldn't fix.

Then, as if yanked up out of my seat by some invisible fist, I was on my feet and running. I started with documents and then jewelry. Last but not least, I needed cash. I tore through every old purse, book bag, briefcase, winter coat, and junk drawer in the house, which netted a whopping grand total of $4.16. It was pretty bleak.

Then, I remembered Darren's jeans from the night before. They were by the bed and covered in urine since they had been well inside the golden splash zone. It was disgusting, but I was determined. Carefully tweezing the wet denim between my fingertips, I gingerly rooted around in the pockets. There, in his piss-soaked jeans, I hit pay dirt. Between three of the five pockets, I found a twenty and forty-eight one-dollar bills.

Admittedly, I was a little irked by the denominational breakdown. The twenty, I understood. Darren had been out at the bars and probably stopped at an ATM at some point. The forty-eight ones, however, had to be a different story. It seemed pretty clear that he and Rizzy had been to a strip club, but I couldn't be sure if he forgot to tip his stripper after she slid her vagina down a pole for him or if forty-eight one-dollar bills were all his hairy ass could muster at amateur hour. Either way, the money was there, and since the $4.16, three unused tampons, two hair ties, and five half-melted cough drops that I found were barely enough to buy a good cup of coffee, I had no room to be prissy about it.

In less than two hours, everything I thought I couldn't live without and $72.16 in cash were piled on the urine-free part of the bed. The pile was remarkably small. I kept thinking, *this can't be it*, to myself as I shoved it all into a single 9 x 12 manila envelope. It seemed like there should have been more.

My mind scanned the rest of the house for anything that was mine, alone. There was the desk my parents had bought me when I started chiropractic college. There were photo albums and scrapbooks filled with all of the shows I had done and pictures of friends that I didn't have anymore. There were the fabric shears and the sewing machine my grandparents gave me for my 14th birthday.

There were all of my notes and books. There were all of the knick-knacks and trinkets I had collected. There was the stuffed rabbit my mom had given me for my last show. There was still so much stuff…all the beautiful junk of my life was smashed into rotting cardboard boxes in the basement.

I felt all of it squarely in my gut. I hadn't thought about what belonged to me in a very long time. It wasn't just junk or things. It was my life. I hadn't thought about my life like that in a very long time. I put my life aside when I went to school and when I married Darren. Everything that had been mine became ours. From the minute we took our vows, there really wasn't any separation between us anymore. I was not me. He was not him. There was only us. The notion was so romantic at the time. I felt like it was the two of us together against the world, and nothing would ever change it. It was totally saccharine…and completely unrealistic. I relinquished everything I had ever been over to a childish, fairytale notion of love. It wasn't realistic, and it had never been real. Now here I was, wavering, unsure of where Darren stopped and I started.

Uncertainty was creeping in around the edges of my plan. "Now what?" I said out loud to myself. I had been so angry and so sure, just minutes before. I had been so completely done with the whole thing that I was ready to walk away and never look back, but the uncertainty short-circuited all of the caffeine and adrenaline. It was making me weak.

All I could think about was what tomorrow would be like. How would I feel when I woke up in my parents' spare bedroom if I even made it that far? What then? If I ran away, that would be it. There would be no going back. And what about my practice and my patients? I hadn't thought at all about them. I couldn't abandon them. I could be sued for that. I could lose my licenses for that. Darren had disrespected me in a way that I could not have concocted in my mind on my most creative day. On the other hand, my marriage had been my choice. No one had forced me into it. I picked this. I had made this bed. Now, it was my lot to lie in it, for urine or not for urine.

Fatigue was melting my resolve into a puddle of rationalizations. My life, good or bad, was here. I was not a quitter. I was married. I had taken a vow. Just because I didn't visit God every weekend at church, didn't mean that my promise didn't count. A marriage was worth fighting for. Everything that was worth anything took work and sacrifice. At least that's the way I had operated the rest of my life. If I left now, I'd be giving up. I'd be leaving everything behind me. It wasn't just about the things. It was the whole thing. My childhood home was gone. My friends had faded away. Dance and art were my past. This was my present.

The screen door clanked and screeched open, and my window of opportunity closed. Darren was home. I had lost track of time somehow. I thought he would be gone for at least a few more hours. Adrenaline shot through my chest.

I grabbed the envelope and shoved it into the rusty black filing cabinet under the computer desk. That filing cabinet was full of old bills and statements. He would never look in there. He never dealt with any of that stuff. It would be safe. I would be safe and ready to go when I needed it.

Darren called out as the front door closed. I didn't respond. His heavy footsteps hit the stairs. Without thinking, I ripped the covers off the bed and started stripping the sheets.

"Oh man," Darren groaned, "I was going to go back to sleep."

"Sorry," I said without looking at him as I threw the mess on the floor at his feet. It wasn't an intentionally bitchy move to pile it all there, it just seemed like it.

"Did you have to do that right now?" he asked with more than a hint of irritation. "You knew I was coming back."

"Yes, right now. Were you really going to sleep on that?" I pointed to his side of the bed where the stain was still visible on the mattress pad.

"Oh," he chuckled, "yeah, that. It's fine, I can get it later."

"No, you can't," I said tersely. "It needs to happen, now."

"Okay, okay, it's just the sheets. It's not a big deal," he insisted.

"It's a big fucking deal," I said with unexpected force as I ripped at the mattress pad with more aggression.

"What the fuck," Darren said sanctimoniously.

"What the fuck? What the fuck? I'll tell you what the fuck. You fucking urinated on me last night!"

"On the bed, not on you," he said as if it was perfectly reasonable.

"It was on me!" I yelled. It was like the top of my head flipped open and angry word lava poured out, "And either way, you still did it right on the bed! Our bed! And then you slept in it! And then you left! Fuck!"

"If it bothered you that much, you could have cleaned it up by now. It's been hours," he said flatly.

A guttural "eeeyyahh!" uncontrollably flew out of my mouth. I grabbed the laundry basket from the closet and furiously flung the piss-sheets into it.

"Wait," Darren said rather quietly in comparison to his previous decibel level.

I grabbed the basket off the floor without looking at him and headed for the stairs. My head was throbbing. *Leave-leave-leave!* repeated over and over in my brain like a screaming death metal waltz, *Leave-leave-leave!... Leave-leave-leave!... Leave-leave-leave!... Rrraaahhhhh! Leave-leave-leave!... Leave-leave-leave!... Leave-leave-leave!... Rrraaahhhhh!*

"Wait!" Darren said with angry desperation as he grabbed my elbow and pulled me back hard. My shoulder seared with pain.

"Don't!" I yelled, wild-eyed and panting. I yanked my arm out of his grasp which sent the piss sheets tumbling down the stairs.

He had touched me like that only once before. We were at my parents' house not long after the notebook fiasco. There had been lots of crying and arguing in the dark about how my parents had disrespected him, or some nonsense like that, right after we went to bed. As I got up to leave, he grabbed my flannel pajama top and yanked me back toward the bed. I was strong and pretty good on my feet, at the time. I held my stance and heaved my entire bodyweight away as hard as I could. He pulled. I pulled. He whisper-shouted at me to get back in bed, and I whisper-shouted, "No! No! No!" right back. We went on like this until the flannel gave out and ripped open around his grip sending me crashing to the floor. The ripping and the crashing and the bruise that it left on the side of my neck with the flannel PJ garrote sent him into spasms of remorse. He said he was sorry that night, the next day, and every day for a week after it happened. He swore he would never do it again. He swore he didn't want to be that guy, and I believed him. I thought it was a fluke. I assumed it was an aberrant reaction to the situation with his mother and the notebook. I let it go as much as I could and buried the rest deep in my memory. It stayed buried until now.

Here we were, again. He stared at me with a panicked, gape-mouthed expression that I had never seen on his face before. I stared back with an equal measure of shock and fury.

Leave-leave-leave... leave-leave-leave... leave-leave-leave... aaarrrgh! Leave-leave-leave... leave-leave-leave... leave-leave-leave... aaarrrgh! Leave-leave-leave... leave-leave-leave... leave-leave-leave... aaarrrgh! Leave-leave-leave... leave-leave-leave... leave-leave-leave...

aaarrrrgh! hammered on loudly in my head. I let the laundry basket fall to the floor between us and headed for the stairs.

"WAIT!" Darren said with even more panic. "Wait…please, wait."

I stopped and turned to face him. "You said you would never do that, again."

"I didn't mean it," he said pleadingly.

"I don't care!"

He looked wounded. "I just didn't want you to walk away. I want to work this out."

"You said you would never do that, again," I said flatly.

"I know. I know. I'm just tired. I haven't slept," he responded like it was a reasonable excuse.

"Neither have I."

"I know," he said with remorse, "It was stupid."

"What part?" I asked.

"Huh?" he shot back with irritation.

"What part of it was stupid, Darren? I need you to be specific," I said.

"Damn it, Alane," he said forcefully, "You know."

"Yes," I said with increased calm, "I do. I am well aware of every stupid fucking thing that has happened in the last few hours. I need to know that you do, too."

"All of it. All of it was stupid," he shot back with frustration. "I'm sorry. I was drunk, and I didn't know what I was doing."

That wasn't even half of it. I wanted him to say so much more than that. I wanted to unload. I wanted to make him listen to every last detail of every last stupid fucking thing that he had done. I wanted to force him to listen to all of it, but when I opened my mouth all that came out was, "Okay."

"That's it? Okay?" He sounded frustrated.

The pause that followed was long and painful. That wasn't it at all. I hadn't even scratched the surface of the sea of shit that I wanted to get off my chest. But I couldn't make the words come out. All I could get out was, "That's it. That's all I can do right now."

After another eternal pause, Darren said, "Okay."

I turned and walked down the stairs collecting the laundry as I went. The morning had been a wild ride. In that moment, I made my choice. I was staying. If I was a coward, then so be it. It just wasn't the right time. If I was leaving, it couldn't be a big show, in a fit of emotion. It had to be a clear-headed choice. I had to be sure about it. If I left, that was it, end of story.

We never really talked about any of it after that. I cleaned up the mess and got the death-metal waltz to stop playing on a loop in my head. Darren fell asleep on the tiny sofa. He never said if Fat Nicky's at 5:30 in the morning was worth the effort. I never told him that I almost left him or about my manila escape envelope. We argued a lot. I think we both sensed that things were different. Our whole world seemed to be a slightly different hue. Food tasted different. What passed for laughter was tinged with hesitation and dissatisfaction.

Work was less interesting. Four months earlier we threw caution to the wind and left our jobs. We bought a small practice in an older Pittsburgh suburb across the street from a Wal-Mart for $35,000. Theoretically, we should have been able to pay back the loan we took for it in about a year and still make as much for ourselves as we had been while working for other people. This was the first time I learned that our theories were nothing more than fantasies with poorly researched business plans attached to them. We were so excited and so motivated, but that didn't last. By month four, chiro-practicing on our own was just as monotonous as it had been working for other people, only without a guaranteed paycheck.

The holidays came and went. The practice was a ghost town for over a month. While people were assaulting each other in the Wal-Mart parking lot with cheap DVD players, we sat alone in our office just across the street. I endured another Christmas with Charlene. That year, my Christmas present tower was almost nonexistent, and she wrapped what was there in festive paper that was the perfect solid shade of chemistry notebook green. Everyone else got presents wrapped in paper covered in candy canes and cartoon Santas. I thought maybe she might sing some journal entry Christmas carols for everyone or send highlights from my journal out with the Danky family Christmas card so that all of her friends could see what she had been up to, but she didn't. At least that year, I got to go home to my own bed every night when the festivities were over.

As for our bed, we were still sleeping on the same urinal cake mattress. We were way too broke to afford a new one, and I had two choices—live with it or sleep on the floor.

Winter that year was almost soul crushing. The dreary cold seemed never-ending. Everything was covered in a layer of grime that was some combination of salt, ash, and exhaust mixed with a little perma-soot left over from the last century. I had never missed Florida as much as I did that winter. I preferred my salt in the water and in the air and occasionally on the rim of a cocktail glass.

Darren and I kept on arguing. They were a little different in the aftermath of Piss-a-palooza. They were quieter but heavier. The jabs were deeper and more personal. What we argued about specifically, I can't really recall. All I remember is that every argument ultimately ended in a fight about me and my need for independence. I guess I had been asserting myself a little more than before. I had always prided myself on my ability to speak my mind and make my own choices, but somewhere in the time between saying I do and hiding my escape envelope in the filing cabinet, I changed. It felt like I deferred everything to Darren and to what would make Darren and everybody else happy…and by everybody else, I really think I just mean Charlene. Darren, on the other hand, felt like I disagreed with him at every turn.

"When we got married, we became one," Darren would say, raising his eyebrows so forcefully that his forehead looked like an accordion. "We are husband and wife. We are one." He hadn't started his "manifest-your-dreams" phase, yet, but his tone was the same as what I would later come to think of as his "life-coach" voice.

"I agree," I would say, "but that doesn't mean I stop being me."

"Yes, it does," he would insist like I was saying the dumbest words ever uttered by a human. "We are like one person. We are the same. Two halves of the same whole."

"Yes," I would say, "two halves, my half and your half. My half doesn't have to always agree with your half. My half has its own opinions, and your half is free to have yours."

"No," he would continue in the same irritating tone. "We are one. We do things together. We think things together. We have to be of one mind. That's what marriage is."

He would get started on this over just about any topic from work, to food, to movies and books—anytime I didn't share his opinion on something. He said I was infuriating. I thought he was absurd.

"So, I can't have my own thoughts about things. I can only have 'our' thoughts about things. Is that right?" I would ask.

"Yes!" he would say with excitement, like he had led me to some sort of spiritual epiphany, "That's exactly right!"

"But what if I don't agree with you? What happens then?"

"That doesn't matter because we are one," he would insist with excitement.

"So, you'll agree with me when I'm right?" I asked. I thought maybe we were on the way to making sense.

"Sure, if I think you are right," he said earnestly.

"What if you don't?" I asked.

"Then I'd be right," he said like it was obvious.

"But what if you're not?" I pressed.

"We have to be together. We're married," he insisted.

"But what if you're wrong?"

"You said you're already wrong."

"But what if you're wrong?"

"You should just trust me. In our vows, you promised to honor and obey me."

"No, I didn't. We took that part out. Remember?" It took a lot to get the reverend to take that part out, but I made it clear that it was a deal breaker and at the time, Darren said he totally agreed.

"Maybe we shouldn't have," he offered with unreasonable arrogance for the situation.

"Doesn't matter. We did, and you agreed to it," I was getting worked up. "You knew what I was like. This isn't new."

"Why are you like this?" he said dismissively.

"So, you're saying that I should just agree with you?" I said ignoring his question.

"Yes, that's what it is to be married. There's no you and me," pointing to me first and then himself as he spoke, "there is only you and me, together, as one."

"I agree that we are 'one,'" I actually used air quotes (for the record, I hate air quotes,) "but we are still two separate people. We're supposed to make each other better, not stop being ourselves."

"Not separate. One," he would insist, holding onto life-coach tone with all his might. “One,” he would say again as he slid his fingers together and slowly shook his interlocked hands up and down like it meant something profound. I always thought he looked like a stoner trying to play “here’s the church and here’s the steeple,” when he did that.

“That’s not what I signed up for. I’m still me. You married *me.* The rest of this is some bullshit. You want me to do whatever you want and never complain about it. It sounds like I am supposed to just do whatever you say. Is that it?”

“There’s the problem, Alane. You’re still talking about you. You haven’t really let yourself be really married. We are not one. This is why we fight so much.”

His bullshit would instantly become more than I could stand, every time he got to this point, and every time we repeated this exchange, I got angrier and angrier. I didn’t want to yell. I had already done that too much, and it solved nothing. I didn’t want to pretend that this was rational. I had tried that, too. By the end, I would start bawling. I didn’t want to, but I couldn’t help it. It made me look weak. I was just so damned frustrated.

“It takes both of us to fight, Darren,” I said the last time we rehashed this fight.

“I’m not fight-fighting, I’m just talking to you about what you need to do…”

…and then I lost it…

“What I need to do?! What I need to do?! What about what you need to do?” By then I was yelling, crying, hyperventilating, and spitting all at the same time. “Fuck you…you know, Darren, just fuck you. If you don’t like me, then let’s end it. I am not going to just roll over and do what you what want me to do and think what you want me to think. You said you married me because I was strong and smart. You said that you loved that about me. But, if you don't, then I can't do this. I can't be here."

"Are you saying you want a divorce?" Darren's voice instantly dropped into his manliest yelling voice. "'Cause once you say it, there is no going back!"

I sat down on the radiator crying with snot dripping consistently out of my right nostril. I kept wiping it with my sleeve.

"Is that what you want? Huh?" he yelled as he paced back and forth in front of me.

I couldn't speak through all of the crying and snotting.

"Oh, so now you have nothing to say," he yelled with disgust, "that's perfect!"

"I don't want a divorce!" I forced the words out in a raspy scream, "I just can't keep doing this! It's like a fucking bait and switch. You never told me that was what you expected. I don't even know where this is coming from! Where did you get this shit?"

"Why do you have to make everything so fucking hard? Why can't you just agree with me?" he yelled.

"Agree with you about what? What are we talking about, here?" I yelled back.

"Anything! Anything at all...just fucking agree with me! Just let me have one, every once and while!" he yelled louder.

"Just let you have one? You mean that I should agree with you when you are factually incorrect? You just want me to let you say whatever you want and not think for myself? Why, Darren, why should I do that? Why would anybody do that? You won't do that!"

"Because I am your husband!" he screamed at the top of his lungs.

"I should just keep my mouth shut and walk ten steps behind you? Is that what you mean?" I kept getting louder.

"Ten steps behind me? Don't be ridiculous!" he spat.

"But I should keep my mouth shut, then" I wiped my nose with my sleeve.

"That's not what I said," he said in a calmer voice.

I was worn out from this one. I was worn out from all of them. "Maybe we should separate," I said flatly, "I can go to Charlotte. You can stay here and keep the practice."

"You can't go. I can't do the practice by myself," he said as though it just hit him that I might actually be done.

"We barely have any patients," I said. The crying had stopped, but my dripping nostril wasn't letting up. "Maybe we just need to be apart for a while."

"Is this what you want?" His voice wavered, and his eyes welled up.

I took a long pause while I thought about how I really wanted to answer him. This was the moment. If I was going to do it, this was the time.

"Please don't do this," Darren said quietly as he wiped his eyes.

I looked up at his face. All of the false pretense was gone. The anger was gone. For the first time in a long time, he just looked sad. "Do you still love me?" I asked, looking him right in the eye.

"You know I do," he replied pleadingly.

"No, I don't. Answer the question," I said firmly. He said nothing, so I asked again, "Do you still love me?"

"Of course, I love you," he said quickly.

I held my eyes locked right on his. "Can you accept that I will never just do what you say because you want me to?"

He hesitated, but then said, "Yes."

I hesitated this time. I was hurt. I was angry. I was tired. I knew this was my chance to change things, to start over, but I couldn't make myself say the words. Deep down, it felt like I really loved him, and the thought of leaving scared me. If I left, I would be a quitter…a failure of my own making. I didn't want to be wrong.

I said, "I love you, too, but we have to fix this," but I wasn't really sure what it meant to love him anymore.

He hesitated, again. "Okay, we will."

That was the last we said about it for a long time.

We spent the rest of the weekend together, just the two of us. No homebrews, no frat brothers, and no family dinners. We went to dinner and a movie, and we laughed for the first time in a very long time. We talked about how things had been with his family as if we were friends, and without any prompting from me and only one beer in his system, Darren confessed that he really wasn't happy with the way Charlene had been treating him. They had been talking a lot on the phone when I wasn't around to hear it. I had no idea that she had been going after him just as hard as she had been going after me.

It was like some weird confessional. We talked about things that we had never talked about before. We talked about how much we loved being chiropractors and about how much we really hated our new practice. Neither one of us had been courageous enough to admit it out loud. Neither one of us wanted to disappoint the other. The truth was enlightening, and our conversations flowed like we were back in Iowa when things were new and hopeful. It felt good, but it wasn't enough. Nothing was fixed. It was all just a crack in our foundation with an old rug thrown over it.

That night, as the conversation waned and we were almost asleep, a loud dragging sound in the kitchen shook the house. It was out of place, but neither of us was willing to go look for a source of the sound in the dark.

The next morning, we found the large blue blown glass vase that stood by the door to the basement standing perfectly upright in the center of the kitchen floor. It hadn't rolled or fallen over, and neither of us had been out of bed that night. It was just there like it had always been there, unbroken and a little dusty from neglect. There was no clear cause for its relocation. It had been in that corner by the door since the day we moved in. It never rattled or shifted when we walked heavily across the floor or on the stairs. I rarely even cleaned it. There was no reasonable explanation for it. I thought it might have been the gnome, letting me know he was still there, and maybe, that he approved, but I couldn't be sure. Even Darren thought it might have been a ghost. We moved it back to its rightful place, and it never moved again until we moved out of the house.

◆◆◆◆◆

It's amazing what a little urine, followed by some relentless honesty and snot tears can accomplish. It wouldn't be my first choice for couples counseling techniques, but we had to work with what was available to us at the time. Things held together for a while after that. I'd even be willing to say that things improved. The practice got better. (Translation—we started making some money.) Our home life got better. Even Pittsburgh, itself, seemed better despite the fact that winter had hit full-force and the city was already running out of salt for the roads. It was weird.

Darren took a break from the beer for a while. He took a break from Charlene, too and focused all of his energy into the practice and into us. It was his New Year's resolution. It all seemed like a wonderful idea.

...and it was for a while...

But as with all good things, it ended. The end of our happy streak was abrupt and painful. The winter was hard. Self-employment was even harder. Add in a little sprinkling of Charlene on top of all of that, and it was a recipe for catastrophe.

Darren started wavering on the hard line he had drawn where

his mother was concerned, and as a result, Charlene started creeping back in, little by little. First, it was the phone calls. Then Darren invited her to our house for dinner. Thankfully, she declined that invitation.

As January continued on, the two of them talked more and more. Charlene was always in some kind of crisis. That month, Darren's grandfather had met "some gold-digger floozy" down in Florida, and it was getting too serious. Charlene's main concern, as she described it, was her inheritance which she insisted on detailing when we went over to their house for Sunday dinner. Darren had insisted that I give them a chance, and I begrudgingly complied.

At the first opportunity, Darren and Earl abandoned the kitchen, leaving me there alone with Charlene while she smoked and tended to food. Once again, there was nowhere to run. The whole thing seemed like some perverse flashback as I sat there listening to Charlene complain about how a gold digger had done her wrong. I listened to all of the things that were wrong with the floozy and how she was ruining her father. I listened to her yowl about Wall-Cat who had recently abandoned her by moving to Florida, and who had spent time with the floozy and seemed to like her. Charlene's words were awful, even the ones about her own daughter. My only consolation was that none of it was directed at me that time.

A part of me felt compelled to defend the two of them. After all, they weren't there to defend themselves. That was a horrible mistake on my part that resulted in a torrent of disgruntled, exasperated looks from Charlene that I was certain were nonverbal journal threats of some sort. After that, I just let Charlene bitch and puff without burdening her with logic or an alternative perspective. The last thing I needed were poster-sized copies of that stupid journal plastered to the front window of our office over the weekend when I wasn't there.

I let Charlene smoke and bitch and smoke and bitch as I sat there taking it all in. I'd interject an occasional, "Oh my God!" or, "No!" when it was clear that she needed a response. Every now and then, I'd throw in a, "No way!" to mix things up and let her know I was really following along. In fact, I listened to every last detestable, selfish world that rolled out of her mouth. I hated it, but I couldn't help myself. Maybe I was feeling particularly masochistic that day, or maybe I was afraid she'd turn on me if she felt ignored. Maybe I just wanted to hear every foul thing she could come up with to prove to myself that she really was that vicious—as if I needed proof that she was a foul and hateful, self-serving creature and that it hadn't been my imagination.

I got what I wanted…

I hadn't made any of it up. It was all right there. Charlene ran down the same list of bullshit about that "bitch homewrecker" that she had used against me. It was fascinating…and it brought it all right back.

The kitchen timer dinged. Charlene crushed out her cigarette as she barked, "DEAR!" into the air. She heaved her body out of her chair, "DEAR! Dinner's ready!"

Darren and Earl came in from the living room where they had been watching the playoff games on TV. They had been close enough to hear the whole thing. There was only one thin wall between them and us, and it wasn't like Charlene was soft spoken. Darren looked at me and rolled his eyes. Taking it as a look of solidarity, I smiled back at him and went on about setting the table.

Charlene kept going even after we sat down to eat. Earl gave her a "yes, dear," and then quickly redirected by asking me directly how the practice was going.

"Fine," I said as looked at him and smiled. To my right, I could see that Charlene had stopped in mid-bite and was glaring at Earl like he had betrayed her.

"That's good," he said in his usual monotone.

There was silence. Charlene was still frozen and glaring.

Darren broke in with an embarrassing story about a patient who hid behind a plant and how we learned an important lesson that day—never assume the office is empty. Three of us laughed about it. Charlene glowered and chewed her food. Dinner went on in awkward silence, and then we went home.

In all, the dinner was a success. I endured three grueling hours of Charlene and her nonstop bile-spewing about a woman neither of us had ever met, but that was all. I survived it. Darren seemed happy, Earl seemed at peace, Charlene was Charlene, and all seemed right with the world.

And that lasted for about two days.

As the next week progressed, Darren sank into a dark and seemingly idiopathic black funk. From where I sat, he looked downright despondent with a supersized side order of self-loathing that manifested as anger toward me. I guess calling his funk idiopathic wasn't really fair. Things were better than they had been, but the spectrum of improvement above a "complete shit-trastrophy" still includes "super shitty," "shitty," and "overwhelmingly crappy." Honestly, things were pretty bleak, and the lack of liquid psychotropics had Darren down a bit of a hole.

The state of our practice wasn't helping. The improvement we saw after the New Year was only temporary. Despite Darren's initial burst of energy on practice building, our waiting room was like a desolate wasteland, and the patients that came in were becoming the epitome of high maintenance—demanding after-hours appointments and house calls for non-emergencies and never having their wallets with them when it was time to pay their copays. They knew we needed them. They could sense that our schedule book was light. They were like vultures picking away at a mostly dead road kill pizza. The rancid smell of blood and fear drew them in, and the more we rotted, the harder it was to shoo them away. They would linger and talk about absolutely nothing sometimes for over an hour. I always felt guilty as I gently pushed them toward the door. I knew that most of them were lonely. I was supposed to be helping them. I was supposed to be grateful for their trust in us. I think they thought they were helping us, but they weren't. They just made our days harder and longer. We became prisoners in our own practice.

To make things worse, Charlene would call, and Darren would disappear into the back room, leaving me alone at the front desk. She had stopped coming into the office for appointments, but she called almost every day. Then she would call again almost every night after office hours, and Darren would skulk off to the farthest corner of the house to talk to her. I didn't want to hear any of it. Whatever her problem was, I didn't want to be caught in the middle, so I gave him a wide berth.

On my side, I was fighting and losing the battle of the winter blues. I have never wished for sunshine as much as I did that winter. Back in Florida, I had taken the sun for granted and had often wished to see the snow or longed for a cold, cloudy day. What I fool I had been. That winter I would have given just about anything for some palm trees and a sunburn. Darren didn't say it, but I think the Pittsburgh winter was getting to him, too, and he was neck deep in his New Year's resolution and struggling. It's hard to sell wellness for a living with a pickled liver and stale beer breath. It was harder than either of us expected it to be for him, but he stuck it out…at least until his birthday rolled around the first week of February.

As a general rule, Darren made every effort to enjoy his birthday as much as possible. Up to that point in our lives, it hadn't been terribly unreasonable. We were still young. We didn't have kids yet. As long as there was a designated driver (i.e., me), there was no real reason for him not to celebrate to his heart's content. This year, other than our lack of discretionary income, his only real obstacle was his own New Year's Resolution, and since that was self-imposed, a night off for a little celebration was no big deal. He could get back to it the very next day.

Theoretically, it was a perfect plan…

This year, for his birthday, Darren chose dinner and karaoke with Charlene and Earl. It wouldn't have been my first choice, or my millionth for that matter, but it's what he said he wanted, so it's what we did. We had done it before, and Darren and Earl really seemed to love it. Truthfully, I didn't mind. I loved the applause. It wasn't the perfect replacement for my old life on stage, but it was better than nothing, even if everyone in the room was blitzed out of their minds. Most of all, it was also a great way to avoid conversations with Charlene. It was hard to hear her over the amplified caterwaul of drunk forty-somethings and their passion for 80's hair bands.

Darren's birthday was the day after Earl's, so this night was a two for one celebration. Right away, it seemed to be going well. We all seemed to be getting along. Charlene even seemed to be having a good time. She loved fawning over Darren when he sang and reminding me of how talented he was and how successful his public high school musical career had been.

Under normal circumstances, with a normal person, this would have been the perfect topic of conversation. I wanted to talk about dancing and singing and performing. I wanted to talk about dancing in New York and Paris and performing at the Kennedy Center and how different it was from the silly theme park gig I had for two summers when I was in high school. Inside, I was bubbling over with things about my life before the Dankys. I missed myself. I wanted to talk about something, anything, that was even remotely related to my life before chiropractic and before I met Darren. I wanted her to know me. I wanted to let her in…

…but I didn't…

Instead, I sat there, smiling and nodding, agreeing with her about how talented Darren was and how proud I should be of him as he sharply warbled his way through "Piano Man." It was clear to me that my stories weren't for Charlene. What I wanted to talk about was my past. It wasn't even that impressive. If I let her in, it wouldn't make her like me or respect me. It would just give her more to despise about me. It would make me an arrogant asshole who had to one-up her own husband to make herself feel better. So, I said nothing. I just kept smiling and nodding as I ground my teeth together and sipped my beer.

When it was my turn at the mic, I gulped down one last swig of beer for courage and walked up to the front. I held the sticky mic in my hand and belted out some Bonnie Raitt with reckless abandon. She wasn't my first choice, but she always played well to a room full of half-soused NASCAR fans. (About the singing, to be fair, I should point out that I was never really a singer, intrinsically speaking. I was a dancer who could sing. Still, I was pretty good, and I was even better when the audience was completely tanked. It was like being graded on a curve. As long as there wasn't a professional ringer hiding on the other side of the bar—which actually happened a few times—I usually got an automatic "A.") When the song was done, I made my way back to our table as the bar applauded. It felt good and familiar, but I kept my head down and sat down in my chair without giving much more than a smile and a nod.

"Way to go, Alane!" the DJ said enthusiastically. "We've got a live one in the house tonight! Give her a hand!" The applause swelled to the point of embarrassment, and I loved every second of it. I couldn't help myself. I stood up on the rung of my chair and gave my best theme park smile and a wave, mouthing "Thank you!" to the room. It was fantastic and utterly ridiculous...but mostly fantastic.

When I sat down in my seat, Earl and Darren were smiling and congratulating me. Charlene scowled in the corner. Earl turned around and said, "Dear! Wasn't she good?"

"Yes, dear," Charlene replied dryly as she rummaged around in her purse. "She was wuu-nderful. I'm going out for a smoke. Darren, come outside with me." She stood up and grabbed her coat.

"Sure! Be right back," Darren said cheerfully. He kissed me on the cheek and followed Charlene out the door. For the first time in a long time, he looked genuinely happy.

To this day, I don't know exactly what happened outside. I know that Charlene and Darren were out there longer than the length of a single cigarette. I know that Earl and I were alone at the table long enough to run out of small talk. They were out there long enough for Darren to miss the DJ calling his name for his next song. They walked back inside while I was singing another song. From the look on Darren's face, something had happened.

After that, Darren drove us home. He probably shouldn't have. On the way, he stopped and bought two cases of Iron City. (Iron City was Pittsburgh's hometown beer, and it was just about as far at the other end of the beer spectrum from microbrew as it gets.) That was a bad sign.

I asked him if he was alright. "Fine," was all he gave me. I asked him if he enjoyed his birthday. "Yup," was all he said. He never took his eyes off the road. When we got home, Darren cracked open the first beer before he got his coat and shoes off. Then he flopped himself on the couch and turned on the TV.

"You staying up for a while?" I asked cautiously. It was a stupid question, of course, but I didn't know what else to say.

"Yeah," he said staring at the TV and aggressively flipping the channels.

"Okay," I said. I lingered in the doorway, wanting to say something, wanting to fix whatever it was but with no idea what had happened or what he needed. "Are you alright?" I asked tentatively.

"Yeah," he said tersely.

I hung out in the doorway for a while wishing I knew what to do or say. Eventually, I said a cautious, "Goodnight."

"Good-night," he said emphasizing both halves of the word individually and not taking his eyes off the TV.

I waited a little while hoping for something to change, but it didn't. I went up to bed, alone. I didn't bother to turn on the lights. I stared at the ceiling in the dark for what felt like forever, telling myself it was nothing and I was overreacting. My gut knew otherwise. Something was up. Something had happened.

Charlene had done something. My gut was certain about that. I reran the whole night over in my head trying to figure out what I might have done to set her off. To the best of my recollection, I had been polite and conversational. I let her guide the conversation. I didn't argue or correct her when she said something patently inaccurate or personally offensive in any way. I couldn't understand it. I also couldn't get over the horrible feeling that something was brewing again, and it was about to explode.

I fell asleep sometime after three o'clock that morning. I didn't wake up when Darren came to bed, at least not enough that I could remember it. When I got up later that morning, I was greeted by a sea of empty beer cans in the kitchen. Darren's New Year's Resolution had come to an abrupt end rather than a brief pause for a single birthday celebration. Looking at the aftermath, I knew that my suspicions from the night before had to be right, but I still had no clue of why. The only thing to do was wait. I made coffee, cleaned up the mess, and went in to watch what was left of the Sunday morning news cycle.

When Darren finally rolled himself out of bed, I was braced for a big blow up. There wasn't one. He got up like there was nothing wrong. We spent the day together like there was nothing wrong. It was like there really was nothing wrong. It was creepy.

It wasn't until later that week that the arguments started. We argued about everything—the practice, food, beer, my hair, the cat, the car, the computer—everything except whatever happened with Charlene that night. We couldn't agree on anything other than the fact that we hated it and that we were barely making enough money to live off of, let alone making enough to pay our insanely large student loans bills or starting anything that remotely resembled a retirement plan. We revisited every stupid thing we had ever argued about and more, including the ongoing battle over my name.

The issue of my name had been a problem since the beginning. Simply put, I didn't want to change it. I never did, and I never said that I would. But the week after our honeymoon I thought the world was going to end at Charlene's fucking kitchen table. We were staying there until it was time to return to school. I had all of the paperwork there to fill out to change my status from single to married. I was happily chattering away with Darren and filling everything out when Darren said, "I wish you would change your name…"

...and then Charlene started...

Actually, Charlene lost her mind. No matter what I said, she wouldn't stop. I had been clear about it from the very beginning with everyone, but it didn't matter to her, and once she started, Darren piled on. He claimed that he had never been okay with it, but he didn't think that he had to say anything about it. He thought that I would just do it anyway because that's what married women are supposed to do.

It would have been nice to know this in advance. I was generally averse to being told what to do at that point in my life, and the idea of being branded with his name was beyond nauseating. He might as well have tattooed "Property of Darren Danky" across my forehead. I wanted no part of it.

The two of them were relentless. Darren used my own mother, who had taken my father's name without complaint, against me. He complained that I just had to be different. Charlene chimed in by saying that I should have said something about it before the wedding and that Darren would never have proposed if I had been honest. Of course, we had already covered that more than once by the time she said it. I had already explained that Darren knew all about it and he had said that he didn't care. She actually called me a liar and then glared at me like I was a criminal. Then Darren said the following:

"If you don't change your name, then you're not really committed to me. It's like you're planning our divorce before our marriage has even started. Is that what you want, Alane?"

His words were shocking. We had only been married for a week and a half, and he was mentioning the D-word and accusing me of commitment issues. All I could think was, *Would I sit here and take this shit from the two of you if I weren't committed?* But I didn't say it. Instead, as my last defense, I asked the following:

"So if it's no big deal, then change your name to Gray."

You'd have thought that I'd asked Darren to scrape his mother's face off with a butter knife. Charlene emitted a string of snorting grunts, squeals, and huffs the likes of which I had never heard before. Once Darren finished his own series of coughing guffaws, he let out an emphatic "No!"

The fight then went on and on, right there at the kitchen table. A hyphenated name was out of the question on the grounds that it would confuse our future children. I argued that any future child of mine would be smart enough to handle it, and if they had something to confess about intelligence, it was a little late.

They remained unmoved. Hyphens, they claimed, were indecisive. It was their last name or nothing.

In the end, to make it all stop, I conceded. They had worn me down. The honeymoon was over, and I caved. The precedent was set. I gave up the first real fight of our marriage, and more importantly, I surrendered a piece of myself and what I believed to placate the two of them.

As a consolation, they agreed to a ridiculous compromise—I got to keep the last name I wanted (a.k.a., my maiden name) but as a second middle name. After a quick and incredibly anticlimactic trip to the social security office, I became "Alane, Catherine Gray, Danky," and that was that. The Gray part of me was now no longer a surname, or an honored maiden name. It wasn't even my middle name. It was a second middle name hanging there like a vestigial tail. It didn't even get its own initial on anything legal. I was now Alane C. Danky. My life, my history, culled with the stroke of a pen at Charlene's kitchen table.

Darren said that it was a small thing. He also said it was an honor to become a Danky. Tradition or no tradition, honor or no honor, it wasn't small at all to me. It was huge on every level. It was total bullshit. It was a bait and switch. He lured me in with promises and then changed the plan. The great Darren—the self-proclaimed hater of all liars—lied to me from the start. This was a year and a half before the notebook debacle. If I had been wiser, maybe I would have cut my losses that day and told them both to shove their name and our fledgling marriage up their honorable asses.

...but I wasn't wiser...

That small thing came back with a vengeance once we were practicing in the same office. The problem was simple. There were two Dr. Dankys in the same place. It was hard enough to make people understand that I wasn't Darren's receptionist just because I answered the phone. It just meant that we were broke and couldn't afford employees and I wasn't about to tell a new patient that we were nearly destitute, under-experienced doctors who could barely afford lunch let alone pay some bimbo to answer the phone for minimum wage. It wasn't exactly a selling point.

All of the practice management advisors we found said the solution was easy—be "Dr. First Name." It's a big thing in chiroland. Even some solo doctors go by "Dr. First Name" because they think it makes them more approachable and less medical. As far as I was concerned, it was ridiculous and not an option. Darren thought it was demeaning and refused to be Dr. Darren on principle but insisted that I be Dr. Alane because "it was just easier." It was either that or be "Dr.-Mrs. Danky"—which I hated even more than "Dr. First Name." Begrudgingly, I tried it. "Dr.-Mrs. Danky" morphed quickly into "Mrs.-Dr. Danky" and then "Mrs. Danky" or just some version of "uh, hello" or "hey, um" which invariably was followed by the question, "When is Dr. Danky going to get here?"

To this, I would say jokingly, "Well, Dr. Danky is right here!" with my best theme park smile on my face, which was usually followed by, "No, the Him-Doctor, when is he going to get here?"

...it was too much...

And after that, I decided the solution was to dust off my vestigial tail and become "Dr. Gray."

Darren was not amused and refused to play along. He would only call me "Dr. Alane." Our patients just called me "Alane" because they were either confused or they were a hundred years old and didn't like to call youngsters "doctor." Darren's family and friends would call the office and say "Who?" or "Who's that?" when I answered the phone with "This is Dr. Gray, may I help you?"

I was pushed to the limit. When Darren tried to bring the name thing up, again, in the aftermath of his birthday, it was too much. I lost my mind a little. The whole argument exploded into an aggressive rehashing of our entire marriage culminating with the dreaded we're-supposed-to-be-"one"-not-"two" thing all over again, which was nothing more than a massive condemnation of my need to continue thinking for myself and the insistence that I am not fully committed to our marriage.

This time, my response to this line of bullshit was, "Yes, you are right! I do need to have my own opinions. I am my own person! I can't be some fucked up Darren-Alane Marriage Monster! And I worked too hard to be your fucking secretary!" I then promptly started blubbering uncontrollably. It was the kind of blubbering with dripping snot and spittle flinging and everything. It was horrifying.

To make it worse, Darren laughed. I don't know if he was laughing at me or what I said or of the flinging spittle or if it was just an involuntary defense mechanism that spontaneously developed. Whatever it was, it stopped the argument, cold. Nothing was resolved, it was just weirdly and awkwardly over.

Darren and I didn't talk much after that. We worked. We ate. We slept. We lived around each other. He was on the phone with his mother for hours at a time each night that next week. That Saturday we spent another evening with Charlene and Earl. Darren drank an entire case of Iron City while we were there. I had to pour him into the car and prod him up the back steps to the house when we finally got home. He drank two more beers and then fell asleep. As he slept, I lay awake with visions of my escape envelope filling my head.

The next morning over breakfast, Darren dropped a bomb.

"Let's move," he said flatly.

I nearly choked on a wad of French toast that was occupying my mouth at the moment. A muffled, "What?" was all I could get out.

"I wanna sell the practice and move," he said again. I stared at him, stunned. "We can move to Charlotte and start over. I can't take it here anymore. You'd be happier."

"Are you sure?" I said, avoiding the treacherous but highly pertinent "why" question. I didn't want to spook him.

"Yes, I'm sure," he said. "I can't stay here. I hate the practice. I hate the cold. My parents are driving me crazy…I'm sure."

"Okay," I said trying to mute my excitement, "let's do it."

We spent the rest of the day making escape plans together. We put the practice up for sale right away. We were warned that selling a practice can be a slow process and we should be prepared for it to take at least a year and maybe more. We devised our plan accordingly. We would both look for jobs in North Carolina and whoever got one would move down and get us settled while the other stayed behind to run the practice until it sold.

We got an offer for the practice in less than 30 days. I took it as a sign. Even the Universe wanted the madness to end. I was thrilled, and so was Darren. In fact, he was the happiest I had seen him in forever. We probably should have been terrified; we were completely unprepared for what was happening. We had no jobs and no place to live. Our licenses weren't even up to date anywhere but in PA. It was wonderful.

...and then Darren told his parents...

Thankfully, I wasn't around for that conversation. Darren's version of the event was abnormally calm and eerily upbeat. My gut said it was bullshit, but I wanted it to be true so badly. I wanted Darren to get the support he needed from Charlene. I wanted him to be able to be really, genuinely happy about our future and our prospects, so I went along with it like it was the truth, which of course, it wasn't.

Charlene's phone calls stopped cold for a week and then returned with actual vengeance. Every time she would call, Darren would find the farthest place from me he could find to talk to her until the constant running and hiding became too much. After that, he just stayed wherever he was at the time and tried to get through them as quickly as possible.

The calls mostly involved Charlene screaming. Some of it was hard to decipher but when she got to the "That bitch is the DEVIL!" part, it was always crystal clear. Her eardrum rupturing howls were so loud that Darren had to move the phone away from his ear which helped.

The last time he let it happen was the most memorable for me, personally. We were standing in the basement organizing our old boxes and repacking most of it for what I hoped would be the last time for a long time.

Darren rolled his eyes and said, "Ma, stop it!"

Rage started to build in the bottom of my gut. As it shook its way up through my chest and throat, the rage morphed into a wave of uncontrollable tears that came out so forcefully that they arced out of my eye and splattered onto the cardboard box in front of me.

Charlene kept going. "That bitch is the DEVIL!" she shrieked. "She's tearing our family apart! DIVORCE HER! I want you to divorce her right now! She's the DEVIL! She's THE DEVIL!"

"MA!" Darren bellowed into the phone. "She is not the devil! The only one tearing this family apart is you!"

"Yes, she is! Aaaaghhh!" Charlene wailed through the phone. "Why are you doing this to me? Why are you letting her hurt me like this? Aaaaagghh!"

Torrents of tears were streaming down my face. Darren was crimson and soaked in sweat. "That's it, ma! I've had enough! I am not divorcing my wife! She is not the devil! You can't do this to us anymore!" and he hung up.

Hanging up a cell phone was not nearly as emphatic as slamming down a landline receiver, but it was still incredibly gratifying. Darren put the phone down on a box and stared at it as he hyperventilated. "I can't do this anymore," he said. He was talking about Charlene. That much was clear. He walked over and pulled me into his chest. "I'm sorry…I love you."

I cried on his shoulder, overwhelmed by an odd mix of relief, love, and rage. This nightmare was ending. Darren had finally manned up and cut the umbilical cord. He felt like the Darren I fell in love with. e felt like the DarrenHe HHe was finally acting like the husband I wanted him to be.

Less than a month later, the practice sale was final, and we had moved into my parents' house, once again. It was stupid to go back there. I knew it when we did it, but we had nowhere else to go. We would move twice more before we landed in what I would come to think of as *our house*, the place where our real marriage started and where it ended. As for Charlene, it took over a year for her to have a real conversation with Darren again, but it happened. A mother's love never really dies, and neither does her hate.

Chapter 13

When we finally stopped wandering, we had been together for 9 years, 2 months, and 12 days. We had been married for 6 years, 355 days, and 2 hours. I wasn't particularly aware of the passage of time as it was happening. My need to assess and chronical the exact amount of time of—and between—notable events didn't develop until much later when I realized that time was an ever-morphing blur that expands and contracts at random and can only be controlled by obsessive accounting (and even that is usually pretty futile). In that particular moment, it seemed like we had been married for decades, like my life with Darren was the only life I had ever known. Everything that had been before faded into obscurity except for a single box of photo albums and scrapbooks that I had managed to save from the trash bin.

It was probably a good thing that I wasn't focused on my past, considering the way it all played out. There was no time for reminiscing. There was no room for sentimentality or frivolity. There was only work and Darren. On the surface, it looked perfect. We opened our own practice, this time from scratch. We bought a brand-new starter house in a brand-new neighborhood surrounded by lots of other young couples who thought they were upwardly mobile. It was a real stepping stone. We could see where we were and where we were going. We were on our way to the enigmatic somewhere that we had told ourselves we wanted.

It seemed like everything was coming together. It felt really good to stop wandering. I unpacked all of our moving boxes for the first time since graduation. Our practice was growing steadily. We could even afford an employee, so there was someone there to answer the phone other than just Dr. Alane. (Yes, we both settled on "Dr. First Name" to avoid confusion and to avoid the whole last name issue altogether.)

It was in this seemingly idyllic world that Darren found his next big thing—his "authentic self." It might seem like a rational, educated, human being who literally held the health and safety of other human beings in his hands on a daily basis would already have been acquainted with his "authentic self," but as I came to understand through hours and hours of seminars, webinars, books, breakout group sessions, and daily inspirational emails, he wasn't. According to the enlightened souls who were driven to liberate the world from egocentric blindness and who really wanted us to keep paying their tuitions and monthly membership fees, I wasn't either.

...and so began the *Life Actualization* phase of our marriage which featured a toxic slurry of self-actualization, success visualization, "living as if," and practice management that consumed nearly every aspect of my existence for the next two years and then lingered through until the end like a festering boil.

It started with Darren's first taste of chiropractic practice management and then really took off the day he found the Culmination Center.

The Culmination Center is as hard for me to explain now as it was then. It was supposed to be a safe place to shed my insecurities and gain personal confidence so I could more effectively communicate with—and market to—potential patients. It was supposed to be our ticket to personal and professional success. In reality, it was dangerous, free-range, unlicensed psychotherapy packaged as adult-learning workshops and corporate-style team building. It was like The Secret, Scientology, and Tony Robbins had a baby and abandoned it in a low rent business park just outside of RTP (a.k.a. the commercial real estate equivalent of the wrong side of the tracks.)

Don't get me wrong, the Center was full of faithful followers willing to pay their hard-earned money to get emotionally fucked one weekend at a time by a bunch of self-appointed life coaches who thought recruiting for new Center prospects was the perfect homework exercise. They swore it wasn't a religion or a cult, but it was hard to believe them after the Daybreak Gratitude session at a nearby lake—all-white attire was mandatory, and towels were optional.

Their personal growth (a.k.a self-empowerment building) exercises were torturous and usually involved a lot of crying. Their goal was to reveal the most painful, regrettable, or embarrassing moments of each person's life and then emotionally flog them in front of the group until they broke. For me, it took over two days of repeated insults, calling me out as an "aging Barbie doll," and insisting that an obsession with physical appearances blocked my success and the formation of deep interpersonal connections. Honestly, I think I was a little frustrating for them, and it took them a while to get a handle on my personal brand of emotional baggage. While physical appearance was a thing for me (I had spent over a decade battling my weight for dance and hating the post-pubescent body I saw in the mirror every day after the age of fourteen, for God's sake), they missed the mark with the Barbie doll type, and I certainly wasn't driven by the need for male approbation or attention. I got that whether I wanted it or not. I think I was more the Courtney Love type (minus the heroin and the bipolar disorder, of course) than I ever was a Barbie.

They kept at it, though. They insulted and belittled and humiliated me until I broke down and cried out of sheer exhaustion, and once the crying started, they had me. There was no stopping it. Every exercise that followed ended in some form of degradation and more crying. When I was finally too dehydrated to cry and too beaten down to fight back, I stood there and took it until they decided I had broken through. I must admit that it was a pretty brilliant psychological manipulation. By the time they were done, I was convinced that my whole life had been an illusion and that everything that had ever happened to me was the result of my own actions. The good, the bad, the horrifying—all of it was my own creation which meant that I could make my life into anything I wanted it to be. The universe was mine…

…and then the endorphins wore off. When I sobered up from my three-month psychobabble bender, I was in the exact same place as I was when I started, minus about $6,000 in Culmination Center tuition fees. The basic premise of the training was still intact in my mind—I was responsible for everything in my world. I was the master of my own destiny. I could make my world into whatever I wanted it to be, and it was great…until what I wanted in my universe didn't match what anybody else wanted in their universes, which was particularly poignant when it came to Darren and his universe.

Darren got something else from his time at the Center. In a way, it was a highly successful experience for him. He learned that he created his own reality. He also learned that his reality should be everyone one else's reality, too, which meant that it was his duty to teach the world the truth and to coach everyone in the world on living his truth. In other words, he walked away from the Center as a self-appointed Life Coach.

Very few people in the world are cut out to be a life coach. Life coaching is an insidious disease that spreads one stupid inspirational meme at a time. Really, no one should ever seek out a life coach, let alone try to be one. Asking for help from a life coach is like asking a drowning man for swimming lessons. It's pointless, and it usually ends badly.

While Darren never openly claimed the title "Life Coach," exactly, he did actualize two very important things about his life. One, he was more than just a doctor, he was a *wellness coach*, whose mandate was to save the world from itself. (As JT put it, he was going to save the world one spine at a time.) Two, I needed a coach and he, Darren Danky, was the only man for the job. Somewhere along the line, he determined that he was smarter, better, and more evolved than I ever was or could ever possibly be. For the sake of our marriage and for the sake of our practice, I needed a coach, and he was it. He could see all of my blockages and how they had been holding us back. He knew exactly what I needed to do about them, too.

For the record, I didn't feel particularly blocked or held back by my own mind. I will admit that I was frustrated and largely unfulfilled, but I was more blocked by circumstance than anything else. I was isolated, again. Every person I met was a potential patient, which didn't leave much room for friendships. In the practice, I had been sidelined, again. While we were at the Center, we "lost" our receptionist, which really meant that we fired her for gross incompetence and inappropriate behavior in front of patients. It also meant that I was answering the phones and carting files around the office, again. Soon, I started morphing from Dr. Alane back into front desk "Alane." At the same time, Darren decided he couldn't stand being "Dr. Darren," so he started calling himself "Dr. Danky" (again). It was overwhelmingly confusing for all of our patients and made me look like I had been demoted in my own office.

Life Coach Darren swore that it was all in my head, that it was a reality I was creating for myself. Actually, I agreed with him in a way. I had chosen to quit my other job. I had chosen to move to that podunk, backwards town that was full of evangelical half-wits and light-blue-collar, Northeastern transplant victims, and I had chosen to answer the fucking phone because The Almighty Dr. Darren refused to do it…but, I didn't think that meant I had to like or want to keep doing it. Regardless, he was determined to coach me into a state of greater fulfillment and success, because my lack of fulfillment was bringing him down.

…which brings us to FSP…

Along with the Culmination Center, Darren had signed himself up, and by extension me, with Full Schedule Practice, or FSP, which was a full-service chiropractic practice management system that claimed to be the blueprint for chiropractic practice success. It mapped out everything—from what paperwork to use, to how to answer the phone, to what to say to patients, and even how to treat them. If a wayward chiropractor needed help, FSP had the answers. There were coaching sessions over the phone at least once a week. There were endless videos and webinars to watch. There were quarterly conventions held in cities around the country. The system was available in almost every format available at the time. Just like the Culmination Center, it worked best as a total emersion program, only this time, it was total emersion in everything chiropractic (except for reviews of standardized research or anything based in actual evidence. I'm not suggesting that everything FSP taught was wrong, just that they weren't terribly concerned with teaching the *why* behind the *what*, nor did they leave room for anything that didn't fit into their narrow view of the profession…and they notoriously cited statistics that didn't really exist.)

FSP's primary goal was to help Doctors of Chiropractic (DC's) the world over find their inner awesome. FSP's Grand Poohbah, JT, had built an entire system around his own personal awesomeness using nothing but his wits, some pilfered intellectual property, and an evangelical megachurch/Florida timeshare business model. By the time Darren got to FSP, JT had turned his solution for poor, struggling, awesome-deficient chiropractors into a giant, well-oiled, money-making machine. His premise was fairly simple. First of all, chiropractic wasn't a job, it was a way of life, and without fully committing to the lifestyle, even the best chiropractors were destined to fail. Second, JT's plan was the answer to everything. As long as his plan was followed without deviation, chiropractic practice success was inevitable (but not guaranteed, of course.)

The FSP plan for chiropractic success covered everything in the office and beyond—when to wake up, when and how to work out, what to eat, how to meditate, how to schedule patients, how to train staff members, how to decorate an office, how to appropriately serve tea to a new patient in the waiting room, etc. Then, of course, there were all of the FSP products to buy—videos, handouts, and the x-ray analysis packages, patient communication postcards, office posters, t-shirts, computer software, treatment equipment, and on and on. At the seminars, we watched JT announce the successes of his member doctors. Then they would kiss JT's ring and tell impassioned stories of their transformation thanks to the FSP program. They would say time and time again, "Just follow JT… just follow the FSP system. It works. Have faith in the system."

On the surface, it looked like they were right. It seemed like FSP simplified some of the tedious, day-to-day stuff. It seemed like a perfect way to stay plugged in with other chiropractors and to be held accountable for what we were and weren't doing in our office every day. (Small private chiropractic practices can become isolated and lonely. It's easy to lose touch with reality.)

Darren bought into FSP completely. He was thoroughly enamored with JT. He decided that JT was grooming him as his future protégé after only about 3 months in the program. (JT was gifted at making everyone feel that way as long as they were paying.) Darren was certain FSP was the answer. In fact, he was so certain, that he turned the entire practice over to JT's cult of chiropractic and washed his hands of everything else we had ever talked about.

I, on the other hand, didn't want any part of it. I was a solid clinician, and I wanted to help people. I also wanted to make money, but I didn't want to follow JT's cookie cutter template for patient care. I wanted to be the chiropractor I was trained to be. I wanted to be a doctor. As I saw it, in the FSP system, there was very little difference between answering the phones and treating patients—both followed a script, and we weren't really supposed to deviate from it.

Which brings me to a hard truth. No matter what I thought about JT or FSP or Darren or any of it, it didn't matter. The practice wasn't mine. I was nothing more than an employee in the practice I paid to open. Darren owned one hundred percent of the company. My name wasn't on any of it other than the debt. I had no signing rights. When it got right down to it, I had no control over any of it.

That unfortunate truth happened out of what Darren would have called necessity and what was really ill-considered future planning. When Darren opened the practice, I was under contract in another office about 40 miles away. My job and my credit card funded everything for over a year. We had already borrowed money from my parents and his, and he wasn't willing to take any of the jobs he was offered in the area. He wanted to start his own practice, and it was the only way we could afford to do it and feed ourselves at the same time. The details in my contract kept me from being a part of it, and Darren said that he really wanted a practice of his own.

Only later did he ask me to come and work with him in his practice. He said he needed help. He was certain that we would be more profitable if we worked in the same place. He thought we would be better off in the end if we worked together, and he promised to sign fifty percent of everything over to me.

So, before I finished out my contract, I used my job to get approved for a mortgage, we bought a house down the street from his office, and six months later, we went to work together—again. Darren never officially signed any of the practice over to me, although he was more than happy to use my credit to cover anything and everything he wanted. Not long after we made all of the changes, JT decreed that an office couldn't run without a single, clear leader in the office, and since Darren owned everything and had been there by himself for a year, he was the obvious choice. To top it all off, Darren decided that we needed to invest everything we made, beyond his salary, back into the practice until we were stable—which meant I wasn't getting paid, had no health insurance, and had zero retirement plan. He said all of our money was community money and we would make changes as the practice became more stable.

Agreeing to any of it was stupid. I know that, now. I should never have left the job I had. I should have taken the other job offer that landed in my lap right before I moved into Darren's office. I should have found another job—any other job—no matter how far the commute, no matter how far removed from chiropractic or healthcare it ended up being. I should have gone my own way. I even knew it as it was happening. That's what every cell in my body was telling me to do…well, every cell that was left after accounting for the cells that told me to lock Darren in a closet somewhere and just run the damn thing without FSP all by myself.

But, I did none of those things. I let Darren run with it. He had said that I was too stubborn. I thought maybe he was right—I just needed to relax and follow his lead. It was time for me to start having babies, anyway, and when that day arrived, I would need him to bear the brunt of the practice, anyway. (Technically we had been trying to get pregnant for about four years. It was bound to happen eventually. I thought that the Universe and my body knew that I couldn't handle a baby in the middle of everything else that had happened, and if I just got everything in place—Darren running the practice, a steady cash flow, and a stable place to live—then it would happen.)

…and then there was Melissa…

Melissa had been one of my closest friends in chiropractic college. She was young and energetic and was one of those people who could do seventeen things at once and ace all of them without breaking a sweat. We had some differing opinions on the philosophical side of things, but that didn't matter to me. Melissa was smart and funny, and most of all, I trusted her. We were good friends, and I knew she had our best interest at heart.

Melissa was an FSP devotee. She had been with it since her internship, and her 5-year-old solo practice was one of JT's glittering examples of FSP success. It didn't hurt, either that she was a successful pageant girl who knew how to smile, how to dress, and how to remain graceful under pressure. Simply put, Melissa was killing it in practice. She had two babies and a husband who barely worked, and she was still able to pay off her house, pay off her student loans, pay for FSP, and go to the Caribbean for vacation at least once, if not twice, a year. Clearly, she was doing something right. I thought it would be smart to follow her path. So, where my faith in FSP wavered, my trust in Melissa and her friendship held strong.

So, I agreed to all of it. I let it all happen.

It took a while to see what FSP really was—a revenue-generating monster with little regard for the needs of an individual patient, the specifics of practice, or our bottom line. Once I saw the truth and really understood it, it was hard for me to see anything else.

In the world of FSP, a single scripted formula was the answer for every patient and every practice problem. Every time our practice wasn't producing, there was another seminar that we needed to attend or some new ad package that was supposed to fix it. Every time we went to the next seminar, the thing we bought the last time was obsolete, and we needed to buy the next new thing. FSP insisted that it had an answer for everything, and the answer always boiled down to one of three things: we weren't following the FSP system exactly, we hadn't bought the right FSP products, or (and this was my favorite)…

…we weren't thinking correctly.

We were told more than once that *we* were the reason our practice was struggling. While they were partially right, it certainly wasn't the entire story. Of course, it made perfect sense to Darren who thought that when FSP said *we*, they actually meant *me*. In his mind, he was naturally awesome—just like JT—and was doing everything right. I, on the other hand, was neither awesome nor right about anything, which meant I was the entirety of the problem. It didn't matter that the local economy had blown up, and almost half the population was either underemployed or out of work entirely. It didn't matter that when JT decreed that insurance was bad for business and told us to stop taking insurance, Darren followed his advice like a lemming even though the numbers didn't bear it out. It didn't matter that everything we did made us look like desperate snake oil peddlers. It didn't matter that FSP, JT, and ultimately Darren had reduced over 100 years of chiropractic advancements and progress into a seven-minute exam, a ninety-second adjustment, and a bunch of pseudo-religious brainwashing bullshit that made most people run away like the wind.

Nope, it had nothing to do with any of that. According to Darren (don't forget that he was coaching me at this point) and, by extension, the trainers at FSP, those were just excuses. I was the real problem. I wasn't thinking positive thoughts sincerely enough as my feet hit the floor each morning. I was thinking negative thoughts about money while patients were in the office. I was too focused on errors in our legally binding, financial package contracts and repeatedly shifted The Almighty Dr. Darren's focus to money instead of letting him focus on his patients. (Occasionally Darren would give me a break when a new patient either "wasn't ready to be helped," or was "too afraid to invest in herself," but most of the time, it was me and my general lack of awesomeness.)

Like I said before, they were partly right. I had become a giant vortex of negativity and frustration in response to all of the stupid. I never let a single person see it—not at the office, not at the grocery store, not to my parents over the phone…I kept all of it to myself. I smashed it all down and kept going. (Honestly, it might have bubbled over a few times, but for the most part, I kept a perfect theme park smile on my face and a lid on everything else.)

I hated what was happening in our practice. I hated everything about the FSP practice model. I hated the seminars. I hated the office scripts. I hated JT's fake smile, fake tan, and his wife's big fake boobs. I hated the weekly coaching calls. I hated JT's training videos that looked like they were straight out of 1985 complete with fake ferns, popped-collar golf shirts, and "Eye of the Tiger" playing behind a grainy video of JT's "awesome" golf swing. (Darren made us watch those videos a minimum of three times a day and any time we weren't watching inspirational excerpts from "The Secret.") I hated paying JT thousands of dollars every year to be a part of his cult when it clearly wasn't helping us or our patients.

I had a whole lot of hate toward the thing that was consuming our entire life. On a typical morning, we were up at 4:45a.m. We worked out for about 45 minutes, meditated and visualized for 15 to 20 minutes, and journaled for 15-20 minutes. (Yup, that's right—journaling. When it was JT's idea, it was a perfectly awesome idea that we both should do every day.) Then we showered and got ready, ate breakfast (that I cooked every morning after I fixed lunch to go), watched at least 15 minutes of "The Secret," and got to the office by 7:00a.m. (As a side note—JT claimed that the human body didn't really require as much sleep as the medical community and almost everyone else on the planet claimed. He said that four to five hours a night were plenty. I guess that's true for a bipolar in a manic episode, but even they crash eventually.) Between regular office hours, training, coaching calls, back office paperwork, in-office workshops, advertising, accounting, and marketing events, we were working around eighty hours per week, and when we weren't working, we were talking about work, thinking about work, or working on work-adjacent things.

We worked our asses off, and we were still blowing it. My hatred for it aside, the FSP model just simply wasn't working for us. We did everything they said to do. We did everything that Melissa said to do. We even went together in big, expensive, marketing events with other FSP offices in our area, events that brought them more patients than they could handle, and we were still struggling to get people through the door and to get the people who tried it to stick with it.

All JT would say during our coaching calls was that we should commit more fully to the process. Get up earlier. Visualize more positively. Make the business about "saving lives" rather about "making money." He insisted that if we got our "heads right," all of the things we needed in our lives, including financial success in our practice, would happen.

After one particular call, Darren mediated for 10 whole minutes before coming up with his own solution. To get to the next level in our practice, we needed to connect God to our practice. All of the most successful FSP practices were Christian-centric, and he was certain it would work for us, too. We were in the Bible Belt, after all.

Now, it's important to understand that Darren had tortured me with church off and on since the first year we were out of school. Everywhere we moved, he would drag me into church after church. He said he was searching for one that spoke to him. Over the years, we tried a little bit of every Christian denomination except for Catholicism. (Honestly, I think that one scared him a little. There were too many rules.) For me, our Sunday morning church service tour was usually tolerable and only occasionally so misogynistic that I had to rant about it all the way home.

Church was nothing I wanted for myself. Darren, on the other hand, seemed intent on it. Luckily, I could get by just about anywhere. Like I've mentioned before, my family was a brimstone-fueled combo of devout Southern Baptists (on one side) and Pentecostals (on the other), so I knew how to handle myself, even though at 35, I remained an unbaptized heathen. I also respected the sanctity of church processes enough to stay in my seat when we happened to show up on communion day, which embarrassed Darren to no end. Every time, he would elbow me in the ribs and tell me to get in line with him. I guess he wanted me to lie and denigrate their religious practices rather than draw attention to myself as an apostate. Of course, he hated liars, so where that would have left me in that situation, I don't really know.

That being said, Darren had decided that Jesus was the answer. He was certain that a full-on marriage of chiropractic and Christianity in our practice was going to be the thing that set us apart from all of the other chiropractors in our tiny, unforgiving town, and of course, I thought it was a terrible idea. Despite his penchant for church hopping, Darren was not a devout guy. He never stuck with any church or any spiritual practice beyond weekly beer worshiping for more than a couple of weeks at a time. I was certain it was going to end up being a miserable pit of insincere pandering. Either that, or we'd both be struck down by a single freak lightning strike on some random, and otherwise, sunny day. It wasn't that I didn't believe in a higher power, and it certainly wasn't that I didn't believe in the basic philosophical principles of chiropractic. It's just that there is a certain type of chiropractor that likes to claim that the whole Above-Down-Inside-Out chiropractic thing was a Christian notion since its inception—which it wasn't. I didn't want to be that kind of chiropractor. I wanted to be a doctor of chiropractic, not a dogma-waving chiro-crack monkey. We weren't going to survive if we went that way with it. Our town was too small and too remote. There weren't enough people to make it that way for more than a few years, at best.

Needless to say, it didn't work. Just like I thought, no one really believed it, no matter how much Christian alternative music we piped through the waiting room speakers. The ones who did believe it wanted us to treat them for free or join their church.

The Christian era in our office came to a head the day that Darren tried to actually quote scripture. It was a hideous sight to behold. It was like watching a horrible car accident unfold right in front of my face. I wanted to look away, but I couldn't. The whole twisted, gory mess was heading right for me, and I had no hope of getting safely out of its way. It was flying right into my face.

It happened during one of our mandatory wellness workshops. (That's right, I said mandatory, although we never turned away a single patient who was bold enough to refuse.) Darren decided, out of nowhere, to quote the Bible. It was a fumbling attempt, at best. As the small crowd of our patients grew restless and embarrassed for him and as he realized he was about to tank the whole thing, he tossed it over to me, "As the Lord breathe-eth on my hair… uhm…I believe it was Peter…uhm…or Paul who said that…uh… Can you find that for us, Dr. Alane?"

There I sat, slack-jawed and unprepared in the back of the room, inconveniently next to the waiting room Bible that one of Darren's patients had so graciously given him. I had sat through that lecture at least once a week for the last two months, and there had never been a Bible quote in it before. But there it was. The entire room turned around to look at me after Darren threw that wad of verbal nonsense and essentially said: "go fetch."

I might know how to behave in church, but in the land of Bible quotes, I am of absolutely no use, and that's when we're talking about a real quote. Darren's ridiculous word scramble was not even close to a real quote, which meant that I had no idea what to do. Without thinking, I grabbed the waiting room Bible and started nervously rifling through the pages, searching for anything that seemed even remotely similar to it. I hopelessly flipped through those pages for what felt like Methuselah's lifetime as everyone in the room stared at me. Finally, I blurted out, "If my dead grandmothers are watching this, they are doing cartwheels in their caskets," followed by a long roll of uncontrollable self-deprecating chuckles. "Why don't you go on with your presentation, Dr. Darren?" I said, flashing my best theme park smile. The room broke out in a roar of laughter and turned back to face him.

Sadly, for Dr. Darren, some Bible-y sounding words with a couple of apostles' names sprinkled on top aren't a Bible verse. Sadly, for me, I wasn't quick enough to come up with anything to salvage that awful moment other than an awkward joke. I should have just picked a random passage and blurted it out. It would have been better than what actually happened. For the next month, every patient that had been in the room greeted me at the front desk with a Bible verse of the day, followed by a look of concern and the question, "Have you and Dr. Darren found a new church home, yet?"

I tried every polite response I could think of to deal with that question. We even visited a bunch of them because we were so backed into a corner. I just couldn't bring myself to say the full, horrible truth to their faces. I never said plainly, "No, and we don't want one, because this bullshit is just a put on," or, "Sorry, we don't want to visit your church. I'm really a closeted Pagan, and Dr. Darren prefers to nurse his hangover on Sunday mornings by masturbating to porn on the internet." My dead grandmothers would have brought themselves back from the dead if I had ever actually said any of that out loud, or the townsfolk might have shown up with torches and pitchforks at our door one night.

Dr. Darren, on the other hand, gleefully accepted the invitations when they started rolling in. I just stood there with looking gobsmacked and exhausted. Once he said yes, what else was there to do? These were our patients. I didn't want to offend them. I also wanted the practice to grow, and church was a good way to meet people. But this practice was our whole life, and the idea of living my whole life as a big fat lie was almost more than I could stand. Then again, maybe I'd pick up a useful quote or two…

…So, we went to church…or churches to be exact.

As expected, I couldn't stand it while Darren tried to find a way to be a super church guy without having to do anything but show up. Needless to say, none of them were a good fit, and Darren burned out on Sunday morning services when he realized that showing up smelling like a stale keg wasn't good for his public image. In the end, chiro-Jesus was not the answer Darren hoped it would be and he backed off of most of it. Of course, the Christian rock and the occasional group prayer with a patient who had witnessed the Bible quote carnage stayed for a long time.

…and our bottom line still sucked…

While the Jesus experiment was happening, FSP rolled out its newest groundbreaking protocol, ever—mandatory spouses. Yup, JT decided that requiring our patients to bring their spouses when we reviewed their results and talk about their treatment recommendations was a breakthrough that every FSP practice needed to move to the next level. At first, it seemed reasonable. It's always preferable to have family support in healthcare decisions. Then, JT made it clear that he really meant for us to require it. He wanted it to be mandatory, as in—if your husband doesn't come with you, your appointment gets rescheduled—mandatory.

The minute he said that I recoiled. No way was that going to fly in our office, ever. Being the good little pseudo-feminist that I was, there was no way I was going to suggest that a woman couldn't make a financial decision on her own or that she needed a man's approval to do something for herself. The same thought process applied to the men. They could talk about this stuff at home on their own time, in my opinion, and the thought of turning patients away at the door because they dared to show up alone just seemed like lunacy to me.

Darren, on the other hand, was all in. "Why wouldn't a spouse want to be there? I'd want to be there for you," he would say every time we talked about it. He was fully on board with the mindless JT cattle train. "If a husband really cares about his wife, he'll want to be there. He can support her through it. You know what JT says, that everyone in the house needs to be focused on our patient getting better, and who knows, they might just decide that they need to get checked out, too."

"What if he doesn't really care about his wife?" I asked without the slightest hint of snarkiness. It was a sincere question about a sincerely possible situation.

"Ugh!" Darren shot back, "You're always so negative. If you think that's going to happen, then it's going to happen. The choice is yours."

"You can't be serious," I said.

"Dead serious," he said. "I think you need to spend more time visualizing on this. Really, Alane, I think you need to spend more time focusing on what you want rather than focusing on what can go wrong. You know that when you think about problems all the time, you get more problems."

"I have been doing my visualizations, Darren," I shot back, this time with full snark.

"Not well enough, I guess. We'd have more patients if you were really invested in it. You've gotta trust the process," Darren said smugly.

I was getting really angry about this. He was acting like he was some sort of master who was dealing with an unruly apprentice. "That's great, but I'm the person at the front desk who's going to have to turn people away and endure the backlash when people aren't happy about it."

"I guess you'll get back whatever you manifest with your mind," Darren said dismissively and walked out of the room.

"Hey," I said angrily, "I'm serious. I don't think this is a good idea. I think JT is really off the mark with this one. I don't think it's a good idea to draw such a hard line. You tried it with the mandatory new patient workshops, and that didn't go well at all. We haven't suspended anyone's treatment because they didn't show up for a lecture like JT said to do. I think we should go our own way with this, too."

"That's just your fear and personal limitations talking," Darren was going into full life coach mode.

"Yes, it is," the frustration in my voice was ramping up with every word. "I am afraid that we are not going to be able to pay our bills because we are personally limiting ourselves based on the recommendation of a guy who had never set one foot in our practice, and by the way, hasn't practiced in the real world for over a decade!"

"You need to get right with this," he said busying himself at one of the computer kiosks. "Talk to Melissa, maybe she can give you some advice."

I was so frustrated, I was about to burst. I dealt with the money. I paid the bills. I was the one faced with our patients when there was a problem. I was the one who had to handle the break up when they weren't happy. If anybody had their finger on the pulse of his practice, it was me. You would think that what I had to say about how patients were responding to our hardline evangelical chiropractic line and our monthly stats would have been all the information he needed to know that something wasn't right.

But I called Melissa anyway. Melissa was the whole reason Darren joined FSP, and she was the person that kept him pumped about the possibilities. My relationship with Melissa was a little more down to earth. She would talk to me about the real way that her practice was going. She would talk to me about her frustrations, her concerns, and about all of the very un-FSP things that she had done, especially in the beginning, to make sure that her practice was financially successful. Melissa was a pragmatist. She knew she needed enough money to pay all of her bills, so she took every patient that was willing to show up regardless of their willingness to follow JT's hardline rules. She did what was necessary to survive, and it paid off grandly for her. By the time we joined the club, Melissa's practice was big and getting bigger. She was living the life that Darren and I had been chasing the entire time we were wasting time wandering back and forth between PA and NC. I knew that she would understand. I thought it would be good to get a little guidance and a little commiseration from a friend who had been through it already.

When I called, Melissa was as upbeat and excited to talk to me as usual. Sometimes I felt like the Eeyore to Melissa's Tigger, but our dynamic had been like that from the beginning, and she never seemed to mind. This time, I unloaded the whole thing about requiring spouses and workshops on her pretty quickly, skipping the usual pleasantries about her kids and her busy pageant schedule.

Her first response was to laugh. That was her usual thing. She laughed roundly and said, "Oh yeah, I remember that. Tracy (her receptionist) hit a lot of resistance to all of that in the beginning," followed by another long roll of perky laughter.

"Oh my God, I am so glad to hear that I am not the only one!" I said as a wave of relief washed over me. I knew I had been right about that. "What did you do?"

"Wow, you know? We took everyone. Anybody that would walk through the door. I even took people that didn't like my treatment plans and just wanted to come in whenever they felt like it.

I don't think I would have made it if I hadn't." I could hear in her voice that she was back in the past in her mind. The tone in her voice dropped, and there were hints of tension seeping through her usually upbeat façade. It's the same tone that almost every chiropractor I have ever talked to gets when they talk about their first few years in practice. "You know how JT feels about that, of course," she added.

"I know," I said in agreement. JT had been preaching to us from day one about only offering long-term treatment packages. He said that anything less would drag a practice down and prevent a doctor from helping as many people as possible. I had always thought there was a lot of potential in meeting people where they were comfortable, but then again, no one was coming to me for practice advice, "and look at you, now! You are doing so well."

"I am," she said brightly, "thanks."

I went right into the reason for my call, "Melissa, I just need a little help. Darren is all in with this stuff, and JT is telling us to draw hard lines with our patients. He wants us to turn people away."

There was a long pause on the other end of the phone. The longer her silence went on, the more my throat started to clench. Melissa never hesitated. She never had to think things through before she said them. Finally, she let out, "Well," followed by another pause, "if I had it to do over again, I would draw a hard line from the start. You always have to weed your garden. It's a lot easier if you pull out the weeds out before they have a chance to grow strong roots."

"But, Melissa," I said somewhat desperately, "you said, yourself, that you wouldn't have made it if you hadn't been willing to take everybody no matter what. We need to make more money, Melissa. I'm drowning, here."

"Darren's making the right call, Alane. He's just stronger than I was when I started. I wish I could go back and do it all over again the right way." Melissa had recovered her usual confident tone.

This felt an awful lot like betrayal, but I knew that it wasn't. Melissa was just doing what she was told. I just didn't think she would do that with me. I thought she would drop the FSP bullshit and really talk to me. Tears started rolling down my face, but I couldn't let Melissa hear me cry. It just would have been too much. "Melissa, come on. You don't think we should do whatever it takes to sustain ourselves right now? Would you really tell a patient who is in pain and looking for help that you won't talk to her about her exam results because her husband isn't with her?"

"Yeah. Absolutely!" Melissa said with what sounded like sincerity, "I've decided that we are going to commit to that hard line in my office starting this week."

"I don't know what to say," I said despondently into the phone.

"Don't worry! It's going to work out! Just be all in, and it will be fine. You'll thank yourself when you see the results. Ok, nice talking to you, I have patients waiting. Gotta run! Love you!" Melissa ran together cheerfully before the line went dead. I put down the phone and let out a long hard sigh.

Darren had been listening through the wall. "See. Aren't you glad you called her?" he said in a gleeful tone.

"No, I'm not happy. I'm not happy at all," I said. "She's committing to it now…this week. That means she has never done it before. She's never even tried it, and she's telling me to be all in. Her practice is strong. She can take a hit if it doesn't work out. We can't."

"It'll be fine," Darren said. "There's a patient getting ready to walk through the door. Gotta go." With that he fled to the back of the office, leaving me alone at the front desk.

I wiped my tears, put on a smile, and that was that.

The hard line had been drawn. Just like everything else FSP, I absolutely hated it. For a while, Darren was fully committed to it, so much so that he insulted more than a few of our potential patients—especially the women. He even had a shouting match with one of them right in the middle of the waiting room. By the end of it, the veins were popping out of their temples, and they were pointing fingers in each other's faces. Most of the other women that were pissed off and offended just never came back. This one, however, wasn't going to go quietly. She was well-connected, and the practice took a big hit that day. Who could blame her, really? JT's hard line had officially turned our practice into a public patriarchy. It had been that way behind the scenes for years, but when it moved around to the other side of the reception desk, it was more than many of our self-respecting patients could stand. No amount of smiling social grace could smooth over that kind of damage.

Darren continued to hold the line for a little while, but it wasn't long before he gave up on it. After that, he threw himself into marketing the practice. His entire focus was on getting the right number of spines through the door, and not much else, which brought a whole host of weeds into the office. Not only did he refuse to turn these people away, he started wheeling and dealing to make sure that no one left. Within just a few short months, Darren was practically giving treatment away. On paper, it was all in the name of financial hardships, but in reality, it was all in the name of chasing a higher number of patient visits per week. All someone had to do was say it cost too much, and Darren would scramble to make them happy. Soon, we were working all day in exchange for a couple of bucks, some homemade mayonnaise dip, and a lot of empty promises to volunteer at our marketing events.

I kept saying that we should get back into the insurance

networks, but Darren held his ground. JT had approved financial hardship as a reason to deviate from the program, but never insurance. So, in short, we could work for a plate of cookies but not for money from an insurance company. That would be ridiculous, of course.

The day I accepted my fifth jar of mayo dip and a plate of cookies in exchange for $1,100 worth of treatment, I started thinking that it might be time for me to find another job.

The day Darren decided that I should serve our new patients an assortment of beverages on a tray during their first visit, I lost my mind. What that meant was that it was now my responsibility to carry a tray of coffee and tea around the waiting room while a new patient was filling out paperwork. It was more than I could take. I hadn't spent four years and six figures to schlep free drinks. I could have done that with no degree, and I probably would have made more money at it. After a week of doing it anyway and Darren telling me that I was doing it wrong (to which I said that I would gladly treat the patients if he would rather wait tables) I told him, "ENOUGH! Hire somebody else and let them do this bullshit! I'm out!"

...and, so it was. I quit.

I didn't actually leave, of course. I couldn't. Darren freaked out after one day of being left to his own devices in the office, so I stayed to train the new employee. But technically, I quit. I was free to find my own way. I even found a job. Another office needed a second doctor, and they offered it to me. I even got to hold the contract in my hands and daydream about the possibilities of a life with a paycheck...

...and then I found out I was pregnant.

The day of my interview, I felt a little bloated. My bra didn't fit right. My pants were a little tight. I was kind of dizzy and really sick to my stomach, but I figured that I was just nervous. Good chiropractic jobs didn't come around very often. I didn't want to blow it. A few nerves were reasonable, or so I thought.

I interviewed well that day. I was at least better than everyone else that they had talked to that week since a few days later they made me an offer. It felt marvelous. Someone else valued my skills. They wanted to pay me to do what I had been trained to do. It was perfect. Darren could do his thing. I could do mine. I thought, maybe, we could have a relationship that didn't include JT or our patients. It was the best day I'd had in over two years.

The very next day, I was officially late.

Two days later, after a great deal of freaking out, I was officially pregnant. I wasn't just a little pregnant, either. The urine hit the stick and the second little line appeared before I even had a chance to start the timer.

Chapter 14

So far, I haven't said much about our sex life. I guess that's because the entire topic of sex was such a powder keg for us, but since I'm about to discuss the direct product of our sex life, it might be helpful.

To talk about it with any degree of reasonable disclosure, I probably need to go back to my life before Darren. The truth is, I was pretty good at it when I wanted to be…

…sex, that is…

I don't know why. I just was. The town where I grew up was cinched up tightly by the Bible Belt, and my very Christian, but non-practicing, family followed right along the moral line with it. I probably should have had some moral imperative to be bad at it based on Religious principle, alone, but I didn't. I wasn't "loose" as my grandmother would have said, and the word "slut" is just too inflammatory, in my opinion. I like to think of myself as having been "occasionally free."

So, what led me to be so good at sex? I don't really know. Maybe it was just some genetic proclivity handed down to me from my distant ancestors. I'm sure my mother would die if she ever heard me say that. It's been suggested that I had self-esteem issues that lead me to equate sexual attraction with self-worth. All I can say to that is, of course, I had self-esteem issues. What teenage girl doesn't? And, who says that self-worth and sexual prowess are equivalent things? Being sexually attractive doesn't necessarily mean one is sexually gifted. It just means it's easier to end up looking like a whore without a healthy dose of personal vigilance. I didn't have any daddy issues or substance abuse problems. I wasn't abused, mistreated, or exploited in any way other than the usual ways that young girls are abused, mistreated, and exploited by the world. All I'm saying is that no one was going to make an after-school special about my sad life because I didn't have one. I was just a normal kid, with a whole lot of dance training. I was taught to use my body as an instrument of artistic expression and occasionally expressed myself off stage as well as on.

... we all have our gifts...

I think I was searching for something that felt as good for me as it seemed to feel for other people. Frankly, I couldn't understand what the big deal was all about. It was a bodily function, just like all of the other bodily functions, and it seemed preposterous that so many people would be so bound up by it.

Don't get me wrong, I wasn't a one-stop shop for anyone who wanted a good romp. Like I said before, I was "occasionally free" which meant I was selective, I was careful, and I was in a relationship most of the time. If I had been a guy, I would have been a super stud. As a girl, the probable reputations were not so nice, but I rejected them as much then, as I do now. I wasn't buying or selling anything with my sexual escapades. I wasn't trying to screw away any hidden self-loathing. I was just an active participant in the carnival of youth. To sum it up, I was a free, empowered, and fully evolved sexual creature, and I had been that way for a long time before I ever even met Darren.

Sex with Darren started out as an entertaining diversion from the stress of school. Actually, we waited a long time before we ever got down to business. When we finally did, it was really good. It wasn't the best, but it was really good. For me, it hit all of the major requirements, and it was good enough. For Darren, to put it bluntly—he seemed really, really happy. It turned him into a stupid drooling lump, which I found thoroughly entertaining. The entertainment value usually wore off after a few months. This time, it didn't. To be blunt, the effects of my apparently magical pussy, which he fondly dubbed The Pussy of Life (or the POL for short), were so strong on Darren that it seemed it would never wear off.

In the past, when this sort of thing happened, I was paying close attention. I didn't buy into the fantasy. I enjoyed it as long as I could, and when I saw that the effects were about to wear off, I promptly ended things. Sure, it got ugly. Sure, it hurt, and sure, I cried and played lots of sad, whiny, chick music alone in my apartment with a bottle of wine.

...I'm not a soulless monster...

I was just aware of where things were headed. I knew that things like that weren't meant to last forever. They were casual and fun, and most importantly, temporary. There was no reason to draw it out and make it worse for everyone involved.

With Darren, this is where I messed up. It was just sex. He didn't really love me. He was just under the powerful whammy of my POL, and somehow, I must have whammied myself in the process. I'm still not exactly sure how that happened. I thought by that point in my life, I was immune. I wasn't. Instead, I got stuck in my own trap. I thought it was true love, too. Looking back on it now, I don't think it had anything to do with Darren, specifically. I was the right age, it was the right time, and I was distracted. It probably could have been anyone.

At the very least, his proposal should have been the thing that ended it. Darren proposed during sex. I should have known, right then and there, that it was just the pussy whammy. Like I've said before, it's not like I ever envisioned my wedding day. But honestly,

I should have held out for something better. I should have insisted on something more fully considered than an orgasm induced outburst of a proposal. Why I said yes, I'll never understand. It was out of character for me. But in that moment, those three breathless words, "Let's get married," seemed like the best thing he had ever said. I was all in.

One thing I knew for certain was that Darren was attracted to me. His attraction was always very apparent. In the beginning, he would watch me get dressed and would always be looking at me from across the room. In the beginning, it seemed intimate and exciting. It wasn't until much later that it got weird. For the longest time, he wanted us to shower together. It seemed sweet and sexy until after the wedding when he made it clear that showering together was mandatory and threw tantrums when I took one without him. When it was for fun it was one thing, but as a requisite part of a daily routine, it became something else, entirely. One of us was under the water while the other had soap in their eyes, or as in my case, I froze in the dry end of the tub while Darren preened under the water like a teenage girl. When I decided that I simply couldn't take it anymore, we settled on me showering first as Darren stood outside the glass shower door to watch until I was done. That got creepy fast, so I started to the shower as fast as I could in hopes of finishing before he made it into the room.

Sex, itself, changed early on in our relationship. It turned out that Darren had some serious self-esteem issues (a.k.a. penis size insecurities) from his teenage years that would crop up from time to time. It seems that some girl in high school caught a glimpse of his penis, under circumstances that were never fully clear to me, and then proceeded to spread small penis rumors about him around the school. Knowing that teenagers can be cruel and psychologically eviscerating creatures, I was quick to support him and spent a great deal of effort to ensure that he felt adequate and confident. It was, in my mind at the time, a loving gesture toward the person that I was about to marry.

I thought my words mixed with our shared activities as an engaged couple would be enough to reassure him. At first it seemed like they did, but eventually, he started repeating his tale of woe at least once a week, and at least once, he broke down into tears about it. I continued to console him and underscore his physical adequacy, fully expecting my words and loyalty to heal the decade-old wound once he felt certain I was with him for the long haul. For some reason, they didn't. Instead, he spun wildly out of control and turned his mistrust toward me—specifically, my past. To be blunt, he was obsessed with penises I'd known before and eventually demanded a "dick size" comparison.

Frankly, I was horrified. I had no idea what to say for a whole host of reasons. Ultimately, I told him the truth. He was not the biggest. He was not the smallest. He was, in my opinion, above average, and most of all he was what I wanted. (I thought that last bit was particularly important for him to understand.) Alas, no matter how truthful and reasonable my answer was, it was not enough. He asked and re-asked the question in an attempt to catch me in some sort of lie. After several rounds of this questioning, which took place entirely in the dark one night after we had just had sex, he decided that he needed a visual aid.

It was an absurd request, and I told him so. I couldn't remember the specific sizes and dimensions of my previous lovers on a good day. It simply wasn't something I thought about. It was especially not on my mind when I was in bed with him. I told him all of this, but he pushed and pushed, holding up his hands at different distances apart, each time asking, "This big? Or this big?"

Ultimately, I relented and just held up my hands at random

distances for the largest and the smallest. It was crazy, but it seemed like it worked. I thought he let it go.

...but he hadn't...

Over a year later, something sparked the same question and the same crazed need for visual aids. By this time, I was less willing to indulge him for more than just a few minutes. So, I held up my hands and showed him the lengths as I thought they might have been. I then reminded him that it was a very long time ago and something that I never thought about.

Again, I thought that would be the end of it, but it wasn't. Darren flew into a rage about how different the two demonstrations were. He told me that he hated liars and that he couldn't believe that I would lie to him about something like that. After much crying and yelling, I finally convinced him that I was not lying to him, that he was holding me to a ridiculous standard that could not be quantified. He hadn't measured the sizes that I demonstrated the first time, just as he hadn't measured the sizes that I had just shown him then. This was an absurd conversation. If he was going to hold me accountable for precise descriptions of all of the penises I had seen in my lifetime, then I needed an equally precise accounting of every vagina he had ever seen. I demanded that he draw them out to scale and that he be as anatomically accurate as possible.

He didn't appreciate that at all, but it did bring the argument to an end. The Dick Offensive didn't come up again until many years later. In fact, the whole matter had been put to bed, but when we moved back to Pittsburgh the last time, Darren's penis fascination reared its ugly (and genuinely average) head. We didn't really argue about it like before. Instead, he started leaving little penis surprises for me randomly around the house. For example, I sat down at the computer one day to find that the mouse pad had been replaced with one that held a picture of Darren's limp member shoved through a nectarine. It was a shock for so many reasons. I mean, what happened to that poor nectarine, exactly? Why did he wait to take the picture until he was flaccid? Was there really nothing else that he had to do that day other than waste food and our color ink cartridges? So many questions…

It explained why were had been running out of produce faster than usual. It also explained why the keyboard and mouse were so gross and sticky. I shared my displeasure with him as I cleaned up his mess, to which he only laughed. I could see no reason for him to violate what was to have been my lunch the next day. Our sex life was still really good at the time, or so I thought. We averaged about three times a week. It was weird. As far as I know, he didn't do that again. If he had, I am sure that I would have found evidence of disemboweled fruit somewhere around the house or a sticky thumbprint on the camera, at least.

He also developed a fondness for random games of Peekaboo Penis. It was a terribly annoying game. Darren would randomly expose his unit and then wait for me to notice. For instance, I would come downstairs to find Darren sitting leisurely on the sofa with his member lolling out of his shorts and an impish grin on his face. I'd be cooking in the kitchen and turn around to find his wang flopped out of his shorts as he stood there in mid-conversation. At first, I tried to laugh it off. Next, I tried ignoring it like it wasn't even there, but this only made him do it more often. When he finally gave up any inkling of subtlety and just started walking in the room with his pants down around his ankles, I decided it was enough. I went instantly red in the face and started yelling at him. He met my anger with laughter, at first, but ultimately yelled back, telling me that I was a puritanical prude and that I needed to lighten up.

I never knew exactly what brought on Peekaboo Penis. We had sex a couple of times a week back then. It wasn't like he was starved for attention. I'll admit that the more he pushed for sex, the less we had it, but even with that, he still got it more than most and definitely more than he should have. The longer Peekaboo Penis went on, the worse things got for both of us. Sex turned into a miserable obligation for me and a mindless compulsion for him. The passion had waned. It seemed like the love wasn't that far behind it.

For a while, I thought we might be headed for the end. I'd be lying if I said that I hadn't been thinking about it. When I got the job offer, I thought it might be the first step toward a way out for both of us. Then the pregnancy changed everything. It was a shot of epinephrine right into the heart of our marriage. The passion came back, and the penis games went away. Darren snapped out of his sex weirdness. He started acting like my husband again. Everything seemed like it was going to be alright.

Chapter 15

As it had been for me with weddings, so it was for me with babies. I never really dreamed about motherhood. For most of my life, pregnancy was more of a threat than a desire. As good as I was with sex, and as controlled as I tried to be about it, pregnancy was always lurking in the shadows like a ghoul, waiting for the perfect moment to pounce and rip my life to shreds with its pointy ghoul-teeth. While Darren and I were in school, I was so afraid that I was going to get knocked-up that I was almost neurotic about it. It was bad enough that I had already made myself a chiropractic college stereotype by getting married before I graduated. I was determined not to double down and get pregnant at the same time. (Pregnancy was like a communicable disease in chiropractic college. One girl gets it, then it spreads like the plague. And, yes, all chiropractors all know how babies are made, but sometimes "natural contraception"—a.k.a. the rhythm method—doesn't work out so well.)

As far as I was concerned, pregnancy in college was never an option. I would never have finished the program. I needed more stability than that. I needed more money than that. I needed time to let my body freak out. I needed less stress. I needed Darren to be a support system. My need for all of those things made me vigilant.

Seven years later, I still needed it, but there I was, pregnant and worse off than I ever was in school, with no insurance, a growing pile of debt, a floundering business, a new job that I hadn't even started yet, and a husband who was not consistently grounded in the reality of day-to-day living.

The most inexplicable part was that, in spite of all those things, I would characterize myself as happy. It wasn't normal happiness, of course. It was a weird kind of happiness—one that I had never experienced before. It was a bizarre altered state that made everything seem surreal. It even seemed a little dangerous at times. I knew it wasn't real, that it was just a chemical reaction. I was aware that the logical parts of my brain were completely freaking out, but the hormones coursing through my body washed everything in a Gaussian blur. I could, without hesitation, catalog all of the things that were wrong with my situation. I knew that I felt terrible and exhausted. I knew that I was barely holding our fragile financial existence together and that this was the last thing that I needed to add to the shit show that was my life. I knew all of this. I could see it all as plain as day behind the smoothing hormonal booze filter that made it all look pleasant and non-threatening. None of it seemed to matter. I was just happy.

Freakish happiness aside, I was unnecessarily self-conscious about my new condition, too. Like a teenager, I was walking around trying to just be cool about it. I felt like I had done something wrong—like I had let some random jock knock me up in the back seat of his convertible. I felt like I should hide it. Once the truth was out, the world would know beyond a shadow of a doubt exactly what I had been doing behind closed doors. It was ridiculous. Pregnancy was an acceptable, if not coveted, thing for a thirty-six year old married woman. Technically, we were way behind schedule and at risk of "disappointing the Lord" with our insubordination if we didn't procreate soon. (At least that was the Truth that was occasionally lobbed at me across the office reception desk by Darren's Bible-thumping patients.)

What almost no one knew was that Darren and I had started trying to have a baby five years earlier while we were still in Pittsburgh. By "trying to have a baby," what I really mean is that I took a few extra vitamins and stopped freaking out about birth control. After the first month of trying, and as the Charlene complication kept building, the baby plan slipped to the back of the line. We stopped trying, but we never restarted trying not to. We left it up to chance and forgot about it.

...and then it just happened...

Really, I was happy about it. Actually, we were both happy about it. Right away, our marriage problems seemed to vanish, and we were together like we were in the beginning.

We decided not to tell anyone until after the 3rd month which was fine by me. As I said, I was self-conscious about the whole affair, and I wanted a little time to experience it without anyone else's intrusion. Darren barely lasted a week. He couldn't contain himself and started telling everyone, even our patients. He would blurt it out, and I would stand there weirdly embarrassed and inappropriately ashamed. I never managed to match his excitement over sharing the news. Each time he did it, the edges of my reality would sharpen, and thoughts of my irrational indignity, the job I had turned down, and our dwindling bank account would start to take over. "Oh, yes," I would say, "you're right. We're so blessed." I think it might have sounded sincere, but I really can't be sure.

On the physical side, pregnancy felt awful in ways I had never before experienced—and I almost died once in my twenties. No, really, I almost died as in the doctors-in-the-hospital-are-out-of-options kind of dead. That story isn't really relevant here, but it makes my point. Pregnancy felt like hell. My entire body just felt bad. I was tired all the time. My head hurt. My joints ached. I was so bloated that my body felt like it was trapped inside a giant water balloon. I was hungry all the time, but the smell of food made me sick. It was hard to sleep, and when I did, I had nightmares about an alien spawn exploding out of my stomach in the middle of the office.

...It was such a blessing...

Honestly, I couldn't understand why other people got so excited about the whole thing, and I never understood the baby doll obsession that I was expected to go through as a kid. My friends, the baby bridezillas who were so eager to get married to the first guy they could nail down, were equally as enthusiastic about babies. They would spend hours fussing over their dolls with a freakish degree of specificity. They would pretend to feed them and burp them and change them. Then they would pretend that their dolls puked on their shoulders and then say, "Oh, there, there... did-ums spit up a widdle? Let mommy clean that up. I wuv you so much!" and then follow it up with a big kiss right on the dolls' little plastic puke faces.

All I could think was: *Ewe! Gross! Yes, let's get Mommy to clean it up! Mommy, the gross baby just barfed on me!* I mean, really, in what universe is make-believe vomit fun? So, there I was, just like with the wedding thing, faking my way through it to fit in and clearly missing some critical internal biological programming.

So obviously, the real-life baby thing was going to be a challenge for me. I kept telling myself: *This is what you wanted. You did this on purpose. This is what you wanted. It's going to work out.* At some point, I should have started to believe myself. I wanted this, sort of. This was part of the whole marriage deal I made when I said, "I do." I was supposed to have a husband and at least one kid, maybe more. It was expected.

I had no idea where that expectation started. I had been upfront with Darren from day one. He knew my reservations about having children. He said he was good with whatever happened, and it's not like my parents were the pushy type. They hardly ever mentioned it. They already had a grandson. I'm sure they would have loved another one, but they had listened to me blather on about never having children since I was child, myself. I think they got right with it by the time I was about eight. Still, I felt the pressure. I knew that Charlene really wanted grandchildren even if they had to be half me, but I don't think her opinion would have swayed me enough for it to matter.

No, this pressure was from somewhere else—somewhere inside me. It was an experience that I felt like I had to have. It was a basal, physiological urge to do the one thing that only a woman can do—the one thing that would make the decades of cyclical bleeding, bloating, and hormonal swings worthwhile. I wanted to feel the power of creation inside my gut and play my part in the great continuum of human existence. I wanted a genetic legacy that would carry on after my time on this planet and in this body was over.

On every other level, however, it was a different story. The idea of pregnancy was terrifying. It was worse than a tattoo, once it was there, it was never going away, even if I tried to have it removed. My brain knew that pregnancy was a really bad idea no matter how fine the chemicals swimming around in it made everything seem.

Our tangible world was falling apart. Darren's office had declined to the point that it was barely breaking even. We had no money in the business which meant we had no money at home and, importantly, no health insurance. The job I was offered didn't offer benefits, either, but it didn't matter. Thanks to the pregnancy, it was a completely unworkable option for me. It would have been six days a week of physically slinging other people's bodies around from 7:00 am to 6:00 pm with on-call coverage every weekend in an office that was over an hour away from home. At any other time, I would have been all in and ready to go, but at thirty-six with a baby on the way, things were different. Even if I was healthy enough to work through my pregnancy, then what? I didn't have family nearby. It was just the two of us with no support system. I couldn't be gone thirteen hours a day before I gave birth. What the hell would I do after the baby came?

Ultimately, I didn't give them a chance to retract the offer or fire me for some concocted reason once they found out about my condition. I turned the job down before I ever signed the contract. It was the right thing to do, but it meant that I had no choice but to go back to Darren's office.

I just kept reminding myself that other people have babies all the time. I wasn't the first woman on the planet to get pregnant at a bad time. Still, the stress I felt was overwhelming. While the logical part of my brain ticked through the list of everything that was wrong with being pregnant, how bad the timing was, and how unprepared we were for anything of this magnitude to happen, the pregnant part of me didn't care. All of the noise was muted by that enigmatic drunken happiness I talked about. It felt like something really wonderful was about to happen, and none of the rest of it would matter when it was done.

Even Charlene was happy for once. At least, she started talking to me like she almost liked me. I guess she decided that I was her best shot at a legitimate grandchild, so she had to be nice, at least while I was pregnant. After the baby was delivered, I was sure that everything would go back to normal, except for a marked uptick in the amount of time I had to spend with her. I felt certain that her otherwise debilitating fibromyalgia would disappear and she would find the strength to make regular visits to North Carolina once the baby arrived. She had the miraculous ability to recover from her debilitating chronic pain whenever something she wanted was at stake like a Vegas trip or a cruise. I'm sure a baby would rank up there for the first year, at least.

Things even seemed better at the office. Darren was happier than he had been in years. He was actually excited about going to work. Our bottom line was responding nicely to all of the effort. Thanks to the little parasite inside me, we had the best two months in practice we had ever achieved—ever. I finally had a reason for not seeing patients that I could live with. Soon, I would be needed at home and work would be secondary for me. I wouldn't be wasting my education, I would be taking a break to raise our child—or maybe even children. (In utero, I was a twin, but either my twin opted out, or I wasn't willing to share the spotlight because only one of us came out.) By the time I would be ready to come back, the office would be ready for another doctor to handle the overflow. I could slide right in, as Darren's equal, without a problem.

While I am not an obstetrician, I did study the process of pregnancy and childbirth in school. Once I was the patient, however, it seemed like everything I had learned flew right out of my head and left me with a brain full of stupid fears and mindless questions. When it was time to see the obstetrician, I really didn't want to seem uneducated. Chiropractors have enough reputation issues as it is. I didn't want to make it any worse by sounding like an idiot. That being said, I read everything I could get my hands on that talked about the process from beginning to end. I prepped for it like it was a board exam.

I fretted over everything and ultimately chose a reputable women's reproductive health clinic that was associated with one of the major hospitals in Raleigh. I didn't matter that this whole thing was going to send us deeper into debt. I might have been a chiropractor, but I wasn't about to try some sort of self-directed homebirth in my bathtub as Darren wanted us to do. He insisted that women have been having babies since the dawn of time and that we didn't need to go the hospital route. All of the FSP doctors were using midwives for homebirths. It would be fine.

That might have been true for the hardcore FSP acolytes, but it wasn't right for me. The only midwife in our area was a thirty-something pseudo-goth chick with dirty fingernails who looked like she might be stoned most of the time. I was not about to subject myself, my baby, or for that matter, my profession to something as questionable as that. At thirty-six, myself, I was officially considered "geriatric" as a pregnant woman. I needed to consider all of the potential outcomes, no matter the cost and no matter how un-chiropractic it might appear. I would find a way to make it all work out. (This was the one battle over FSP that I won without much effort. I think the potential father and the educated doctor inside of Darren knew it was the right thing to do.)

My first appointment was set during my 14th week. That day was a jumble of anticipation and excitement for us both. We were ready to get the whole process officially started. Our first stop after an hour and a half in the waiting room and a quick dipstick pregnancy test was with our patient liaison. She was a mousy little thing with giant glasses and a scrub jacket with tiny cartoon bears holding balloons who spent most of her time telling me that whatever I was feeling was "all perfectly normal" and reviewing the long list of things that pregnant women should never do. Eventually, she got to the inevitable "so, what do you do?" question. When I said I was a chiropractor, she wrote CHIROPRACTOR boldly in the margin of my intake form and swiped it twice with a bright pink highlighter. I politely pointed out that my profession already was written down on the paper right in front of her and that I had written it in myself when I filled out the form. Darren kicked my foot under the table like I was being obnoxious. The mousy liaison never even looked up at me in response.

...It was all perfectly normal...

Next, she shuttled us into the financial manager's office who said "congratulations" and then shoved pages of cost estimates and payment options at us since we were uninsured. She sat across the desk staring at us until we signed all of the contracts and gave her a check for a third of the estimated overall cost of the entire event—assuming it would be a normal birth with no complications. Complications were extra. They would bill us after the fact for that. Hospital fees were also not included, but we could walk over and talk to the hospital directly about that. After that, they happily scheduled us another appointment in two weeks, handed us a bag full of pamphlets with smiling babies on them, a sample of baby wipes, and a refrigerator magnet with the office phone number on it, before shuttling us right out the door.

It was all very efficient. Regardless of the fact that this was a huge life-changing event for us, this was just Tuesday for them. Most of all they wanted us to know that everything was "all perfectly normal."

We were stunned. We had just emptied our bank account, and we never even saw a doctor walking down the hall. They hadn't prepared us for that. We thought I was getting an initial work up. What we got felt like a marginally polite shakedown.

I thoroughly expected Darren to lose his mind when we got to the car and spout off about the attitude of mainstream medicine and how ridiculous it was for me to go there when we could do it at home for a fraction of the cost. In that moment, I was fully prepared to agree with him.

He started as soon as the car door closed. "See, you shouldn't be so intimidated by asking people to prepay for their care." That wasn't what I was expecting at all. "They just did it, and we didn't even put up a fight." Following JT's instructions, Darren had started insisting on long-term prepaid treatment plans in his office, which meant that a guy who came in with a minor backache got a pitch for 12 months of treatment rather than help for his back pain and a follow-up visit. I couldn't help but feel that this was some kind of healthcare karma coming back on us.

"I don't want to talk about it," I said with agitation.

"No, seriously," he went on, "you've been saying that other doctors don't work like that, but they do. You have your proof. JT was right."

"JT's an ass. It's a totally different thing," I said.

"It's not, you just can't stand being wrong" he shot back arrogantly.

"I'm not wrong." I couldn't believe that my first pregnancy visit was turning into Darren's proof of JT's fucking concept.

"Yes, you are," he replied.

"No, I'm not. It's not the same thing. At the end of this, we get a baby. At the end of a year of chiropractic, you get no low back pain. Something that even a bad chiropractor should be able to do in less than two weeks most of the time." My annoyance was growing.

"We are not selling pain relief, Alane. That's what medical doctors do," Darren spat out the word "medical" like it was a vile, unclean thing. "We provide wellness. That's worth three times as much as a baby."

"Oh my God!" I said on the verge of tears. "I can't do this right now! Do what you want. It's your office." I slumped down in the passenger seat with my hand over my eyes. My head felt like it was going to split open.

"You're right. It is," he said getting in the last word.

We rode the rest of the way home in silence.

Our experience at the OB's office seemed to inspire Darren in a way that JT and his cult hadn't been able. The next week, Darren was on fire with office procedures. He decided that I was done talking to people about paying for their care. In his words, "they could sense my uncertainty." So, he took it on, himself, because only he understood how important it was and my negativity and hang-ups about money were getting in the way.

Even though I hated pitching 12-month contracts and payment plans, having the job stripped away was a belittling, professional blow. To be frank, I hated talking to patients about money. Still, it was my job. I really couldn't bear hearing that I was bad at my job and that I was the sole reason our numbers were bad, especially when there were so many other factors that were contributing to our office problems. I wasn't allowed to treat patients in any capacity beyond weighing them and telling them that "Dr. Darren will be with you in a moment." It felt like Darren was creeping closer and closer to full frontal misogyny every day.

Then one afternoon, I decided it was enough. I was exhausted. My abdomen was tense and heavy, and I kept thinking that if my bad attitude was hobbling our practice, then it might just hobble our baby and nobody wanted that. I needed to be at home. Darren had an employee. She was trained. She could answer the phone and hand out water bottles. He wasn't alone. I wasn't abandoning him or "his" patients, who all somehow suddenly became "our" patients once I declared that I was going home. Nothing was going to implode without me there. He couldn't have it both ways. I couldn't be the cause of, and the answer to, all of his problems. So, I went home and stayed there for the next three days.

At that moment, I decided that my pregnancy was becoming utterly disagreeable. I felt terrible. I felt sick and uncomfortable, and I couldn't understand why anybody ever claimed that they felt their best whenever they were pregnant. It had to be a conspiracy. No woman in her right mind would choose this if the truth got out. I was supposedly a healthy person. For fuck sake, my husband peddled wellness for a living. I couldn't be this exhausted. I should have been healthy enough to run a marathon and a practice and save the planet with a baby on one hip and another one on the way. Good God, what was all of this chiropractic wellness shit for if it didn't turn the act of having a baby into just another bodily function?

I thought maybe my problem was chiro-cult related burnout. I couldn't be sure, really. All I knew was that I felt awful, and the worse I felt, the more Darren's irritation grew. I could see that he was excited about the baby, but he was clearly frustrated by my choice to stay home. I don't know why it was such a thing for him. His front desk chick, Kelli, was more than capable. In fact, she was really good at her job. The patients even seemed to like her a little better than they liked me. From my perspective, it was a winning situation all the way around.

Darren, however, was not in the same place with it. By the end of his first week alone, he was bubbling over with annoyance. Without asking me how I felt about it, he made Saturday dinner plans for us with a fellow FSP doctor, Eric, and his wife who had their first baby the year before, Cathy. Eric had been part of JT's cult of chiropractic for a while as part of his associate position with one of the biggest FSP offices in the State. Cathy was a school teacher. Darren said he thought it would be good for us to get out of the house and hang out with other chiro-parents. I guess he wanted me to see how another woman had successfully handled everything since I was clearly struggling with it. Which made sense considering (twenty-eight year old) Cathy's state-funded health insurance and paid maternity leave along with Eric's guaranteed monthly paycheck. Obviously, our situations were nearly identical.

Even so, I was all for dinner out even if I had to endure it with another brainwashed chiropractic wellness enthusiast. I had been alone in the house for three days, and Darren had barely spoken to me since the day I decided to come home. The thought of getting out and talking to humans other than Darren sounded good to me.

That Saturday, I worked myself up to go all day, or rather, rested up all day. I was determined to go and have a good time despite my ever-present sense of exhaustion and the growing pressure in my abdomen. I was pregnant, after all, and as everyone at my OB's office kept telling me, this was normal.

It was almost time for us to leave when the state of my body started changing. The pressure in my abdomen swelled, and my head swooned. I thought I might pass out. "I don't think I can I can go," I said to Darren as I sank into the couch.

"Sure you can," Darren said. "Just sit for a minute. You'll be fine."

"I don't know," I said with concern. "This feels weird. I don't think I can be in a restaurant right now. Just call Eric and cancel. We'll try again some other night."

"I don't know why you're trying to get out of this. I can't cancel. They're already out and expecting to meet us." Darren was standing by the front door like a kid waiting to go play outside. "You've been at home all week. You probably just need to get out of the house. It'll be fine."

"Three days," I said flatly.

"Huh?" he grunted.

"Three days," I repeated. "I've been here for three days, not all week. I was at the office with you on Monday and Tuesday.

Remember?"

"Fine, three days, whatever. You were home doing nothing while I was at work," Darren shot back with annoyance. "Let's just go. We can sit at the bar until they get there."

"I don't want to sit at the bar," the sensation in my abdomen was building.

"Fine, we'll get a table and wait for them," he offered dismissively, "Let's go."

"If I don't feel well here, then I probably won't feel well there," I insisted. I wasn't even sure that I could stand up from the couch let alone endure dinner in a loud restaurant.

"You're being ridiculous," Darren pushed on, "You're just pregnant. Other pregnant chicks go out all the time. You'll be fine."

"I don't want to go!" I said forcefully, "If you are so worried about it, you can go, and I'll stay here."

"I can't do that, Cathy will be there," he said, clearly irritated. "They are expecting both of us. It would be rude."

"Canceling dinner isn't rude, but showing up and coming off as a bitch because I don't feel well is," I said. I was trying to keep my sense of humor about the whole thing, but I was failing.

"Have you been reading that 'What Happens When You're Expecting' book, again? Eric said that you should stop reading that book. It makes everybody think they're in the worst-case scenario category."

"Wow, there's some attentive doctoring…" I said only slightly under my breath.

"What?" Darren said with clear agitation.

"I said Eric's an excellent doctor," I replied loudly.

"There's no need to be shitty, Alane," Darren shot back.

"Fine," I said with exasperation, "let's go." I hoisted myself up off the couch and headed for the door.

"Don't be shitty while we're out," Darren said at me as I passed through the front door.

"Have I ever been shitty to one of your friends, Darren? Come to think of it, have I ever really been shitty to anyone around you?" I asked with calm defiance.

"You've thought about it," he said haughtily, "and you do that thing where you're really nice to their face but then you bitch all the way home in the car. It's shitty."

"Would you prefer that I just say every thought that runs through my head straight to their faces?" I asked smugly.

"Can you just be nice to people, for once? You know, it's your bitchy attitude that keeps us from hitting our goals."

That hit a nerve with an acid-filled needle. "Yes, I wasn't even in the office, and everything bad that happened was still a direct result of my bad attitude, Darren. Can we just go to dinner?"

"Fine," he said before he piled into the car. As he started the engine, he added, "Let's just drop this and go have a good time."

"Great, let's do that," I volleyed back reflexively, masking my overwhelming irritation with an upbeat, happy façade. For the first time in my adult life, it made me feel a little schizophrenic to hear a pleasant tone come out of my mouth in the face of such blatant disrespect. I was taught to smile and act like nothing was wrong, especially when other people were involved. It was a Southern cultural mandate if not a genetically encoded biological imperative to sweep things under a rug. This time, though, something was different. Things were changing. I was changing. At the same time, I was starting to doubt myself. Maybe Darren was right. Maybe it was me. Maybe my seething contempt for just about everything in my world (except for the baby in my gut) was the single source of everything bad that had ever happened to us. That seemed a little one-sided, if not entirely unjust, but maybe it was true. All I knew for sure was that I needed Darren to be the sole provider for a while. I needed him to make everything work out while I figured out how to handle the alien life form growing inside my body. If that meant that I had to keep my opinions to myself a little better, then so be it. I didn't have the energy to fight over it.

On a good day, the drive to the restaurant usually took about twenty-five minutes. This day, however, traffic was backed up for several miles thanks to an unusual number of fender-benders on the road. A steamy sprinkling rain had been falling all afternoon, making the roads unusually slick. It looked more like rush hour in January than a Saturday afternoon in July. Forty minutes had passed, and we were only halfway there.

"I should have taken the back road. I knew I should have taken the back road," Darren said with aggravation. "Now, we're stuck."

"It's ok, we were an hour ahead of schedule when we left. We have time to spare," I said trying to be genuinely supportive.

"I just wanted some time at the bar before they got there," he said morosely.

"What, you're wanting to pound a couple of beers before Eric gets there? Are you expecting it to be that bad?" I laughed.

"I did want a couple," he said, "They're not bad. I like Eric a lot. They're just really religious, and they don't drink much, I don't think. I don't think Cathy drinks at all, in fact."

"Well, I guess you will just have to get through it without it tonight," I said with a chuckle.

"I don't want to," Darren shot back sternly.

"Oh, come on," I said still chuckling, "you can go without it for one Saturday night. In fact, you could go without it while I'm pregnant. You can suffer through this pregnancy thing with me."

"No way," he chortled.

"Come on," I said, "show a little solidarity. It'll be fun!"

"No," Darren shot back flatly, grimacing at the road.

"Okay," I chuckled on, "wuss."

Darren just stared at the road. I let myself drift off in thought about Darren and his beer brewing obsession, wondering if he was going to give it a rest once the baby got there. A sharp pain in my abdomen snapped me back to the present moment. It felt like distress. I told myself that it was just a ligament stretching or some other soft tissue something happening. *Eric's probably right. That book is making me crazy,* I thought to myself as I closed my eyes and took a deep breath.

It happened again. The sharp pain was more stabbing this time, more intense. Dread washed over me. "Darren, I think something's wrong," I said out loud.

"I'm sure you're fine," he said as he stared at the line of traffic in front of him. "You probably just need to eat."

"No, seriously, something's wrong." As I spoke, the pain hit again, only this time it was in more than one place. "I need to go home."

"We can't. They're already on their way by now. They're coming from the other side of the city."

"I need to go home!" I insisted. The pain was subsiding, but my dread was growing.

"Damn it, no! We made plans!" Darren said angrily.

Tears welled in my eyes. "Something is wrong. I can't go in there like this. I want to go home."

"I can't believe you're doing this. You let us get this far and now you want to cancel and go home?" he said more to the air than to me.

"Yes!" I cried. "Something's wrong! Please take me home." I cradled my stomach as a cold sweat broke out on the back of my neck. None of this was normal. As Darren picked up his phone to make the call, the traffic broke open. "We're right here," he said pointing to the buildings down the road as Eric's phone rang on the line.

I ignored him.

Exactly what Eric said, I don't know, but from Darren's responses, I deduced that he must have been irritated. "I don't know what else to say," Darren offered as an apology, "She says she needs to go home, man. Sorry… (Darren paused for Eric's response) …I know, I know. I told her she should stop reading that book… (another pause) …Thanks, man. I'm really sorry. She's just new to the whole pregnancy thing… (another pause) …I know. I know. Yeah, I'm sorry, man… (another pause) …I will. Thanks, again, man." Then, he hung up.

Darren turned his head to look at me, "He's being really nice about it, but I think he was really upset."

The whole situation was absurd. I wanted to yell at him, "I'm carrying your baby! I just told you that I think something is wrong and you're worried if Eric is upset? Are you fucking kidding me right now?!" But, I didn't. I was too uncomfortable and too upset to deal with it. Instead, I just said, "Thank you," and sank down in my seat for the ride home.

On the way, Darren stopped for a twelve pack of microbrew since, as he said, "the keg's tapped," meaning he was out of his own beer. I sat in the car while he went into the store. He returned with a twelve pack of IPA and two cans of snuff. The snuff thing, which was exactly as contrary to "wellness" as it sounds, was a habit he had stopped years earlier right after we met. He started again right before we got married, then stopped, and started again right after graduation, and then stopped again before we moved to North Carolina the last time. Then, thanks to one night out with his best friend from high school, he started again in earnest and never stopped.

When we got to the house, Darren went straight inside, shoved a wad of snuff into his lower lip, and cracked open his first beer before he even took off his shoes. The rest of the night, we sat in front of the TV together. I slept when I could and stared at the TV trying to ignore my impending sense of doom when I couldn't. Darren sat shirtless on the loveseat drinking beer after beer and spitting snuff juice into an empty bottle.

The rest of the weekend was mostly the same. I stayed on the couch. Darren stayed with me, drinking and dipping his way through Sunday which involved another trip to the grocery store for more IPA and more snuff.

The next week dragged by as I stayed at home. I occupied myself by cleaning out the spare room—step one in my baby-themed makeover plan. I didn't have anything to put in it, but all of the junk we had mindlessly tossed in there had to go. It was a long wait until Friday when I was scheduled to go in for my first real appointment, and most excitingly, my first ultrasound. I was nervous, of course, but at least the stabbing pain and the overwhelming sense of dread from the weekend had abated. I hated to admit it, but Eric had been right. Putting the books down helped.

By the time our Friday appointment time came, Darren and I were both bubbling with excitement. We were ready to go. We were ready to see our baby. We were ready to frame copies of the ultrasound image and send it to the grandparents. The angst was gone, and we were eager to move ahead with it.

My visit went well. Everyone was polite and efficient as they went through my history and set the stage for the big ultrasound reveal. The technician came in the room and completed the task efficiently and without any fanfare and then left me there, feet in still the stirrups and nether regions in the wind.

Darren looked at me and said, “This is a little weird, huh? I leave somebody alone in a gown for five minutes, and they freak out. Here, they just leave you with it all hanging out like it’s nothing.”

I laughed a little, “It’s easier this way. Less talking; more uterus wanding!”

“I don’t know how you can make jokes in that position. I’d be too weirded out,” he said with a shiver.

“I’m a woman,” I laughed, “shit like this happens to us all the time.”

“Christ, Alane…” Darren said like he was mildly repulsed.

I laughed some more, “How do you think I got pregnant to begin with? You should know. You were there. I probably made a few jokes then, too.”

He laughed and shook his head, “Oh my God, you’re not right…”

I was still laughing when the doctor came in the room. She was tall, blonde, and serious, and got right to her work after only a few cursory pleasantries and a quick confirmation from me that it was alright to shove the ultrasound in again. “Even though you know it’s coming,” she said flatly, “I always like to ask permission first.”

“It’s only polite,” I laughed and cut my eyes over to Darren whose face was so red I thought his head might explode from the rush of blood. Darren had never witnessed the indignity of a pelvic exam in person. As close as the dummy forms we used in school were to the real thing, the true invasive nature of the process was lost on him until that moment.

Expressionlessly, Dr. Blonde prodded and shoved, tapping away at the ultrasound console capturing image after image. “Ok,” she said, you can sit up...You can get dressed. The nurse will show you to my office where we can go over your results.”

“Thanks,” I said, dismounting from the stirrups.

"That's it?" Darren said.

"Yes," Dr. Blonde said, "See you in a few minutes."

"That's it?" Darren said to me this time.

"Looks like it," I replied as I wiped down the remaining globs of lubricant and shimmied into my underwear. With Darren in the room, the whole post-pelvic process seemed more awkward than usual. He watched me get dressed every day like it was some kind of peepshow. Today should have been no different, but for some reason, it just felt creepy.

"That was weird," he said staring uncomfortably at the back of the exam room door.

"Eh, not really. It's worse when they stand there and talk to you while your vagina's still whistling in the wind." I said, "Trust me, that's weirder."

"Huh," Darren grunted almost to himself like he was trying to picture the scene differently in his head.

The nurse returned and escorted us down the hall to Dr. Blonde's private office, replete with an over-sized leather desk chair, a giant cork board of smiling baby snapshots and thank you notes, and fern-filled planter stands flanking our markedly less comfortable seats. She closed the door behind her as she left.

Instantly, my nerves started ramping up, and I was having trouble sitting still. "You know this means that something is wrong, right?" I said as I scanned the photos and letters on the wall.

"Not necessarily," he said, "you always assume the worst. This is probably just their version of a report of findings. We do the same thing."

"No, I'm serious," I insisted, "There is something wrong. They should have talked to us more in the exam room. They should have shown us the ultrasound and said congratulations. Something's not right."

"Don't be ridiculous. It's not a TV show. This is real life," Darren said dismissively.

"How many gynecologist visits have you had in your life, Darren?" I said bitingly.

"Oh my God," he said loudly with a chuckle, "you are so melodramatic."

I wanted to be angry, but I was too nervous. Instead, I sat there bouncing my heel rapidly off the floor and fidgeting with my hands to keep them from shaking.

When Dr. Blonde walked into the room, I made myself stop the nervous movement. I had to appear composed no matter what was coming next.

"Ok," she said as she took a seat in the large leather desk chair, "so, I have some difficult news..."

All of the muscles in my body seized.

"The fetus is no longer viable..." She paused for a beat as she robotically shifted her eyes back and forth between the two of us. "I can't be certain, but it looks like it stopped developing somewhere around the eighth week or so..." She paused, again. "I'm very sorry."

I sat there looking at her in stunned silence. I could feel my throat tightening into a ball as I forced myself to take a breath.

When neither of us spoke, she continued, "I can't really be sure why it happened. You have two pretty large fibroids in there that could have caused a problem, but I can't be sure that's what did it. This just happens sometimes. We can always run some tests if you want, but we don't have to. You're not that old, yet. You can try again."

After another long pause, Darren and I looked at each other. I kept hoping he would speak and fill the void in the room, but he was as stunned as I was. Dr. Blonde silently thrust a box of tissues in my face as though it was just code in her bedside manner software program. I took one as a reflex. "What now?" I croaked out as I balled the tissue up in my fist.

"Well…" Dr. Blonde said with a practiced thoughtful tone. "There are a couple of ways to go with this. Your body should evacuate it on its own. Honestly, I can't believe that hasn't happened already. Or, we can schedule you for a 'D&E' which is what we typically do, but I see here that you are a chiropractor. I know how you chiropractors are, so I doubt you are interested something like that. Really, it's up to you."

I could feel Darren getting agitated. "This isn't really about chiropractic right now," he said to Dr. Blonde before he turned to me, "What do you want to do?"

I sat there squeezing the tissue in my fist. There was no way I could make that decision, I was still processing what she said. My baby didn't make it. It had taken so much for me to get right with it in my head, but I was finally ready. I was excited. And now, it was gone—just like that—and worse, I had been carrying a dead embryo-fetus around inside me for weeks talking to it like it was a living thing. What new fucking hell was this?

"Why?" was all I could get out.

"Why what?" Dr. Blonde said, "Why did this happen? I can't really say. It could have been anything. Since you just started trying, I wouldn't worry about it. You can try again."

"There has to be a reason," I went on.

Dr. Blonde sighed as if discussing this was a bother, "No, not really, sometimes it just happens. It's not your fault, if that's what you are getting at. Do you know what you want to do?"

At that moment, a single tear rolled out of my eye. "I don't know…" My brain was locked. I couldn't reason my way through any of it. "Do I have to decide right now?"

"No, you don't have to decide. If you wait long enough, your body might decide for you," she said without emotion.

"What can I expect if my body just handles it?" I asked.

"I figured you would want to do that. You natural health types are all the same. Ok, so you should expect severe cramping followed by heavy bleeding that might last for anywhere between about six to twelve hours. It isn't pleasant, but many women go through it before they ever make it into the office. You can call if you change your mind," Dr. Blonde said as she stood and stepped toward the door.

"I haven't made up my mind," I said bewildered. How could she expect me to make that decision that second? "I just can't think clearly right now."

"Ok, well, I'll have your patient liaison take you to the financial manager so you can go over the financial part of things. Make sure you schedule a follow up afterward so we can check you out. Again, I am very sorry," and with that, she left, closing the door behind her.

The patient liaison took us to the chairs in the hall outside the financial manager's office. "I am so sorry," she said, "It's going to be a few minutes. She is in with a new patient."

All I could do was look at the floor and eke out a "thank you."

Before she walked away, she bent over and put her hand on my knee, "Don't worry. This happens all the time. One in every nine pregnancies ends in miscarriage. You can try again."

I looked up at her and forced a smile as I said, "Thanks." On the inside, I was coming undone. I was devastated. I was furious. I was scared. I was all of it at once, and more. I was pissed that they had just dropped the dead baby bomb on me and now they wanted to talk to me about money. I had already paid them a third of the cost of services that I no longer needed, so I didn't know why I couldn't just leave and talk to them about it later.

We sat through it all, though. We sat through the discussion of how many services had already been applied to our account and how much we should be getting back. Of course, if we chose to get the D&E we would owe them money on top of what we had already paid and then there would be the hospital costs and the anesthesiologist's fees. They couldn't say what that would be, but we could walk over to the hospital and talk to their financial people for more information. Oh, yes, and they were "so sorry for our loss…but not to worry, this happens all the time…"

By the time we got home, I was completely distraught. I couldn't think of anything other than the dead embryo-fetus in my abdomen—the dead thing that I had come to love and plan for and dream about as if it were a real living thing. We even had a list of names…and was it an embryo or a fetus? She said it stopped developing at about eight weeks, so what did that make it, technically? I needed to know so I could think about it accurately.

Darren and I didn't say much to each other for the rest of that day. We just sat together on the couch staring at the TV. Darren brought me one of his beers, and we drank together. The taste of it made me sick, but I didn't care. I just didn't want to feel. I just wanted to be numb for a while.

Most of the weekend was spent in the same state. I sat and stared blankly at the TV, occasionally bursting into tears and then drying it up and staring blankly again. When we could talk, we called our parents, and I cried. We ordered pizza, and I cried. We researched potential outcomes for both options, and I cried. Darren cried a little here and there, but mostly he drank. It wasn't his animated binge-frat-boy-party drinking. It was slow and steady, like he wanted to stay marginally alert but really didn't want to feel much of anything about much of anything.

Ultimately, we landed on our dead embryo-fetus resolution strategy. We would give my body until the next Friday to work things out. If nothing had happened by then, we would schedule the procedure. It felt like my body wasn't going to let go. It took me so long to get pregnant. Then it took me so long to get right with the fact that I was pregnant. Who could know how long it would take for my body to get right with the loss. With my luck, it would stay up there until it necrotized or some other ghastly complication ensued. Still, I needed a little time to get right with things in my head, not to mention the time I needed to figure out how I was going to pay for all of it.

By Monday, Darren was ready to go to work if for no other reason than to get away from the den of sadness that our house had become. I stayed home, and he was fine with it. He had been done with crying by Saturday night. Needless to say, I wasn't. I had been perpetually on the brink of tears for days. Monday was just more of the same for me. The weather made it worse. It set the dismal scene. It was one of those warm, gray, rainy days outside where the ground is so hot that the water steams up off the pavement almost as soon as it hits the ground making everything look like an 80's hairband video. To a fly on the wall, I imagine it looked like I was staring blankly at the TV, but I wasn't. I was staring out the window beside it imagining the guy from White Snake dropping to his knees in the mist covered grass and whipping his big hair around as he mouthed the lyrics to a song I didn't want to remember. I mean, seriously, my brain was choosing White Snake over reality. Things were pretty bleak.

White Snake played on outside the window for a while. At some point it dawned on me how weird it was that David Coverdale's hair never succumbed to elements in any video I could remember—neither rain, nor mist, nor sweat, nor smoke machines. No wonder I had unreasonable hair product performance expectations when I was young.

"Enough," I said out loud. I had daydreamed long enough to call the White Snake guy by name which meant it had gone on way too long. "Time to do something," I continued to myself. I hadn't eaten for over a day. At the very least, I could feed myself. That was a place to start.

With one grand movement, I stood up and turned toward the kitchen. As I took my first step, pain lanced through my lower abdomen. It felt like a metal claw was clutching my uterus and trying to twist it out of my body. It was a pain that I had never experienced before that pitched me over onto my knees. I had to steady myself on the arm of the sofa to keep from hitting the floor.

A few seconds later it subsided. "This must be it," I said to myself with a bit of relief. "Maybe you're ready to let go after all." I straightened myself upright and started toward the kitchen. I made it no more than two steps when the pain hit again, this time with enough force to drop me to my knees.

"Jesus," I grunted as the ripping spasm in my pelvis intensified. I had to get to the bathroom. I got to my feet and shuffled bent forward toward the half bathroom. I barely made it to the door before my uterus let go. It was like an apocalyptic explosion that sent blood everywhere. It was on me and my clothes, it was on the wall and the floor. "Holy shit!" I grunted as the next wave of twisting, searing pain shot through my gut. This time it spread through to my back. A cold sweat broke out all over my body as the room started to spin. I reeled sideways into the porcelain pedestal sink and then ricocheted to the toilet just before the next apocalyptic uterine explosion hit.

Over the next hour, I stayed on the toilet bleeding, clotting, and sweating with searing abdominal pain doubling me over every two minutes or so. Dr. Blonde had said it would be uncomfortable. She said I would bleed. She said nothing about giant chunks of my uterus flying out of my vagina. I was not at all prepared for this kind of pain.

Into the second hour, my legs started tingling from the compression of backs of my legs on the hard toilet seat. "I can't stay like this forever," I announced to the air. There were no helpful supplies within reach. Only a half empty roll of toilet paper and a single hand towel. I didn't even have my phone to call for help. I was going to have to get upstairs to the master bathroom if I was ever going to be able to handle this mess. My plan was to get up the stairs before the next wave hit. As the next round of cramping pain came and went, I stuffed my underwear full of toilet paper. I stood up and reached for the door. Before I had taken my second step, the room started to spin, and my vision started to warp. "Oh…blood loss…" I muttered as I smacked into the door frame. I hadn't thought through the dehydration, the blood loss, the electrolyte imbalance, the hyperventilating…

…some doctor I am…

As I saw it, I had three choices. I could go back to the toilet to bleed out, I could just collapse on the floor where I stood and bleed out there, or I could try to make it upstairs for a clean pair of pants and a maxi pad. (There was actually a fourth option—get to my phone and call for help, but that never even crossed my mind.) Of course, I opted for the most ridiculous option—I decided I had to get up the stairs. I don't know what difference I thought clean clothes would make and it wasn't like a sanitary napkin was going to save me from exsanguination, but I was determined.

I pushed myself out the door and stumbled over to the stairs. I made it up the first three steps to the small landing by gripping the rail and pressing on the opposite wall. Just as my foot touched the next step, the next wave of searing, pain hit like a twisting lightning bolt shooting through my gut and out my spine. I dropped onto the stairs. Another gush of blood rushed out of me. Had to move unless I wanted to add destroyed carpet to my list of horrors that day. The only thing left to do was crawl. So, I did. I crawled up the stairs and crawled all the way into the master bathroom where I must have blacked out for a little while. The next thing I woke up face down on the linoleum. The cramping had stopped. Slowly, I cleaned myself up and got some clean clothes. I found some pads, too, but there were only two of them left.

...shit...

Carefully, I eased my way back downstairs to my phone and a tall glass of water. I dialed the office number. Within two rings Kelli picked up the line, "It's a great day at Danky Chiropractic. This is Kelli. I can help!"

I loathed that fucking greeting, but it was FSP protocol, and Darren was adamant about it. I always thought it made me sound intellectually impaired.

"Hi, Kelli, it's Alane," I croaked out as professionally as I could.

"Oh, hey Dr. Alane! Can I call you back? We have patients right now," she said right on cue.

"No. Can you get Dr. Darren? I need to speak to him," I said.

"I am so sorry, he's with patients right now. I can have him call you when he is free," Kelli chirped back.

"Kelli, I know this is what I trained you to do, but I need you to get him. I need to speak to him." I was still composed, but my voice started to waver.

"I am so sorry, he is with patients," she said back robotically.

That stupid little twit never remembers what I taught her when it's a salesman on the phone. Why is she so good at it right now? I thought to myself. "Okay, fine. Please just have him call me as soon as possible."

"Will do, Dr. Alane! Have an awesome day!" Kelli chirped and hung up.

"Fuck you, Kelli," I said into the disconnected phone. I dialed Darren's cell. He never answered when patients were in the office, but I thought maybe today it would be different considering the circumstances. It wasn't.

Ten minutes later, the cramping started, again. The clotting started, again. I was back in the bathroom, again. An hour passed before I could get off the toilet. Another hour passed before Darren called.

"What's up?" he said casually like it was just another day.

"It started," I said.

"Oh," he said uncertainly, "you okay?"

"I guess," I said back. "There's a lot of blood, and it hurts. I think I passed out a little."

"Holy hell, did you hurt yourself?" he asked with concern.

"No, I was already on the floor."

"What?" he asked.

"It's been a rough day," I said.

"I see that. Do you need anything?" he asked.

"Yeah, I need pads. I am on my last one already."

"Awe, can't you go?" he whined a little. "It's so embarrassing."

"I can't be away from the bathroom that long and the cramping is terrible," I pleaded. "Please, I need your help."

There was an unnecessarily long pause. "Alright," he conceded, "just tell me what to get. I'll get them on my way home."

"Thank you," I said and then proceeded to describe what I needed from the store.

The afternoon dragged on much like the morning only slightly more controlled because I never really left the bathroom. I called the OB clinic to update them on my status and to find out what they wanted me to do next. They reassured me that this was "all perfectly normal" and that it should settle down over the next twelve hours or so. They wanted to see me next week sometime for a follow-up. Other than that, there was nothing else to do but wait it out.

The next twelve hours passed. It didn't stop. Then, the next 12 hours passed. It still didn't stop. As the hours ticked by, the bleeding slowed only a little. It wasn't over, and the cramping episodes were getting closer together. By the middle of the third day, it had been enough. The bleeding and cramping just wouldn't stop, and I was a mess. I called the OB clinic again and got an appointment for that afternoon.

That visit was the first step on a path that I can only describe as a slow walk through Hades. I would eventually go back to the office three more times in the next seven days. Each time, it was a little worse than the last.

The first doctor's proclamation was that there was "tissue" hung up on my cervix which was causing my uterus to continue to contract. So, she extracted it right there in the office—no anesthesia, no pain killers, not even a Xanax…nothing. She said that once it was out, everything should settle down. That was visit one.

…the bleeding and contracting continued…

Visit two was mostly the same but with a different doctor. She said that there was more "tissue" that had been missed and needed to be extracted. She assured me that this just happens sometimes and that the solution was, in her words, "fairly simple." Again, there were no numbing agents, no anxiolytics, nothing was offered to dull any of the pain or calm me down, only repeated vaginal ultrasound wands and some forceps and a lot of painful rooting around inside my angry uterus. And there was no blood work done to see how the rest of me was doing. I asked if we needed to schedule a formal D&E to make sure this was done and the doctor said, "no, this should handle it."

Two days later, when I was still bleeding, I went back for round three. This time I got the same doctor as the time before who said, "There might be more 'tissue' in there, but I just can't be sure. And, you have two large fibroids, one of which seems to be the attachment point for the "tissue." The only thing to do is to try to get it out. This might be a little painful."

"It's all been painful!" I said back.

She said, "I know," and went on about her work. This time, she called for a biopsy needle. "This will only take a few seconds. Try to relax and stay still."

I can say unequivocally that a biopsy needle poking and scraping around in a fibroid in the wall of a uterus is an experience to remember. It was like white lightning inside me. "Please try to relax," the doctor said.

My knuckles went white from my grip on the sides of the exam table. The nurse standing at my left side, grimaced as she watched the procedure. When she saw me looking, she composed herself and peeled my left hand off the table's edge. "Just hold on. You're gonna be alright," she said cautiously.

I squeezed her hand as the needle went in for the last time. "Just once more," the doctor said as it went.

My vision went white, and a cold sweat burst out on my skin, as a wave of nausea hit me. "Aaaye!" I shrieked. I was hyperventilating.

"All done!" the doctor said while cutting her eyes to the nurse. "Take as much time as you need and be careful on the way home. I know you drove yourself, today. Just remember, lots of rest, lots of fluids, come back and see us in a week, and not that you are interested in it right now, but no sex."

"No problem," I said, still panting as I hoisted myself upright. To be blunt, sex was the last thing on my mind at that particular moment. From where I sat on that exam table with its stirrups still raised on either side of me, there was nothing beautiful about sex, about pregnancy, or about the alien spawn it would create. The whole sex thing and everything that came with it was an evil farce concocted by some soulless demon to hold women down, and anyone who said otherwise was probably a soulless demon, too. I knew right then and there that God was definitely not a woman. No woman would have allowed childbirth to be like this. No way in Heaven or Hell.

"Call us if you need anything," the doctor said over her shoulder as walked out the door.

…and that was visit three…

Once I got home, I passed out on the couch.

That night, Darren brought the office billing home for me to do. He didn't have time for it, or so he said. As he handed me the files, he said with certainty, "I need you to come back to the office," he said. "I can't keep up with this, and Kelli's pregnant now."

I couldn't believe what I was hearing. "Fuck," I said, "I just need a little more time."

"Take the rest of the week," he said, by which he meant Thursday and Friday.

I was exhausted, and it had been an awful day. "No rest for the wicked, I guess," I chuckled in resignation.

"What did you say?" Darren's demeanor flipped instantly to muted rage.

Still chuckling at myself and not entirely catching the change, "No rest for the wicked," I repeated without hesitation.

"What is that supposed to mean?" he spat.

I was stunned by the force of his words. "I don't know. It's a saying," I replied.

"How dare you!" he yelled. "Christ, you're unbelievable!" The force of his emotions was fully evident.

"What the fuck," I said in disbelief. I stood up, but the room started spinning, sending me back to my seat on the couch. "What did I do?"

"There you go, criticizing me, again!" Darren boomed as he stormed into the kitchen and pulled a beer from the refrigerator.

"How exactly am I criticizing you? I said, 'no rest for the wicked.' The 'wicked' one would be me." Darren's lack of familiarity with such a common turn of phrase was shocking. I was too exhausted for this.

"Why do you always have to put me down," he said. "What the fuck?"

"'What the fuck' is right!" I said getting louder. "I wasn't criticizing you. I was just talking." The truth be told, I was talking about myself. I had spent the whole day fighting off the crazies and trying to convince myself that the entire pregnancy debacle was not all my fault. I was genuinely depressed which seemed somewhat reasonable considering the week I had just endured. Whether it was hormonal, neurochemical, situational or some combination of the three, I didn't know. All I knew was that oppressive sadness had taken over my waking hours, and I was trying very hard to assess my situation and remain rational.

"You always make everything my fault! I can't believe you called me wicked!" Darren yelled as he sucked on his beer and stared at the muted TV.

"This is insane," I said shaking my head. None of this made any sense.

"Yes, it is," he replied smugly.

"It's just a saying," I pleaded. I could feel what little energy I had left draining from my body. I was still dehydrated and anemic, not to mention nauseated and dizzy.

"Nobody says that," he said arrogantly and without making eye contact.

"Sure they do," I shot back.

Darren looked at me as he spoke this time, "Who says it, Alane? Who says something like that?"

"I don't know, Darren," I was at a loss, "I don't know who said it first. I'd have to look that one up. I don't have a comprehensive list of people who have said it, nor do I know the personality type of a person who might use that turn of phrase. Apparently, whoever they are, they are like me in some way shape or form. The bigger question is, how have you never heard it before? You went to college. And more importantly, why do you think it's insulting?"

"You are so fucking arrogant," he said under his breath.

"What did you just say?" I asked loudly.

"Just forget it," he muttered again.

"Fine, do you want to know how it went today?" I asked.

Darren stayed silent as if he had forgotten about it. "Oh, yeah. What happened? What did they say?" he asked with mild interest.

"She thinks it's all out, now. She used a biopsy needle this time. I've never felt anything like it." Saying the words took me back to the moment. The memory made me sweat and wince.

"Sorry about that." The tension was gone from his voice. "What's the plan?"

"I go back next week for a follow-up," I replied.

"Cool…so we can have sex then?" he asked.

Stunned is not a strong enough word to describe the feeling that shot through my body. "Uh…really?" I asked.

"Yeah, I really need to have sex," he replied bluntly.

"I can't think about that right now." I wasn't sure when my

brain or my insides were going to feel remotely normal again. Sex was the last thing on my mind. After what I had just been through, celibacy was looking like a legitimate option. I hadn't expected him to bring it up so soon.

"Well, when you go in next week, be sure to ask her if it's okay. I can't wait too much longer," he said.

"It's only been a couple of weeks. I think you'll survive," I said.

"Just ask her. I need to know."

There were so many things I should have said in that moment. I should have gone off, but for some reason, I didn't. I just let that be the last word.

"You cooking dinner?" he said next.

"Uh, seriously?" I said in disbelief. "I just had my uterus shredded by a biopsy needle. Dinner wasn't exactly a priority."

"Whatever," he said with annoyance as he stormed off into the kitchen.

Chapter 16

The next few weeks dragged by. I was depressed and uncomfortable. The pain spread from my uterus to my entire body—my muscles, my joints, my head—everything felt ripped in two. I went back to work, but it was awful. I could only make it through half of each day. Thankfully, Kelli was willing to stay longer than she originally planned.

My follow up visit with the OB was unremarkable. They didn't do much other than to make sure the bleeding had stopped and do one last ultrasound to scout for more renegade "tissue." For the record, I did ask the doctor Darren's sex question. She was, by the way, the fourth one from the group practice to see me through this process, and the one who had never been in on any of the other visits. Actually, I liked her the most. She kept looking at my file and grimacing and confirming how many visits there were and what my specific requests had been.

"It's here in the notes that you are a chiropractor, yes? So, you refused the D&E?" Dr. Four said cautiously.

"No, I was a little thrown that day, and I told the doctor that I needed a few days to process everything," I said. Talking about it made me wince. It was still a pretty raw memory. "The plan was to give it a week to work out on its own, and then call if nothing happened," I said.

"Oh," Dr. Four said thoughtfully, "but you refused the medications, right?"

"No," I replied flatly, "I was never offered medications. Trust me, if they had offered it, I would have taken it. I'm a chiropractor, not a masochist."

"Hum…" she said before a long pause, "Okay…I am not your managing doctor, so we'll need to get you scheduled with her sometime soon to figure out where to go from here…you said your husband wants to know when you can have sex again?" She looked at me and then at the nurse.

I'm not really psychic, but I would have sworn I heard her saying "What an asshole…" in her head (or maybe I was just projecting a little. There's no way to know for sure.)

"Yes, I told him I would ask," I replied with embarrassment. Just asking the question made me feel oppressed.

"Clinically, you can have sex again in about two more weeks. But as far as I am concerned, you can tell him whatever you want. You take as much time as you need to take," she said with conviction. I also thought I heard her say, "train wreck…," as she smiled at me, but her lips never moved.

I smiled back and said, "I will," and that was it. I never went back to that office again. Just thinking about it made me sweaty and dizzy. I was done with it. There were other doctors and other clinics. I decided that when I was ready, I would find another.

The next few weeks passed by in a fog. I dragged myself into to the office as often as I could because Darren said he needed me there. Each time I went in, I was dizzy and light headed and too emotional to get anything done, and I was too detached and distracted to accomplish anything that mattered. So eventually, I went home, and I stayed there for more than a month.

On the weekdays, I would sleep at weird times and drag myself into the kitchen to make food for Darren when he came home for lunch and dinner. The rest of the time I stared at the TV. I don't remember much of what I watched. I just remember the feeling of the sofa pressing on the backs of my aching legs and the warmth of our two cats curled up on either side of me. It was as if they sensed that I was lost and stayed vigilantly by my side to make sure I found my way back. In truth, there were times where their warm little bodies were my only tethers to the tangible world. Without them, I might have just floated away.

I know that I cried a lot. It seemed that all I could do was cry and stare and sleep. At night when Darren was home, he would sit with me, even though we had nothing to say to each other about anything. We watched TV in silence, marking time with DVR'd primetime and countless episodes of deep cable biker build-offs and pawn shop reality shows. It wasn't long before Darren started edging away from me each evening, moving a little farther down the couch each time he got up for a drink refill or to go to the bathroom. It took him three days to inch his way past the end of my sofa over to the farthest corner of the loveseat across the room.

Not long after that, the arguments started. They came on gradually at first, usually focusing on little nothings that weren't at all argument worthy—like when I forgot to put out the hot sauce for him with dinner or when he refused to answer a simple question in a reasonable amount of time. (I mean like over a minute or more. I timed him. I had too because he swore I was overreacting. I didn't know that he needed more than 60 seconds to say yes or no to a question like *"Do you want more coffee?"* He had never taken that much time before, and I felt compelled to document the evidence of his cognitive decline if he really needed that much time to process simple questions. He insisted that I was being melodramatic. I insisted that he either had early-onset dementia or he was just an asshole. Either way, we were most likely doomed.)

After that, our arguments mushroomed into full-blown fights.

Once that happened, forgetting the hot sauce turned into a personal assault on Darren's rights as a man, and refusing to answer a simple question became his line in the sand. In his opinion, I asked questions that didn't need to be asked about things that didn't need to be answered. Moreover, he thought that I talked all the time, and he didn't know what it was that I wanted him to say—a premise that I found bewildering since he was never without an opinion whenever there wasn't a question from me preceding it. Consequently, we spent a great deal of time in detached silence, staring at the false truth of reality TV.

I was descending deeper into despair. I was hurting in ways I didn't know were possible. Every joint in my body ached. My muscles felt like they were being stabbed by a thousand skewers. My uterus felt like it had been worked over by a cheese grater. I couldn't sleep, but I wasn't alert enough to accomplish much of anything when I was awake. I felt alone. I felt isolated. I felt an overwhelming sense of loss over something that never really even existed fully in the world. I had loved something that, in the end, amounted to nothing more than disgusting globs of bloody "tissue" that were disposed of by both violent expulsion and brutally inelegant extraction.

…ick…

I had come to love an idea, not a real thing. Furthermore, I had to endure a broken record of sentiments like, "don't worry, you can try again," and "this happens all the time," every time I talked to anyone other than Darren. It was all well-intentioned, I'm sure, but it wasn't very helpful.

At home, it wasn't any better. There was only silence mixed with the annoyingly repetitive requests for sex. I don't mean intimate moments of closeness and connection that might have led to meaningful intercourse. I mean pushy demands for the act with no preamble, no foreplay, no emotional connection at all. There were only questions like, "When can we do it? …Can we have sex, yet? …Wanna do it, now?" Over a very short time, the questions were replaced by random acts of unexpected pantslessness throughout the day, which ultimately devolved down to just his limp, veiny unit lolling out of his unzipped fly. Sadly, for Darren, those random dick encounters only made me want it (and him) less. I felt like I was losing my mind.

As Darren became more and more frustrated, he started drinking more and more often. The weekends were the worst. He would start on Friday afternoon. Sometimes he'd start on Thursday night since he rarely saw patients on Fridays. Those nights, his pace was slow and steady, like he was just taking the edge off of whatever was bothering him. He'd take Saturday mornings off, then get back to it after lunch. From there, it was a steady build from slow, leisurely sips from a pint glass for the first few hours to nearly manic gulping from whatever bottles were around. Sunday's pace was usually a little slower, and he usually stopped after dinner so his liver would have twelve full hours to process it all out before he had to be face to face with a patient at 8:00 a.m. on Monday. Honestly, he almost had it down to a science. The only problem was that he didn't really have drinking buddies. Most of his friends were from FSP, and drunkenness was not a desirable image for them, so Darren was left to drink at home.

While Darren's self-medication plan made him feel better, it only made me feel worse. Alcohol and I didn't mix very well after my miscarriage. Something in my body changed chemically after that horrible experience. The college party-girl who had enjoyed more than a few happy hours and drink specials in her twenties, and then later, drinks with dinner and the occasional set at the local karaoke bar in her early thirties, couldn't take it anymore.

Throwing back a few drinks was no longer worth the searing headache and abdominal pain that came the next morning and then lasted for days afterward. As a result, I spent most of my weekends watching Darren drink his way down a sliding personality scale that was directly proportional to the number of beers he'd consumed.

Off and on over the course of a typical Saturday, Darren would talk to me as he drank. "Did you know?" he would say after beer number two, "You're my best friend…" It sounded like a loving thing a man might say to his wife and the mother of his almost-baby. By beer four, it sounded more like sad commentary on the state of his social life. By beer five, it seemed like it was more of a conversation he was having with himself than with me, and by beer six, it was almost always changed to the following:

"What's wrong with you?" he would say with a disgusted accusatory tone tinged with hints of sincere concern—an attitude combination that can only be successfully accomplished by drunks and geriatrics.

One night, his question caught me off guard, which was ridiculous since it always came sometime after the first sip of beer six. (I think I just wasn't paying attention that day.) "What do you mean?" I asked genuinely. I had been trying to talk to him about my feelings for days, and before that moment, he had mostly refused to acknowledge the fact that I was even speaking.

"I mean, what's going on with you? You are always so sad," he said like it was a revelation.

"I'm really struggling," I said earnestly. I didn't want to sound like a smartass. He was finally showing some interest, "I am not recovering well."

"You look good," he offered.

"Thanks," I said hesitantly, "but I feel like shit…and I am just so sad."

"You know what you need?" he asked confidently, "You need to relax and have a drink with me."

I had hoped for a breakthrough, but I didn't get one. I tried "Thanks, but no thanks," I said sincerely, "I can't drink right now. It makes everything worse."

"No... It makes everything better! You're no fun these days. You just need to relax," he said confidently. There was a hint of a slur, and his eyelids were lower than they were when he was sober.

In that moment, I realized where he was on his sliding scale. "I'm relaxed enough," I said back at him with irritation in my voice, "I don't need a drink. I need a little support, right now."

Darren pretended like he choked as he swallowed and then said with animation, "Support? Christ woman, how much more support do you need? You don't have to come into the office. You spend all day at home doing nothing. I listen to you go on and on about how upset you are. You know that whatever you're feeling you're bringing on yourself. I can't fix it for you."

Ah, yes…Darren the Life Coach was back…

His self-actualization crap always irritated me. This time, it was even worse. "Thanks, that's really helpful," I spat at him snarkily.

"Woah there, no need to get shitty," he said loudly.

"I don't mean to be shitty. It's just that I have been telling you for weeks that I need you. I need your support. And all you can say is that I need to relax and have a drink and that I'm bringing it all on myself?"

"Well, you are," he said smugly.

Tightness gripped my throat, "I didn't bring this miscarriage on myself, Darren." I could feel my anger building. "It just happened…but it was really hard on me. I'm having a hard time recovering."

"You create your own reality, Alane. You have to take responsibility for it and for how you are right now." His smug voice seemed to ricochet around the living room.

"It wasn't my fault!" I said loudly.

"I never said that it was."

"You just did!" I yelled at him.

"Woah!" he said. "There's no reason to yell."

"I will yell if I want to! Why can't you just support me?" I cried, "Can't you just hug me and tell me that you love me?"

"Can't you just stop crying all the time?" he said as he opened another beer. "What do you want me to do, Alane?"

"I just told you what I want you to do." The tears kept coming uncontrollably.

"What is it you really want?" he asked like he already knew the answer.

"I really want you to support me through this!" I cried.

"I am!" he yelled back, "I go to work every day by myself. This was hard on me, too. Don't you think I want to stay home sometimes?"

Hot tears sprang from my eyes, "Are you fucking kidding me?" I yelled at him, "I know that it's emotional for you, but I nearly bled out in our bathroom and had my uterus scraped a couple of times while I was still awake and I drove myself back and forth to all of those horrible appointments because we couldn't afford to close the office. That doesn't even cover the chemical mindfuck that is swimming around in my brain right now. So, I am sorry that you don't get to stay home because you're sad!"

Darren glared at me, "It always has to be worse for you, doesn't it?"

"No, it doesn't always have to be worse for me, but in this case actually it was! Why can't you see that?" At this point, I was blubbering my words through uncontrollable crying.

"Fine!" he yelled back, "Have it your way! It was worse for you! Everything's worse for you. Everything's all my fault, and it's all worse for you! Ya happy? That's what you wanted, right?" Darren waved his arms wildly as he spoke, sending splashes of beer onto the wall and floor.

"No," I cried as I dropped my head into my hands. "I just want you to hug me and tell me that everything's going to be alright." By now, I was crying with full body convulsions.

"Fine!" Darren boomed as he stood up abruptly, sending his beer splattering to the floor as he charged toward the sofa where I sat. He slid himself forcefully up against me and threw his arms around my shoulders. He pressed his body weight into me, forcing my body into the corner of the couch. "Is this what you wanted?" he asked mockingly. He squeezed my arms against my sides with his knee and bracing my lap as he pushed down harder.

"NO!" I yelled.

"What? You said you wanted a hug. I'm hugging you!" "Stop!" I said. It was getting hard to breathe. "Stop!"

"You said all you wanted was for me to hug you!" he bellowed over my head, "What, am I hugging you wrong, now?"

"Not like this! Let me go!" It was hard to get the words out. I couldn't breathe, and I was panicking.

His grip tightened, "No, I wanna give you what you said you need!" He pressed in harder as I struggled against him, "Don't worry! It's alright!"

"Stop it! Stop it! Stop it!" I tried to scream as I flailed against him. He pushed harder with his shoulders until he pushed my ribs through the padding on the arm of the sofa and into its wooden frame. "You're hurting me!" My words came out in weak bursts as I continued to struggle. I was blocked in. My chest couldn't expand enough against the pressure.

"You said you wanted me to support you," Darren said darkly. He moved one of his hands to my head and forced it against his chest. The change in his grip was the opening I needed. I pushed him as hard as I could with my head and shoulders, forcing him to move his leg to keep his balance. I wedged my knees up between us and jammed them into his gut as hard as I could. He groaned and rocked back for just a beat. It was just enough time to get my feet onto his chest. I pushed with all I had left in my legs, sending him backward against the coffee table and sending me up and over the arm of the sofa and onto the floor.

"Leave me alone!" I yelled as I clamored toward the stairs.

"What?" he yelled back with a sardonic laugh, "I thought you wanted a hug?" He kept laughing as I ran.

Upstairs, I locked the bedroom door behind me before stumbling to the far end of the room and slumping to the floor with my back up against the dresser. Darren was still laughing downstairs in the living room. My breathing was labored and erratic as my tears came fast and hard. My spine and my ribs ached. My abdomen was cramping. My lungs burned. I don't know how long I sat there heaving and bawling. I only remember the nonstop string of obscenities that were running on a loop in my head:

Holy shit…fuck…son of a bitch…holy fucking shit dick son of a bitching asshole…

It was some profoundly intellectual shit, to be sure.

Eventually, the tears stopped, and my breath settled. I pulled myself up off the floor, took a shower, and got in bed. As I lay there in the dark, I tried every trick I had ever learned to push what just happened out of my mind. I didn't want to think about it. Every time I did, the tears and the shaking and the nausea would start all over again.

This wasn't just an argument. This was violence. This wasn't a fist slammed against the table. This wasn't a water bottle slung across the room. This wasn't yelling with his face an inch from mine and then punching the wall next to my head. No, this was none of that. This was real violence. That night Darren crossed a line that I never expected him to cross.

We had argued many times over the years—a few times before we took our vows. Most were after. Before when we argued, I was arguing with Darren. This night, I was arguing with someone else. Darren was someone else. He looked the same, but his eyes were different. His words were different. His laugh was different. That night, it was like a person I had never met before was wearing Darren's face. He was not the Darren I married. Before, our worst fights were—at their core—disagreements between two people who loved each other. There was always an undercurrent of our connection beneath all of the shouting. No matter how trivial or terrible the fight might have been, I knew that he loved me. Afterword, we would talk about it. When he flung a glass at the wall beside me, and then again, when he stood in our hall with his fist raised in front of my face. I was clear, if he ever hit me, that would be it. If he ever raised his hand or a weapon to strike me again, that would be it. We would be over. I would leave, and I would never come back.

He never did either of those things again. He threw things across the room. He punched walls and broke cutting boards and beat the steering wheel in my car, but never directed any of it at me, until this night. Technically, he didn't raise his hand, and he didn't actually hit me. He had adhered to the letter of my ultimatum. But he did hurt me. If I hadn't gotten away when I did, I have no way to know if he would have stopped before or after I was dead. I didn't know what to do with myself. I was deep down in a hole before this happened. This just dug the hole a little deeper.

Later that night, Darren let himself into the bedroom with the safety key we kept above the doorframe. In my panic, I had forgotten all about it. He was soused. I could smell it on him from across the room. I pretended to sleep as he undressed and lumbered onto his side of the bed. Luckily, he didn't try to touch me. He didn't even get close to me. As soon as his breathing steadied and deepened, I got up and went downstairs to the couch. I really didn't want to sleep out in the open, but we didn't have a guest bed so unless I was willing to sleep directly on the floor, the couch had to do.

The rest of the night was awful. The fight replayed over and over again in my head, parsing out every word, dissecting every look and every action. He didn't hit me. He didn't throw anything at me. He didn't do any of the things that I explicitly told him not to do, but he had hurt me. He had hurt me and then laughed about it…and then had the nerve to come up and crawl into bed next to me like nothing had happened.

I had to go. I had no choice.

As the hours ticked by, I plotted my escape. I went through everything I would need to do to get out. First of all, I needed a place to go. My parents' house was four hours away, but I would have to explain everything in gory detail to them to get them to understand, and once they understood it, that would be it. Once they were done with someone, there was no chance of reconciliation. While I was fairly certain that reconciliation wasn't where we were going to end up, I wanted to be the one making that decision on my own terms, not on theirs. It would be even worse if I were living under their roof. All of my chiropractic friends' houses were out. They were closer to Darren than to me, and they were all in FSP. The social embarrassment would have been too destructive. Everyone else I knew was either a patient or the spouse of a patient or a friend of a patient, and that was completely off limits.

I thought about a hotel, but the closest one that wasn't teaming with drug dealers and prostitutes was all the way in Raleigh and was more money than I could afford. There was very little room left on the credit card with my name on it. I had been using it to cover our expenses whenever the practice struggled. My credit card funded most of the practice and our personal expenses, and since the miscarriage, it was keeping us afloat.

In the dark, the reality of my situation landed squarely on my head. Technically, I had less than nothing. I had never really considered it before that moment, but it was true. Everything except the house and my credit card was in Darren's name. We had traded my car two years before when Darren got his most recent used SUV. Only his name was then on both of our vehicles. Our bank accounts were joint accounts, except for the business accounts where he was the only stakeholder and the only signer. As it was, the only things truly in my name were our debts. Our house had no equity in it and two loans attached to it, there was the credit card I mentioned that was approaching its maximum balance of $28,000, and then there was my six-figure student loan that was growing daily at the lovely fixed rate of 7.5%. Furthermore, I didn't have a job, which was convenient for the whole recovering-from-the-physical-and-emotional-trauma thing but was horrible for the whole "fuck you, I'm out of here" thing.

The only thing I had for sure was my escape envelope. I never got rid of it, only now I stashed it in my underwear drawer instead of the filing cabinet. Every now and then, I raided the paltry amount of cash in it when I needed to tip a delivery driver or needed cash to pay for something weird at the door. (I never could say no to a box of Girl Scout Cookies.) I would always return what I took whenever I could. I wasn't consciously preparing to leave one day; I just never felt comfortable being completely out of cash. Usually, Darren snatched up whatever cash was lying around for his snuff habit, so whenever I got to it first, I stashed it out of sight. (I think he thought that paying cash for it made it less memorable for whatever sales clerk gave it to him at the gas station next to the office—it didn't.) Before that night, I had never considered how fucked up it was to keep something like that or to feel the need to hide it from Darren. That night I understood exactly how fucked up it was. I also had to admit that it wasn't enough to be of any real use.

The living room was eerily quiet. Even the cats were nowhere. They scattered when the yelling started, and they hadn't come out since. I couldn't blame them. I should have been hiding myself.

"Oh my God, I'm stuck," I whispered quietly out loud to the darkness. After that, I was done with thinking. I closed my eyes and willed myself to go to sleep.

Later that morning, the sun woke me up. Consciousness was unwelcome. My eyes burned from all the crying. My muscles ached and my ribs and neck throbbed. I wished I could go back to sleep and stay that way indefinitely. It would have been easier.

Darren was still asleep. The kitchen was trashed. The remnants of last night's dinner, a throng of empty beer bottles, and Darren's plastic water bottle spittoons were littered around the room. All of the fighting must have made him extra-spitty since there were no less than three disgusting bottles of snuff-spit scattered across the counter. One of which was on its side, its contents pooled on the counter with a sticky puddle on the floor beneath it. The smell made me wretch. I should have spun around and walked away from it. I should have left it all just as it was and forced Darren to clean up his own mess, but I knew that would never happen. If I didn't do it then, I would just have to do it later.

As I cleaned, I weighed my options. None of them looked good, let alone doable. I had already checked the bank accounts and reconfirmed what I already knew. There was no money. Even if I wanted to siphon money out of the business account for my getaway, there was nothing extra to siphon. I could have drained the accounts to zero, but that would have closed Darren's practice in less than a month. That would just make things even worse financially, not to mention all of the potential patient abandonment issues and potential malpractice complaints. I couldn't do it…not to the patients and not to either of us. No matter what happened to our marriage, we each needed a way to earn a living. We needed our licenses, and we needed some semblance of a reasonable reputation. If he wanted to wreck those things by himself, that was his choice, but I wasn't going to do it to him or myself.

All of the frantic ramblings in my brain from the night before were still true. Unless I was ready to blow our marriage up entirely and go home to my parents, I was stuck. I should already have been in the car on my way to Charlotte after what he had done, but every time I decided I was ready to go, I pulled up short. My parents had been married for 45 years. They were what I thought Darren and I were going to be. They loved each other. They respected each other. They were friends first, before everything else. To bring them in on this, I would have to admit failure. It would be messy, and even though it was probably the best choice, I just couldn't make myself do it. I wasn't ready to accept that kind of defeat. Once they knew what happened, the entirety of the last 10 years of my life would be devalued. The good memories would be negated. Everything in my life would be up for judgment, and everything would become Darren's fault. It would be open season on anything he had ever talked about or touched, which would have been great, except for the sad fact that we had done everything together. We had lived together, worked together, traveled together, eaten together, worked out together, and on and on throughout our marriage. Denigrating his life choices meant that they would be denigrating mine, too. I would be thrust into a position where I felt compelled to defend him. At the very least, I would have to defend myself, which would be just the same as defending him. I didn't want to defend him, and I didn't want to be forced to justify myself either. It would have been more than I could stand.

Thinking about it was making me crazy. I wanted to run. I didn't care where, I just wanted to go. When I ran out of dishes to wash and counters to clean, I tried to distract myself with email. I have never been a particularly digital person, generally speaking. I usually found it to be more of a burden than an escape. Often, I would neglect my inbox for days, sometimes weeks, at a time. Plus, there was only one computer in the house, and it was riddled with viruses thanks to Darren's not-so-secret obsession with porn and his penis. Spread eagle vaginas and naked boobs would randomly take over the screen before the whole operating system would lock up. Honestly, I got pretty good at working around most of the viruses, and I think the vaginas and breasts ended up working fairly well as not-so-subliminal conditioning…

…but, that's a story for another day, too.

Anyway, there was a lot in my inbox to work through, and the distraction worked, if only for a moment. Tucked in among the spam and the nauseous quasi-inspirational forwards that most of my email contacts were so fond of sending was something completely unexpected—an email from my old arts school friend, Laura. We had reconnected two years earlier when I looked her up on a whim. She and her husband, Jeff, (also a friend from school) lived less than two hours away down in Wilmington. Laura had stayed with us two times. Darren and I had driven down to visit them a few times. We even stayed in their guest bedroom once when we had to be in town overnight for a continuing education seminar.

Laura and I weren't best friends in school, but we were close—close enough to know all of the best and worst of each other's teenage dalliances. We understood things about each other in a way that only someone who had been there in the moment could understand. It was an old friendship forged in the smoky halls of an arts school dormitory rife with eating disorders, underage drinking, self-loathing, and wanton sexual exploration.

In her email, she wanted to know what I was up to, and if I wanted to come down for a visit. She had a week off and was looking for a distraction. I replied with a "Yes!" Since she was better with her email, she called me almost instantly, and within 30 minutes, we had a plan for the next day. I didn't tell her what had happened, and I had no plans to. I just wanted to be somewhere else, listening to someone else's life story for a while.

Laura's invitation mixed with my obsessive cleaning of all of the surfaces on the ground floor of the house had lightened the energy in the room. When Darren finally pulled himself out of bed that morning, however, the dark oppression returned. We didn't speak. We didn't make eye contact. We moved around each other like we were two negative magnet poles repelling our bodies to the edges of the room. I dressed and left as soon as I could.

That day, I stayed out of the house as long as I could. When I finally came home that evening, Darren was there on the couch, shirtless, sipping beer and spitting snuff juice into another empty water bottle. He was the picture of a healthy chiropractic lifestyle. I wanted to take a picture and put it on next batch of his appointment reminder cards.

He didn't say hello or ask me how I was feeling. Instead, he asked me where I had been all day and why I hadn't told him where I was going.

I told him plainly that I had needed some time to myself.

He said that I should have stayed home and talked to him.

All I could do was stare blankly back at him. I had no words. There was no sense in debating the point. It would only be another fight.

He managed to say he was sorry, but he didn't apologize for what he did. He said he was sorry that I didn't like the way he was with me the night before. He said he was sorry that I didn't understand his brand of emotional support. When I told him that it wasn't support—that he physically hurt me and I wouldn't stand for it, his only response was that I wasn't really hurt. He said that I was just overly emotional.

To that, I bowed up and started to yell. He sat there silently and told me that he wasn't willing to discuss it if I was going to start yelling.

That made me temporarily insane. "I will speak to you in whatever tone I wish!" I yelled even louder.

"I'm not gonna do this" he replied with unsettling calm.

"Fine!" I yelled and turned away from him to face the TV.

"Fine," he said calmly back.

There was a long uncomfortable pause.

"It's not fine, by the way," I spat out.

"Whatever," he said with disgust.

"Fine," I said, again, lowering my tone to match his.

He let out a smug, contrived little laugh.

"What's your problem, now?" I said, unable to keep my attitude in check.

"You just can't help yourself, can you?" he shot back.

"That's almost funny coming from you," I said without looking at him.

He inhaled sharply and then bellowed, "You always have to have the last word, don't you?" It was instantly clear that his self-control had only been a false manipulation.

"No," I said flatly.

"You do! You can't let anything go, ever, can you?" he boomed as he sat up to the edge of his seat.

"I can let things go," I turned my head to look directly in his eyes. "I just won't let your bullshit be the last thing that hangs in the air!"

"Oh!... You have to push it, don't you?" he said louder.

"No," I said calmly.

"You are ridiculous! Are you proud of yourself?" he spat.

"No, I'm not. In fact, this whole thing is completely mortifying, but if you keep asking me questions, I'm going to keep answering them."

"I'm not asking you questions!" he yelled.

"You literally just asked me at least three direct questions!" I was starting to lose it, again.

"They were just questions, you didn't have to answer them!" He was still shouting, but I could tell that he was starting to wear out.

"How am I supposed to know when you are asking me a question and when you are just being rhetorical?"

"Forget it," he said shaking his head and pushing himself to his feet. "It's a mute point."

"Moot…" I said back with exasperation.

"Huh?" he grunted with irritation.

"You meant *moot* point, but it's not a *moot* point at all! I really need to know when you are legitimately asking me a question."

"Fuck off," Darren said and went into the garage for more beer.

I let him have the last word this time. To his credit, Darren rarely uttered obscenities directly at me when we fought. That was more my shortcoming than his, a weakness he regularly used to his advantage when we fought. He knew that when I reached the "fuck you, you fucking asshole" point, he had won. He could claim that I had crossed a line and insulted him beyond reparation. He would point out that he never said words like that to me and go on about how disrespectful it was. His arguments lost some of their power whenever he slipped up and started calling me a "fucking bitch" when he was drunk. To back out of it, he would claim they were slips of the tongue, reactions to my bad behavior that couldn't be held against him. I always assumed that they were what he really wanted to say, and it only came out when the beer had eroded whatever self-control he had as a filter between his head and his mouth. When I said something similar, it usually meant I had burned up my final reserves of energy and intellect and was just lobbing verbal grenades into the room to try to blow the whole thing up to make it stop.

No matter who dropped the f-bombs and attendant vulgarities, they were horrible things to say. I always felt guilty afterward, and he usually used my regret to his advantage. As far as I was concerned, he never seemed adequately guilty after lobbing a hate-filled "fuck off" at me. This time, he seemed especially guiltless. We had entered into a new phase of our marriage, one that I wasn't sure I wanted to be part of anymore.

◆◆◆◆◆

The next day was Monday. Darren went to work. After he left, I packed a bag, wrote him a note telling him where I would be, and headed for Wilmington.

It was a glorious road trip. I felt like I was 25 again—unencumbered and excited about my immediate future. I hadn't felt that way in a long, long time. I drove the way I wanted. I sang with the radio. I ate gas station potato chips and drank a coke—things that I hadn't done for years either because I was living the "chiropractic lifestyle" or because of JT's (and therefore Darren's) "optimal wellness" mandate of the moment. (The rush I got from putting a pile of junk food on the gas station checkout counter was intense—like FSP snack police would descend from the rafters and whisk me off to jail.) I drove and sang and stuffed my face full of toxins, and for a few minutes, I remembered what I felt like before I married Darren. I remembered the freedom and the happiness I used to feel, even on my worst days. It was electrifying…

…and it lasted for about three whole songs…

…and then reality came rushing back in a wave that sent me into a fit of tears that forced me to pull off the road before I caused an accident. It wasn't about junk food or driving or singing. It was about freedom. It was about happiness. As it was, I had become a prisoner in my own life. I was supposed to be married, not incarcerated.

With that thought, my tears morphed into rage. "I am so sick of fucking crying!" I yelled spastically, sending a spray of tiny potato chip bits flying off my lips. It was everywhere—my hand, my shirt, the steering wheel. Some even made it as far as the windshield.

"Ugh…gross!" I said out loud as I stared at the greasy, salty mess. This was a new low. This was just too much crazy. I had to get my shit together. I had to stop crying. I had to stop being like this. No matter what happened, whether I left Darren or stayed and tried to work it out, I had to stop whatever this was. I was coming unhinged and the only person who could re-hinge me… was me.

When I was steady, I got back on the road. At the nearest rest stop, I cleaned myself up, cleaned all of the potato spray off the inside of the car, and made up my mind that the crying was done. I was visiting a friend, not admitting myself for inpatient therapy. That had to be it.

Chapter 17

Laura was probably one of the prettiest of my friends from arts school. That was a notable distinction in a school filled with girls who had all spent most of their lives trying to be the most beautiful and graceful thing in the room. In dance, it's just part of the deal. For Laura, much of it was just her natural state of being with her long wavy blond tresses, tall thin frame, and steel blue eyes. Her husband, Jeff, was tall and equally as handsome.

On this day, Laura welcomed me into their home warmly, as always. It was, as it tends to be with old friends, easy and familiar. The conversation flowed effortlessly about a wandering array of topics—movies and music and dance and philosophy. We talked about Laura's work and about her most recent choreographic endeavor which was about to send her on tour.

It was so refreshing to talk to someone about something other than chiropractic and bogus self-help philosophy. It was equally invigorating to feel the pull of my past life with people who had been there with me, and who hadn't given up on it.

After school, Laura and Jeff had gone to New York as so many young artists do. They had lived there for years and had intended to stay there until 9/11 happened. That made a lot of working artists reconsider their plans.

In Wilmington, dance was different than it had been for Laura in New York. Companies were few to none depending on the year. Auditions for work were even more sporadic. She compensated for the lack by making her own work for herself most of the time. It was enough to keep her connected to her art and to the local art community, which seemed to embrace the two of them with open arms.

Laura knew about the miscarriage. She had loaned me her entire library of pregnancy books the minute she found out I was pregnant, and she was one of the first people to hear that it didn't work out. She broached the subject with compassion and genuine concern, and I was able to discuss it with a degree of detachment that was not my current norm. I was proud of myself. It was a step in the right direction.

She shared with me her own battle with the subject of pregnancy. Like me, she wasn't as motivated to have a baby as some of the other women in her life and was a little trepidatious about the whole thing. It was obvious that deep down she wanted the experience and that she wanted Jeff to have it, too. It was only a matter of time before she would join the mommy club, and I didn't want my bad experience to bring her down. So, I tried to keep it contained. She kept at it, though. She was a good friend and all of the time and distance in the world couldn't change her intrinsic tendency toward helping a friend.

By the second day, my resolve to keep quiet about it started to erode and by the second afternoon, the dam broke. Laura took me to a wine bar downtown for some pinot and tapas. We sat at a narrow bar by the window looking out on the street as we sipped and ate and talked. As the first glass emptied, the conversation gradually started shifting. It went from dance…to chiropractic…to chiropractic and Darren…to Darren and the miscarriage…to just Darren. As I talked, I could feel myself unraveling. It might have been the wine. I hadn't been drinking much at all for the last year. The effects hit my brain like a hammer. It might also have been my emotional exhaustion mixed with a little liquid relaxation. Whatever it was, it came on fast. The next thing I knew, I was unloading the whole shameful story. I detailed everything, including the events of the weekend before, in graphic detail.

I couldn't stop myself. There was no filter between my brain and the outside world. I knew that it was too much as it was happening. It was too much for me to hear, again. It had to be too much for a friendship that had an eighteen-year intermission between acts.

In spite of her horror and probable disgust, Laura remained gracious and compassionate. She was also openly angry and concerned. We left the bar and went to her house where we talked through the rest of the day. She cried with me and told me that she would be there for me no matter what I decided to do. I had stripped down my entire life in front of her, and she was still there. It was like the weight of a hundred sumo wrestlers had been lifted off my chest. I had never experienced so much appreciation for another person in my life until that moment. For the first time in years, I was genuinely and truly grateful.

That night when I went to bed, I slept. I mean I really achieved the deep and restful sleep that had eluded me for longer than I could remember. It was glorious. Once in the night, for no reason that I could name, I woke up. The moonlight streamed through the bedroom window sheers. The room was calm. I was finally calm. I closed my eyes and just breathed, soaking in the feeling of relaxed nothingness.

As I lay there listening to the gentle murmur of Laura's shelf-top waterfall, I heard a small exhalation from the far corner of the room which caused me to open my eyes wide to the moonlit room. In the corner, a small human form stood enveloped in a swirling pale blue ball of light and mist. Its form waxed and waned in slow waves. For just a flash, I thought I saw a face, but it was gone as quickly as it appeared. As I gazed at the tumbling light and mist, a warm, peaceful feeling washed over me. There was no fear or panic. My sense of loss and pain was gone. It was like I was staring at someone I had known and loved my entire life. In my head I heard a voice say quietly, *I'm still here…*

…and then it was gone…

After that, I slept for the rest of the night and woke up hopeful.

Early the next morning, Laura and I went to the beach. We walked for a bit and then sat silently looking at the ocean for over an hour like a meditation. There was nothing left to say. We had talked everything out, and all that was left was the silent comfort of friendship.

Later that morning before I left for home, Laura handed me an envelope. In it was a single key—the key to their house. She told me that she knew that there was not much that she could do other than listen, but that if I ever felt unsafe, or if I ever needed a place to go, their door was always open to me. She said that all I had to do was call from the road and let them know that I was on my way. That was it. At the time, it was the most meaningful gift I had ever received in my entire adult life from another human being, but I couldn't find the words to say that to her in the moment. I just hugged her and got in the car.

I left Wilmington that day, feeling better than I had in weeks. I clutched Laura's key in my hand the entire drive home. Although I never intended to use it, that little silver key was empowering. It meant that someone was there. It meant that I wasn't alone. Laura took in all of the horror and didn't run away. Whatever her opinion of me was, she didn't openly judge me for my weaknesses or utter any ultimatums as conditions for her help. She was just there. That little key held all of that power in its shiny metal form. With it as my new talisman, I headed back to the house and to Darren.

Our house wreaked of oppression when I got home. It was like anger and sadness were oozing from the walls. I felt it the minute I walked through the door. When Darren came home that night, he was on edge and distant, but I could tell that he was working hard to be present with me. He even seemed interested in how my visit with Laura and Jeff had gone. I was pleasantly surprised by the effort. It only took a day, though, for it to regress back into dissonance. The verbal contests were just as I had left them, cutting and demoralizing. Thankfully, the violence didn't return with them. With my key talisman in hand, I made a deal with myself. If he laid one more violent hand on me, that would be the end. I would leave for good. I had a new certainty on my side, and I think Darren could sense it.

That Friday night, we were back at it. By Darren's third beer, the verbal battle was fully underway. As I said, there was no hands-on violence, even late into the evening. What's more, there was no crying. I shed not one tear. There was plenty of hurt and anger, but all of my tears were gone. Instead, I kept my wits about me, meeting his verbal spears with fully cogent responses, soaking up every word he said, and making it difficult, if not impossible, for him to run the game. It wasn't my goal to best him. Winning was not my endgame. I only wanted to hold my own and hash things out once and for all without ending up in a useless blubbering pile. I thought that would be forward progress for us both.

As it turned out, it only gave our fights a totally different tone, and I wouldn't call it progress. The more Darren drank, the more he lost his place. The more he lost his place, the more I would remind him of exactly what he had said. He would follow that up with a string of denials, and as a result, our arguments would either end in volatile stalemates or degrade into a tangle of Darren's side steps and deflections. Eventually, he would just leave the room. To claim that I didn't reap a little pleasure out of his frustration would be a lie. It wasn't how I wanted the rest of our marriage to be, but at the time, it was empowering to be solidly in the fight instead of (figuratively) drooling face down on the ground after the first punch.

Those nights, after Darren had gone to sleep or passed out, I would put myself in bed next to him. In the dark, I would lie there, listening to the loud, steady snores emanating from his open mouth. As I stared at the ceiling, I would wonder how much longer I could take it. I knew it was unsustainable, even in my new self-possessed state. The toll would be too great. The mornings after, I was more exhausted, more restless, and more cynical. Neither of us was winning anything, and eventually, one or both of us would break. For the time being, this would do, at least until I had a clear plan. The Key of Empowerment was in my possession. It unlocked an escape hatch door. It wasn't a long-term solution. It was a last resort. More importantly for me, it was a symbol of hope, something that I hadn't had for a long time.

The next Monday, less than a week after Laura had handed me her key, she called and asked for it back. I could tell from her voice that this was a call she didn't want to make. As it turned out, Laura made the offer on her own, assuming Jeff would agree. I imagine when he heard the whole story, he must have lost it—at least as much as the unflappable Jeff was capable of losing anything. She said that he didn't want any violence brought into their house, and if I used that key, he couldn't be sure of what Darren would do.

"Of course, it's not about you," Laura said earnestly. "It's Darren. We don't really know him and after what you told me… Jeff doesn't…I mean we don't feel safe."

"I understand…" I said into the phone trying not to give away the hot pang of despair that shot through my chest. My heart sank into my gut as my throat constricted. "I will get it in the mail to you in the morning."

"I'm so sorry, Alane, I…" Laura said next.

"It's no problem, really," I interrupted.

"You know we are concerned about you," she continued.

"I know, Laura, please don't worry about it. You helped me so much last week. You have no idea." My voice was tight and shaky.

"We just can't put ourselves in the middle…" she went on with growing hesitation.

"Really…I understand…" I cut in, and I did. The weight of what was happening was crashing down on my head. She had offered too much, and I had selfishly taken all of it. I was ashamed that I had ever even put her in that position. This was my problem, not hers, and Jeff was undeniably right.

"Okay," she said like she wanted to end the conversation, but didn't know how. After a long pause, she added, "Are you alright?"

"I'm fine, Laura. Please don't worry about it. I'll send it tomorrow." I said, trying desperately to sound upbeat and unaffected.

"Okay…" she said hesitantly, again.

"Okay…" I said followed by a long pause, "please say hi to Jeff for me and I'll talk to you soon."

There was another long pause. "Okay," Laura said quietly and then hung up the phone.

…and that was it…

Such was the end of the empowerment key, more importantly, the end of two more relationships. I was crushed. I never meant to put them in jeopardy. I never meant to make them feel mistreated or unsafe. I had no intention of using that key…but, to be fair, they had no way to know that I wouldn't. For that matter, neither did I. The road to Hell might be paved with good intentions, but

Hell's welcome center is built out of the unconscious ones. After I cycled through multiple waves of hurt and abandonment, I realized what I had done by taking that key. I had been selfish. I had carelessly thought only about myself and thought nothing of what it could do to Laura and Jeff, my friends. It was all just too uncertain. It was my uncertainty that made Laura offer me the key to begin with, and my uncertainty should have been enough to make me refuse it.

I had become *that girl*—the girl that I had previously had nothing for but disdain. I had become the girl who was living with violence—the girl who wasn't strong enough to leave—the girl who was willing to drag everybody else down with her. I couldn't blame Laura for making that call. I couldn't blame Jeff for demanding it of her. They were right. This was not their problem to solve. This was not their fight. In fact, they needed to be protected from it. In that moment, I realized that I needed to protect everyone that I loved from it. I had to handle this by myself. Whether I stayed or I left, it didn't matter. This was my mess, and I either had to stay and clean it up or walk away from it and suffer the consequences alone. That was all there was to it.

I heard from Laura only twice more after that. A few months later, she sent me an email to say hello and to ask me to mail back her pregnancy books that she had loaned me back when I was newly pregnant. She said she needed them for a friend. Actually, she and Jeff had finally gotten pregnant. I guess she wasn't comfortable talking to me about it. I boxed them up and sent them right away. I never intended to keep her books in the first place.

Laura sent another email after her son was born. I sent a card, and that was it.

The only real friendship I had at the time had been annihilated. I knew that she thought that I should leave Darren. In her own way, she told me to get out, but I wasn't ready. I couldn't hear it. In the end, I killed that friendship all by myself—and I never even told her I was sorry. I just kept on going down the same road I had been on for years, leaving a trail of both literal and metaphorical dead things behind me.

Chapter 18

Grief is a tricky thing. Despite all of the educated tomes that have been published on the subject and all of the vapid self-help drivel that has been spewed into the ether about surviving it, no one has ever fully been able to capture its true nature and every awful thing that comes with it adequately enough for me. For all of its predictable hallmarks, the specter of grief manifests uniquely in each iteration, leaving its target utterly and completely alone in it. From the inside of grief looking out, it's hard to tell what's worthy of grief and what's not. Everything looks bleak and the same.

I've learned to cast no aspersions on what other people might deem grief-worthy. Genuine grief might be possible over something as mundane as a tube of lipstick. I know girls who have collapsed at the trauma of a discontinued seasonal color, or worse, the loss of an entire cosmetic product formula. I know that I, personally felt a pang of sadness once, when my local grocery stopped carrying Ben and Jerry's Chunky Monkey because it wasn't very popular. I think I even lit a candle that night in memory of its frozen deliciosity. It was at least two months before I was willing to drive three extra miles to another store with bad lighting to buy some. It was tragic. (I really hated the color palate of that grocery store. It made me look peeked. However, the loss of that overpriced, waistline wrecking ice cream was too great. I would have crossed the Rubicon, or driven across town, to assuage my grief.)

Honestly though, I have grieved for real things at times in my life. I've lost family members. I've lost friends. I've even lost a few pets. My family tree is riddled with stories of cancer, heart attacks, strokes, and Alzheimer's. There's been a lot of grieving over the years for dead and, in some cases, the not yet dead. My generation grew up during the dawn of the AIDS epidemic. That was back before the bigots of the world realized that heterosexuality didn't grant them immunity and before the drug cocktails worked well enough for the young to forget how serious the disease really was…and still is.

Of course, there is plenty of grief I have yet to experience, too. So far, I haven't lost my parents. I haven't lost a spouse to illness or injury. I haven't lost my home to a natural disaster or to the ravages of terrorism. In all, I would say that I have been pretty fortunate, but my point is that grief comes in many forms. Almost every situation is rife with the possibility of grief. There are as many kinds of grief in the world as there are people, and what's crippling to one might be nothing to another. It's not for me to decide for another what is grief-worthy and what's not. I can only pass judgment over my own grief.

…and I was grieving…

My grief was over lost possibility. I lost an embryo-fetus, not a baby, not a child, not a person. What I lost was a parasitic mass of marginally differentiated cells. It wasn't a child yet. I can't claim to know the depth of that kind of grief. It could have been far worse for me. As so many people have so dismissively pointed out, spontaneous abortions (a.k.a. miscarriages) really do happen a lot. Worse still, there are women who lose their babies later on in the process or at birth when there is literally a tiny person to mourn rather than just the conceptualization of a child. Nevertheless, the loss of my physically manifesting concept undid me.

It seems like it shouldn't have been the end of the world. Based on the facts, it should have been just a hiccup of sorrow. The mourning period should have been, at most, equal and opposite in duration to the pregnancy itself. My grief and mourning should have neatly expanded and contracted along a tidy sliding scale of intensity in direct proportion to the amount of "tissue" there was to extract, like having a tonsillectomy or removing an epidermoid cyst. So it seemed, based on the reaction of the people around me.

...but it wasn't like that at all...

My grief was deep and murky. It waxed and waned and permeated everything around me. The more I heard that I should just get over it, the deeper my grief became. The deeper it got, the more distorted my perspective became until the whole thing morphed into a self-perpetuating machine of despair.

A normal person would have talked to someone. A normal person would have found someone to listen. I had Darren. At least I thought I had Darren until he told me that I should have been over it already. After that, I looked for a psychologist. I thought getting professional help would be the best next step until I called and discovered that I couldn't afford it without insurance and I couldn't afford insurance, either. Darren also reminded me that he didn't "believe in psychology," and said that I shouldn't waste my time. (I always thought that was pretty funny coming from a guy with a bachelor's degree in Psychology who earned his living as a chiropractor. If I had a nickel for every time someone said they didn't "believe in chiropractic"... I could have afforded a shrink, at least.)

Out of desperation, I tried confessing it to an unlicensed church counselor once. She was "our" friend, a sometimes patient, and a freelance massage therapist who had talked Darren into joining the local megachurch. That didn't pan out either. She said that it probably happened because I had been "prideful in the face of the Lord" and pointed to my neatly framed doctorate degree and state licenses on the wall in our office as evidence. I didn't bother to remind her that I was required by state law to display my pertinent degrees and licenses in a prominent place. She was also an RN. She knew the rules. I also didn't bother to point out that her God was kind of a dick if what she said was true. Babies are made through straight up "sinful acts" all the time...premarital sex, adultery, lust, and the like. Plenty of those babies make it through just fine. I really didn't think God would be that bent up about some certificates in some cheap frames. I decided that her Religion (rather than an actual God) must have rendered her impervious to logic, so there was no point. I also left the friendship gasping for air in my wake. It died eventually, too.

I left the concept and practice of Christianity behind me, too. It wasn't for me anymore. Places like her megachurch obscured their true agenda of hardline fundamentalism with a brand of pop psychology that is best described as Christianity Lite. That vacuous little massage therapist/frustrated RN/unqualified outreach minister served the final death blow to my relationship with organized Christianity for me. It was clear that in her Christian dogma, a healthy baby was God's blessing and my miscarriage was my fault—not bad luck, not divine intervention, but her God's judgment. If her God was going to exact such harsh judgment over mandated degrees on a wall, I wanted nothing to do with it. I was clear that her God cared nothing for my grief. If I officially joined her church or tithed enough, He might have changed his mind, but I wasn't willing to find out.

My grief went on a long time. As a means of survival, I tried to marginalize my grief as best I could. I went back to the office. I had no choice. The practice was falling apart again. It was our only source of income, and we had to keep the practice afloat. We had to make it through no matter how broken I felt.

Darren had lost his patience with my grief. Since, in his opinion, the whole experience had been equally as hard (if not harder) on him as it had been on me, and since he was "over it," He thought that I should "just get over it," too. If I said anything about it, he would say, "Aren't you over that, yet?" or "Are you still talking about that?" He asked as though I were being ridiculous. As if a spontaneous abortion was the same as losing a sock in the dryer or running out of potato chips on the weekend.

Obviously, he had handled his emotions like a champ. He drank it away every week from Thursday night to Sunday afternoon. Not long after my trip to Wilmington, he bought himself a brand-new Harley and started riding, which introduced a whole new group of people into our lives, including our neighbor from around the block, Travis. In Travis, Darren finally found his perfect match. Honestly, they seemed more like soul-mates than Darren and I ever had. If Travis's man-boobs had been big enough for a bra, I think Darren would have proposed.

…but I digress…

So, Darren got a motorcycle, and I went back to work. Kelli stayed longer than she intended after she gave her notice, but eventually, she had to go. Darren hired and lost two more people after that. In the end, he invited me back into the office full time. Things at the office were dire. I finally agreed after several weeks of deliberation, a persuasive FSP seminar, a few intense conversations with Melissa, and Darren's agreement to a few non-negotiable demands: I would treat patients based on my own best judgment, not FSP's, I would go by "Dr. Gray" instead of "Dr. Alane" or "Mrs. Dr. Danky" or any of the other demeaning titles I had previously been given, I would get paid for my time, and finally, we would hire a replacement for Kelli because I was not his receptionist.

Darren even took it a step further. Together, we outlined a plan for the office to meet the needs of all of the patients that walked through the door, not just the ones that met his narrow criteria and were willing to pay for long-term care plans. When we were done, he proclaimed that we had just come up with our "Million-dollar Idea." I wasn't sure about that part of it, but it certainly seemed like a plan that could keep all the bills paid. We drank to the idea and planned to put it into action later that week.

Five days later, Darren changed his mind about our "Million-dollar Idea." He had discussed it with JT on a conference call, and JT told him he shouldn't. Darren killed the plan without a second of hesitation. After that, I was back at the reception desk. At least he tried to call me "Dr. Gray," even though he usually said it with a condescending smirk on his face most of the time. The patients were confused, of course. Mostly when I introduced myself, they'd come back with, "What's your name?" like they hadn't heard me.

I'd say, "Dr. Gray," with a smile.

They'd usually respond with something like, "No, what's your first name?" or "No, what's your real name?" Sometimes they wouldn't even ask, they'd pick up my business card and then call me "Allen." That was usually the end of "Dr. Gray."

Two months and a new receptionist later, I decided I needed to find a job that paid actual money. (He still wasn't paying me for my time, by the way.) I found one, too. One of the other FSP offices needed an associate. It wasn't perfect, but it was something—and they were interested in me. For my last interview, they took both of us to lunch to, as I understood it, make sure that everyone was clear about the arrangement and to make sure that it wasn't a plot to steal their patients and send them to Darren's office. In the middle of the entre, Darren suggested that he might be a better fit for the job since he already knew the FSP scripts and had been working directly with patients for the last year and a half while I had been more of a receptionist. Believe it or not, they went for it, and the guy who wanted to be the only doctor in his practice and be my coach took my associate job, leaving me alone to run his office and to treat his patients.

Not long after that, he adopted a Pitbull puppy and traded in the SUV I drove for a used Jeep Wrangler with a soft-top and no backseat. Six months later, he quit the job that should have been mine, spent four grand on a road trip to Sturgis, South Dakota for a motorcycle rally, and then started another job at a competing office less than three miles down the road from the job he quit. To cap it off, he took in a stray border collie less than a month later.

I stayed through all of it. I stayed after all of the conflict and disrespect and after Darren's night of violence. We kept on fighting, but not all the time, and our fights were just words. To be fair, I got pretty good at slinging verbal bile right back at him, and I discovered that I could intellectually best him without even breaking a sweat most of the time. Although I had always been smarter than Darren, he had been able to keep up in the beginning, but by this time, his persistent alcohol consumption had flattened the topography of his intellectual landscape.

As much as I hated running his office alone and dealing with the mess that he left behind, at least I had some autonomy. Slowly, I started molding the office into my vision of a reputable chiropractic practice. It was a challenge working in the shadow of the reputational destruction that Darren and the FSP model had created. Actually, it wasn't as much the people he had pissed off that were the problem as much as it was the patients that he left behind. The ones that liked him and what he did were as resistant to change as he was and would regularly point out what I was doing "wrong" or "not the way Dr. Danky did it." Even in his absence, it was still his practice, and his patients were quick to remind me of that. In spite of that, I actually started to enjoy my work. After a while, most of Darren's patients had either gotten right with me as their doctor, or they had moved on, and the new patients that came in chose to stay based on what I presented them. The practice was slowly becoming mine, and after a few months, it started to take off.

Of course, Darren had a hard time with my brief window of success. As things started to look better for me, he unraveled. It started with an uptick in Peekaboo Penis. Eventually, it morphed into a new game—Peekaboo I'm Jerking-off My Penis. It was a more advanced version of the game. I would find him jerking it in the shower, and in the living room, and in the kitchen. Wherever I found him, he always seemed to be there, penis in hand and a squinty-eyed grin on his face.

He was still downloading porn to our computer and leaving the images open to greet me when I turned on the screen. He would message full frontal pictures to me while I was at work. One time, an action shot of a fully naked chick hanging backward off of a Harley popped up on my screen while I was talking to a patient. If the patient saw what it was (and I don't see how she couldn't have), she was at least polite enough not to say anything about it at the time. She just never came back for her follow-up appointment. Thankfully, she didn't give me an online review either. Talk about reputational devastation. That would have been a nightmare.

Darren was drinking more then, too. He swore it was all in good fun and tried to prove that he didn't have a problem by drying out for a few weeks here and there, but every time he did, he would inevitably go right back to it and would inevitably drink even more than he did before.

...and then, of course, there was the motorcycle...

Darren's Harley wasn't the first motorcycle that he had owned.

He spent some of our money on a used Yamaha when we were in school out in Iowa. Believe it or not, I actually liked riding with him out there. We would ride out into the cornfields on a Saturday afternoon and stop for Mexican food or ice cream. I would photograph the butterflies and flowers, and we would talk about music and movies and our plans for conquering a little piece of the world. We would stay out all day and ride home at dusk, watching the fireflies light up the open fields like a million twinkling Christmas lights. The time we spent together riding around Eastern Iowa was part of what bonded us together early on. I had hoped, even though we couldn't afford it, that maybe Darren's new Harley would help us get some of that back.

That's not what happened with this motorcycle, at all. The grief bike brought out something completely different in Darren and in our relationship. It gave Darren a sense of freedom. It gave him a new identity in his head. It gave him something to do other than chiropractic and an ability to make small talk with strangers in Harley t-shirts. It gave him a new measure for assessing the people we met, either they liked bikes, or they didn't. It brought more monthly expenses into our world (and the H-D lifestyle isn't cheap.) Most significantly, it brought Travis and all of Travis's friends into our lives.

In Travis, Darren found the adult equivalent of a childhood playmate. He, his wife, and his two kids lived on the street behind ours. Travis had been a military guy for most of his adult life and was riding out the rest of his military career as a recruiter for the National Guard. Travis was, for the most part, a nice guy most of the time. He was rarely rude to me unless he was particularly inebriated and suffering from a bad case of inferiority that day. He was Darren's friend, and he was one of the only people that Darren never criticized. I think Travis was what Darren had always wanted to be—the guy that was revered as a hero by strangers just by walking around in his work clothes.

Darren latched on to Travis right away. He had a Harley and a group of ex-military friends to ride around with on the weekend. Travis seemed to like Darren, too, if for no other reason than the free-flowing homebrew that came out of the refrigerator in the garage.

With Travis around, Darren's weekends swiftly became all about his motorcycle. Most of his weekdays did, too. He rode his bike everywhere he could, even to and from work, which made me thankful that he was working somewhere else. Riding made him smell like he had been dragged behind a truck on his way to work. Personally, I didn't think the aroma of gasoline and exhaust smelled like healthcare. He didn't care, and he never owned up to it if anyone at his work ever complained.

In the midst of all of that, Darren decided that he needed a career change. Two options he set for himself were as follows: 1.) pharmaceutical sales rep…after years of openly bashing "BigPharma" and the "AMA" and shouting from the rooftops that mainstream medicine was actually "sick-care" and not healthcare and actively encouraging his patients to stop taking medications because they didn't need them, he actually thought he was going to get a job peddling pharmaceuticals to medical doctors…or 2.) Special Agent with the FBI…that's right, the United States Federal Bureau of Investigation. He was a thirty-four year old chiropractor in marginal physical condition with no applicable skills or experience, but he was certain that he was a great candidate. To get ready, he trained for the four whole weeks leading up to the initial application examination. Needless to say, he didn't pass it. He was shocked by the news and told himself that he must have been too smart and educated for the FBI. He said that they must have wanted a candidate with more of a "midlevel intellect" instead of higher intelligence and an education. He said the same of the pharmaceutical industry when he couldn't even land an initial interview. That's right, Dr. Darren thought he was too smart and educated for the FBI and Big Pharma.

...I'm going to let that thought just hang out there for a moment...

Obviously, he decided it was better to stay where he was.

A month later, he quit his job and decided that he should be running his own office. It was, after all, the one place where he would be fully appreciated and would reach his full potential.

When he got back, he was shocked at the changes I had made and converted the office back to what it had been before he left. The office faltered under the stress of the change. Darren decided that his office had been ruined, and we were back at each other's throats again.

He claimed that I forced him out of his practice and pushed him into that first associate job. He actually said the words, "You stole my practice from me."

Obviously, that led to a whopper of an argument that lingered for weeks and weeks after that. Darren drank and rode his way through it. I receded from everyone and everything and retreated to my journals. I wrote in them a lot during those days. I didn't even try to hide them. I kept them in my nightstand. If Darren had wanted to read them, he could have. Nothing in them was a secret. I had already yelled most of it to his face most of the time.

Thanks to all of my journaling, I finally saw my life for what it had become. My life was unhappy and unfulfilling. We were married only in the sense that we were legally, financially, and professionally bound and co-dependent. There was no love left. There was only chronic animosity marked by intermittent waves of socially mandated tolerance and clumsy attempts at rekindling the spark of lust that we had mistaken for love so many years before.

I was ready to leave. There wasn't much planning involved in my thought process, but I was resolute, the consequences be damned. I was just going to go with no job, no money, and no prospects. I was going to pack what I could into one of the cars and drive off into the sunset. I had a place to stay. This time I had told my brother about it. All he said was, "Great. Come on over." He told me I could stay with him and he would help me out until I got on my feet.

...I was ready...

I planned to take the next week and tie up a few loose ends because I just couldn't let all the consequences be damned, of course. (There was no need to be entirely reckless.) I could leave knowing that my patients would be cared for and that the dogs and cats were managed until I could come back for some of them. That was all there was to do, and I would make my move. It was time.

That Wednesday, I missed my period. The next day, a pregnancy test confirmed what I had completely missed—I was pregnant, again. I had thought the chances of that happening again were next to none. The first time had taken years to happen. My uterus was a craggy, desolate place with giant fibroids and scar tissue from my run-in with a wanton biopsy needle. Beyond that, I thought that I had been careful. I made Darren wear condoms most of the time when I thought it might be dangerous. We weren't even having sex that often...

...but all it takes is once...and in case I wasn't clear before, the rhythm method is complete bullshit...seriously...

The pregnancy news made Darren ecstatic. The next day, Darren announced that he was going back to work at his old job in Raleigh. He was leaving the practice to me—again.

With that, my plan was blown out of the water. There was no way I could leave. I was thirty-seven (soon to be thirty-eight) and pregnant. I couldn't start a new chiropractic job. Someone had to run the practice. Someone had to pay those gigantic practice bills and all the debt. We still didn't have health insurance. There would be new medical costs. Darren's paltry new salary wouldn't be enough to cover everything. I was backed in a corner.

I couldn't understand why this was happening. No matter how much I journaled or how long I meditated, I couldn't get my head wrapped around why. Eventually, I decided that it must have been the Universe's way of telling me not to leave, that it was a mandate for me to stay, that I had taken *The Vow* and I still had to make good on it. It had to be what I was supposed to be doing. That was the only explanation for such horrific news and such horrible timing.

So, once again I stayed. I changed my plans and squished my desires into a tiny box at the bottom of my brain and left it there. I had no choice. There was a baby involved now. It wasn't about me anymore, it was about destiny.

Chapter 19

This one didn't work out, either. This time, I knew it was over without even having to see the third ultrasound. Darren said I was just being paranoid right up until the moment he saw the images on the screen.

This one made it a longer than the first one. My body looked more pregnant this time. When we got the bad news, this time in a different clinic and with a different doctor, there were no disparaging remarks about chiropractic, and I was scheduled to have a D&E a week and a half later.

The procedure, itself, was easier than the way it played out the time before, although Darren's presence in the pre-op room was not exactly comforting. He passed the time by snapping pictures of me with his new phone as I waited to be wheeled into the operating room. He said he couldn't understand why I didn't want him to take my picture and, as of the time I was taken out of the room, he still hadn't deleted them. I don't know if he ever did.

The aftermath of the procedure wasn't so easy. My body didn't respond well to the postop medications they gave me. The pain, headaches, and vomiting wouldn't seem to stop. Emotionally, I was a wreck, too. Regardless, I was back at work the Monday after the procedure. I couldn't afford to hire a temporary coverage doctor, and there was no way I could afford to close for a week. So, I bled and puked for the next two weeks while I worked and cried my way through my work day. I felt like I had no choice.

As a couple, Darren and I reacted much the same to this miscarriage as we did to the first one. I cried. Darren drank. We fought. The only difference this time, other than meaner fights and deeper sadness, was that Darren had Travis and his motorcycle friends, and I didn't have anyone or anything beyond our ever-expanding debt, two destructive adopted dogs, and my crushing reanimated grief.

As time went on, Darren pulled even farther away. He barely spoke to me and barely spent time with me other than to sit in the corner every morning and ogle my naked body while I changed clothes. At another time in our marriage, it might have been exciting and flirtatious, but then it just felt dirty and obligatory. If I dared to change for work without waiting for him to take his place in the chair in the corner of the room, he would get angry and storm out of the house. The rest of the time, he went out of his way to make me feel inadequate and crazy. When I tried to talk to him about it, he would tell me that I was overly emotional.

I desperately tried to tell him what I needed even though I wasn't sure I really knew what it was, myself, but it only led to more arguments.

"I need this to be okay! Just tell me everything is going to be okay! Please!" I insisted at the climax of our biggest post-second-miscarriage blow-up.

"I can't tell you that," he responded smugly. "I don't know what's going to happen. But I do know that what you think about is what you manifest, so if you want to feel better, you need to stop thinking about all of that negative bullshit." Darren had a knack for spouting the most obnoxious self-help tripe at the most irritating moments.

"I am not being negative! I am just upset, and I don't feel well!" I insisted. I was in no mood for any of his self-help, Culmination

Center, FSP crap. I just needed my husband to talk to me like he would talk to any one of his stupid drinking buddies.

"Well, what do you want me to say?" he asked snidely.

"I don't know! Just say something!" I pleaded.

Darren was perched in the peepshow chair in our bedroom, sipping a pint glass of his most recent homebrew. I was sitting on the floor in front of the dresser, putting away the laundry. The smell was so pungent that it was giving me a headache.

"Fuck!" I exclaimed as I looked up at him. "Why won't you say something? I just told you what I need, and now you refuse to say anything."

"I don't know what to say to you. Nothing I say is good enough. Why should I say anything? You're just going to tell me that it isn't enough!" His self-righteousness was palpable.

"I don't know," I started to cry with giant heaving sobs. "Just put your arm around me and tell me everything's gonna be alright…just…just something."

Darren pushed himself out of the chair and sat down next to me on the floor. He put his arm firmly around my shoulder and said, "Everything's going to be alright."

…Finally!…

I turned my face into his shoulder and unloaded more sobs. I wanted to punch him in the gut, but he was doing what I asked for once, so I didn't want to wreck it. It was a wonderful moment.

…but that's all it was…a moment…

Over the next few weeks, we regressed right back to where we had been, like that moment never happened. Darren spent more time on his bike and more time with Travis, and he was less and less interested in me and anything I cared about.

Then one weekend, the whole thing came to a head. I was on the floor putting clothes away, again. He was in the peepshow chair with a beer in his hand again when he announced that my grief should have been long over and became enraged over my lack of happiness. (I never did figure out what he had against clean clothes.)

"How did you think it would be?" I said. "Did you think I would just be fine with it like it was no big deal? Like I should just say, 'Hey, I just had a dead baby suctioned out of my uterus. It's no big thing, want to get some lunch?'"

"Jesus, you're so melodramatic," he boomed. "Don't be ridiculous!"

"I'm not. I'm not ridiculous. Just let me be sad about this. Okay?"

"You need to just get over it," he said arrogantly.

"Just get over it?... Just get over it?... Are you fucking kidding me?" my anger and my voice rose quickly as I spoke.

He snorted a disgusted chuckle out of his nose. "No, I'm not kidding you. Just get over it. It's not like it was a real baby. It happens to lots of people, and nobody complains about it except you."

"Oh my God!" I wailed, "Why is this happening?"

"It's happening because you are making it happen." Darren looked at me flatly as he spoke.

I tried to slow my breathing and speak like a rational person, "Darren, this has been really hard on me. I don't know why, but it has. I've been sick for weeks. I can't think straight. I can barely make it through a day at work because of the headaches and the fatigue and all of the cramping..."

"It's been hard on me, too, Alane. Christ, why don't you ever consider how hard it's been on me?" His voice became more pressured.

I understood that the loss of the baby hurt him. I knew that he was grieving again, too, but that wasn't my point. "I know that it emotionally hurt you to lose another baby, but that's not what I'm talking about. This has been really physically hard on me, and I don't know why. I need help."

"It's always about you, isn't it," he spat back, "and how hard everything is on you, isn't it? You never consider me for one minute. It was just as hard on me, Alane. It was just as hard on me!"

"No, it wasn't!" I insisted. I thought I had been clear about my point. It wasn't just about the grief. I was physically torn up and falling apart.

"Yes, it was!" he yelled as he sat forward and slammed his hand on the arm of the chair. His face flushed and the veins in his temples bulged.

I couldn't control myself anymore. "Why are you being like this?! This is insane!" I screamed back. "Darren, I was pregnant, with all of the shit that goes with a pregnancy and a bad one at that. Now, I'm not. I had the procedure this time. I didn't react well to that or the medication. Now, I'm still cramping. I'm still sick. I'm still anemic. This is not normal. You are a doctor for fuck sake!"

"So are you!" he boomed and slammed his fist, again. "You're only sick because you want to be. Fuck! Will you just admit that this has been just as hard on me as it has been on you?"

"No…I won't! I won't because it hasn't. Yes, it was hard for you emotionally, but not physically at all! Why are you being like this?"

Darren sat back hard in his chair and stared straight ahead. "It was just as hard on me," he repeated with a growl.

"What the fuck? What the fuck is wrong with you?" I yelled. None of this was making any sense.

He turned his head toward me. His face had changed. He glared at me through narrowed eyes and said coolly, "What do you want me to do, Alane? Hum? What, exactly, do you want me to do?"

"I don't know." I doubled over the open dresser drawer and bawled into the stacks of clean t-shirts. "I don't know. I just need help. Please…please help me!" My words were laced with heaves and sobs. It was all pouring out uncontrollably.

"If you can't tell me exactly what you need, then I can't help you," Darren said coldly as he gazed down his nose at me.

"Can't you just put your arm around me and tell me that everything is going to be alright? Please!" I wailed.

"You just said it isn't alright. Do you want me to argue with you?"

"No!" I cried back at him, "Just do something. Please."

"I'm sitting here, aren't I? I'm listening to you. Isn't that what you want...me to listen to you?"

A massive gurgling sob rolled out of my chest. "Yes, that's what I want, but…"

"But I guess that's not enough for you, now, huh?" Darren growled.

I looked up at him. "Why are you doing this?" I sobbed.

"I'm just trying to give you what you always say you want," he said turning his head up and away from me.

"This is not what I want. You're distorting everything!"

"Of course, Alane," he snorted, "this is all my fault. It's always my fault. Losing my baby had no effect on me, and I am just being a selfish asshole."

A loud cracking sound ripped through my head. What little control I had left was gone. I pushed my hands into the drawer and reared myself up. "That's not what I said!" I shrieked at the top of my lungs. I could feel the spit flying out of my mouth and the blood bursting into my face as I screamed it. "I said that it *was* hard on you emotionally, but it was *harder* on me physically! You are a fucking doctor! You know this!" If I had sprouted horns and demon wings at that moment, it would not have been a surprise. I had never heard my voice come out of my body like that before. It was nearly inhuman. Then again, so was everything else—the pain, the loss, the sadness, the loneliness and now the utter betrayal.

"I'm done with this," Darren said in an offputtingly calm tone. "When you can talk to me like a normal person, let me know." With that, he stood up and walked out of the room.

"That's it?" I screamed. "Seriously?" There was another loud cracking sound in my head. It must have been the last fragment of control crumbling to bits in my brain. "Fuck you!" I let out in a blood-curdling howl, "Fuck you! Fuck you! Fuck you!" Darren had gone downstairs. Through the floor, I could hear the refrigerator open followed by the familiar hissing pop of a liberated bottle cap.

I let out a weak "asshole," as I dropped my head back into the drawer and sobbed. I stayed there, dripping snot and tears into my t-shirt drawer until the shooting pains in my knees and feet were too strong to ignore.

Darren left on his motorcycle not long after that. Eventually, I crawled into bed. I just wanted to sleep. I wanted to sleep and wake up somewhere else where none of this was happening.

Sleep didn't come right way. When I did, I mostly dreamed that I was lying in bed unable to sleep. It was weird. I woke up for real when Darren came home that night. I heard him rev the engine of his motorcycle as he came down the main road and turned into the neighborhood. (I am sure the neighbors appreciated that.) I heard him open the garage door. I heard him rummage around in the kitchen. I wanted him to stay downstairs and sleep on the couch. I didn't want to be anywhere near him, let alone sleep next to him.

Of course, he didn't stay away. It wasn't long before he lumbered up the stairs. I could hear his shoulders ricocheting off the walls on either side of the stairs. His footsteps were unsteady and stumbling as he made his way into our room. The pungent smell of stale beer enveloped the room. His dense body pinballed around among the bed and dresser and nightstand as he tried to undress. I even heard him giggle to himself a few times before flopping into bed next to me.

I pretended to sleep through all of it. I needed all of it to end. I had no thoughts on how it could end or what to do to make it end. I just wanted it all to stop, so much so that I was completely paralyzed. I just stayed there pretending to sleep. I didn't know what else to do. Eventually, I slipped into sleep. It was shallow, fitful sleep, punctuated by giant waking gasps. My brain thought I was suffocating. In reality, I was only violently choking on my own anxiety as I confronted my mortality alone in my sleep. Each time I woke, I looked to my right, and there Darren was, snoring away and sprawled a little farther across the bed. After a few hours of this cycle, I got out of bed. Sleeping was turning into work, and I really wanted to be as far away from Darren as possible.

The next day, we avoided each other which was an impressive feat in our little starter house. When we passed through the same room, there was nothing but silence and some notably emotive breathing. I didn't know it was possible to be that physically close to another human being and yet feel so far apart.

Darren went out on his motorcycle by mid-morning. Travis was waiting for him outside when he left, and they stayed out most of the day.

Around five o'clock that evening, I heard their bikes turn into the neighborhood and quickly retreated to the bedroom. The last thing I wanted was to deal with Darren in front of Travis. He was not exactly a sensitive guy, but there was no reason to put him in an uncomfortable spot, and I was in no mood to fake a smile and vomit up pleasantries while Darren ignored me in front of his friend…and they were probably drunk…and they were probably just going to keep on drinking.

Maybe it would have helped if I had stayed downstairs and thrown back a couple of cold ones with them. Darren probably would have seen it as some kind of olive branch if I had, but drinking just made me feel worse all the way around, and I wasn't in the mood to gloss things over with some alcohol and some small talk.

Up in our room, there was nothing to do. There was no TV or computer, and I was out of books to read. All I could do was sprawl on the bed and try to scribble in my journal. Even though journaling was now an FSP approved activity, I still felt subversive when I did it. The whole debacle back in Pittsburgh left an impression. I know that bothered him, but there was nothing he could say about it since it was one JT said was a must. And if that wasn't enough, Darren knew that I would unleash a monsoon of tears and yelling if he uttered a single word about it.

Below in the kitchen, I heard the refrigerator open and beer bottles clank together as they were pulled off the shelves. I told myself that I wasn't going to eavesdrop. It would just be Travis complaining about his wife or talking about some "asshole on the road" who cut them off while they were riding. It wasn't anything I wanted to hear, and it would have been impolite, anyway. I tried to keep my focus on my writing.

…that lasted about two minutes…

Then my name vibrated up through the floor.

"Where's Alane?" Travis asked loudly.

"Don't know," Darren said with mild disgust, "upstairs I guess. She's probably sleeping, again."

"I'm sorry to hear that. What's up with her?" Travis asked.

"No clue," Darren replied. "She complains all the time and

never wants to do anything."

No clue? I thought to myself. Is that some kind of joke? That son of a bitch just said he has no clue…

"I hear that," Travis said. He and his wife, Pam, had been struggling for the last few years. Darren and I had listened to Travis go on about Pam many times. He called her selfish and complained that she was unwilling to do anything to help herself. He resented her for gaining a bunch of weight since their last child and for constantly chasing diagnosable illnesses. She had undergone several surgeries and seemed to be on a downhill slope since the day I met her. I never really heard much of her side of the story except that she was genuinely sick, and her doctors had run out of treatment options. It wasn't that I doubted her at any point. She was just standoffish and judgy and never really liked me much. Maybe we were just too much alike to get along.

"I spend so much time trying to be supportive of her, and all she does is cry and tell me that everything is my fault," Darren said next.

"Dude, this is how it starts…" Travis said with a chuckle. His voice carried up through the floor with a tone that sounded like derision with a heavy salting of disgust on top.

"I know, man," Darren said, "I can't believe that's what I have to look forward to. I thought she was gonna be different. It's fucked up."

"I don't know, man. It's just how it goes. Get ready. It's all downhill from here." It was like I could hear Travis shaking his head through the floor as he spoke.

"I know, dude. I know," Darren commiserated.

The loud cracking sound went off in my head again followed by a cascade of insanity that ripped through my head like a meat hook. *Are you fucking serious?! Oh my God! Oh my GOD! I am going to lose my fucking mind! That fucking piece of shit! Asshole! He hasn't even told Travis about the last miscarriage! Selfish prick! It's not the same! It's not the same! Fuck! Fuck! Fucking! Fuck! Fuck you! Fuck you! Fuck you!* I held my tongue as my brain raged on, *Fuck…fuck… FUCK!!! I fucking hate you, you son of a bitch!!!…*

We had, in fact, kept the second pregnancy to ourselves. We learned our lessons the first time and did it to spare ourselves the embarrassment if it didn't work out. When I was around, Darren told his friends that I wasn't drinking because I was on a cleanse. Who knows what he told them on the days I stayed home. Most of his friends thought I was a bitch, as it was. They probably didn't even miss me, let alone ask about what I was doing. Now, he was pouring his guts out to Travis without telling him the whole story.

…and I couldn't stand it.

Torrents of tears burst from my eyes. I was trapped in my own house. If I tried to leave, I'd have to pass right by Darren and Travis to get to out. I didn't want to look at them. Their bikes were blocking the driveway. I would have to ask them for help. No way was I going to speak to either one of them. If I tried, the offensive stream of word bile that was flowing through my head might have flooded out. That would only make things worse. If I called home, it would be terrible. Coherent communication was gone, and I had no idea what my parents would do if they heard me in such a state. I didn't have the strength to manage their reactions and my own at the same time, and I was in no mood to defend Darren to them if they took their reactions too far.

That was it. Those were my options as I saw them at the moment. There was no other place to go and no one else to call. All of "my" friends were actually "our" friends. I didn't want any of them to feel like they had to choose a side. And moreover, I didn't want to find out how many of them wouldn't side with me. And, of course, there was what happened the last time...

...things were bad enough already.

All that was left was to stay right where I was and do nothing. So, that's what I did. I stayed right where I was and tried to sleep to the dulcet tones of their misogynistic vitriol. It was torture. I heard everything, every last wretched word of it. It was now so much more than betrayal. It was humiliation.

The next day was Monday. That morning, the house reeked of stale beer and tobacco spit. Travis's words and Darren's response rang in my ears as I surveyed the scene. The kitchen was wrecked. Empty microbrew beer bottles (21 of them to be exact) and no less than three beer bottle spittoons littered the counters and the sink. I even thought I smelled faint notes of cigarette smoke in the air as well, but I still had pregnancy induced hormonal dog nose. There was no way to know if the smell was coming from inside the house or if someone a block away was smoking a cigarette on their front porch. I would have smelled it either way.

I looked at the mess with disbelief. There were dirty dishes on the stove and in the sink. Darren's jacket and half of his clothes were scattered on the floor. It looked like a fraternity had broken in and had a party overnight. Travis might have been an asshole chauvinist, but he had never left a mess like this behind in our house. This had to be Darren's handiwork.

As a doctor, I probably should have been frightened for him. I was sure that they had been drinking all afternoon before they came back here. It was impossible to know who drank what, but anyway I divided it up, it wasn't good for either of them. That much beer in a single day was dangerous, and it wasn't like they were drinking watered down 3.2 beer. This was microbrew. If they had any of his latest homebrew, it was even worse, and the dirty pint glass teetering on the edge of the living room coffee table seemed to support that possibility.

I probably should have checked on Darren to make sure he was still breathing, but I didn't. I was too filled with rage. He had done this kind of thing before and survived it. If he died, there would be a justifiable explanation for it, and if he left a puddle of urine in the bed, at least it would be the last one. For a while, I pondered if I would be able to cry if he never woke up. I decided to practice crying on demand in case I had to call the police. I thought no tears might have looked a tad suspicious.

Alcohol had been a part of our relationship from the beginning. We had gotten to know each other over food and wine, and we usually celebrated everything with a cocktail or a beer. In fact, Darren's romance with "snooty beer," a.k.a. crafts and/or microbrews (his nickname for it, not mine,) started largely because of me. That's what I liked, and Darren regularly teased me about it until the day he finally admitted that he actually like them better, himself. It was on from there. He left me with my seasonal ales and unfiltered Heffeweisens in the dust and ultimately found his true love inside a draft glass of IPA. No more IC light and certainly no more beer brewed by a large American commercial brewery. That wasn't good enough for his refined, drunken palate. He needed the real stuff. Luckily for him, it was getting easier and easier to find.

Now, he was officially out of control. As furious as I was about the way he had treated me and the things he said the night before, the truth of his drinking problem was staring me right in the face. It didn't matter who had the harder time with the miscarriage. This was unacceptable, and I was furious. He was jeopardizing our reputation, his job, his license to practice, and ultimately, our financial future.

In that moment, I decided that I wasn't going to help him. If he overslept, then so be it. If he was still drunk, then so be it. If he lost his job, then so be it. I couldn't fix things for him anymore.

I went on with my morning, working around the mess and trying not to look at it. As I was finishing my breakfast, Darren appeared. He didn't flinch at the mess. He, too, moved around it like it wasn't even there. He moved through the motions of his morning routine like there was nothing wrong. He went to work. I went to the office. When I came home for lunch, I cleaned up the mess. I couldn't stand it. Darren didn't say a word about any of it when he got home. We just moved around each other in silence until we went to sleep.

The next few days were about the same. We saw each other in the morning for about 20 minutes and in the evening for about 3 hours. Occupying the same space was silent torture. We didn't speak. There was no eye contact. Thankfully, there was no physical contact. It was like I was a ghost in my own house. As the gulf between us got wider, the stillness around me grew. It was a strange and unfamiliar state. I couldn't sense our menagerie of cats and dogs. I couldn't feel the phone before it rang or a visitor at the door before they rang the bell. I couldn't feel Darren. As weird as it was, it was also its own kind of relief. It was as close to gone as I could get.

It was around that time that I realized the rest of the truth. Now that I was the ghost, all of my ghosts were gone. The spirits and mists and lights and visions that had been with me my entire life weren't there anymore. They hadn't faded into the background. They weren't just less visible than usual. They were completely gone. It was like they had been erased, or worse, like they had never existed to begin with.

There was no one hanging out in the bedroom upstairs. Nothing was floating over the couch beside me like it was watching TV. The comforting feeling of an intangible guardian over my shoulder wasn't there anymore. They all were gone, and I was enveloped by silent isolation, possibly for the first time in my entire life.

With this realization, my relief turned into a radical emptiness. It was an odd empty feeling. It was more loss. It wasn't the same as it had been with the miscarriages. It was more pervasive. It was an overwhelming absence within my life as I had always known it. They were not me, but they had become a part of me. I desperately needed them, and they had been wholly wiped away. It was as if all the oxygen had been inexplicably sucked out of the room.

Guilt washed over me as I thought about the beings that used to populate my world. I had rarely tried to communicate with them directly. They usually came to me. When they did, more often than not, they scared me. I'd be walking down the stairs and, bam, there one of them would be, just hanging out and staring off into space. Did I just ignore them so long that they finally left? Were they only there to make sure I had those babies? Had they been called on to bigger and better things since I failed at that so epically? Had Darren lied to me when he said that he saw some of them, too? Later on, when he changed his mind and called them figments of my imagination, was he right? Were they all just a product of my own crazy mind?

I didn't even know how long they had been gone. I had been wallowing so far down in my self-pity hole that I hadn't noticed when they left. It was terrible. The Darren that I thought I married was gone. The spirits that had been with me my whole life were gone. The babies that I let myself want died before they even got started, and that was it. Everything was gone, and I was alone.

I was alone.

I was alone with my thoughts and the mindless droning of the TV. I was alone with the threat of our endless debt that just kept growing on as Darren drank his way around the Carolinas…and I was alone with my own crazy mind.

The only things I had left were my journals. That desperate green notebook journal had been the chisel that sunk the first undeniable gouge into my marriage ten years earlier. Now, the pile of journals in my nightstand was all I had left. Their pages held the burdens that my weak human mind could not. They called to me like a siren song. Their blank pages ached for the touch of my pen.

I found myself turning to them more and more often. I wrote in them until my pen ran dry and returned to them as soon as I could find a replacement. I wrote until my hand cramped and then wrote a little more in a desperate attempt to understand how I had come to be in this place…how a life that had held so much promise could have ended up like this…how a life that had been filled with so much art and science and wonder could have been reduced to such pointless nothingness.

Even my ghosts had abandoned me. So much for the stress reaction theory. I was more stressed than I had ever been in my entire life, and there were no visions, no hallucinations, no warm spiritual blankets of consolation borne out of cognitive dissonance. There was just nothing. I was utterly aware of it, and I wrote about it almost compulsively, in my scrawling hand, like it needed to be preserved for future generations to discover. But there would be no future generations, at least not from me. That was clear.

Everything was right there in the pages of my journals, yet I still had no clear understanding of how to change it. It was a hole of words. A deep, dark hole…and that was it.

◆◆◆◆◆

Other than writing, all I wanted to do was sleep. Metaphorically speaking, I had been asleep for a long time, already. Unfortunately, my metaphorical sleep didn't translate into useful physiological sleep. I envied people who could slumber their way through their emotional black holes and reset their brains, but real, restorative sleep never came for me. In fact, I didn't sleep solidly through the night for a couple of years thanks to two twitchy, diarrhea-prone dogs with acute storm anxiety. Add to that my stress about the office, my stress about bills, my drunken sprawling husband consuming most of the bed, my burgeoning case of parasomnia, and the result is a brand of physical and psychological dissonance that was nearly inexplicable.

I was exhausted. My body was giving out under the strain. During the Fall after my last miscarriage, I got sick. I had a sore throat, swollen lymph nodes in my neck, and fatigue that wouldn't end. I thought it was just a virus. As it went on, it progressed to a fever and rash. Since I had almost died from a poorly managed bacterial infection in my twenties, I took myself to an MD for help. She took a brief look and a little blood, offered me a round of antibiotics, and said that should do the trick. Five months, three MD's, six rounds of antibiotics, and a foreboding case of SIBO later, I was no better. My last mainstream medical option came from a local ENT who, after palpating my neck and jaw, declared it to be an infected salivary gland. He stated that this kind of thing only happened to "old people," but he was willing to surgically remove it since that was my only option. He actually laughed at me when I disagreed. He shrugged and left the room. I paid $350 at the front desk, and that was it. I stayed sick for months. (Actually, it didn't fully resolve for another three years. At one point I even named the giant lump in my neck "Nodine" since it looked like a second head was sprouting under my jaw, but I backed off from that pretty quickly. It was too gross and disturbing, even for me.)

In the meantime, Darren met an entrepreneurial chiropractor in Pittsburgh named Denis who claimed to have created a proprietary concussion protocol. According to Darren, all he had to do was go to Pittsburgh to meet with him to get in on the ground floor of this new million-dollar idea. So, he did. After one meeting with Denis, Darren was rapt. He quit his job, reapplied for his license in Pennsylvania, and announced that he was coming back to my (I mean his) office to work until Denis was ready to launch. So, he came back, changed everything, and sent the office into yet another spiral of confusion.

Denis dragged Darren around by his chiropractic balls for over a year before deciding that Darren needed to buy his practice from him for $400,000 instead of working with him on the concussion protocol. That would free him up to work on developing his million-dollar idea full time. (It was hard not tell Darren, "I told you so," but I didn't.) A few weeks later, he took a job in a chiropractic office outside of Pittsburgh, packed up the dogs, and moved in with his parents.

I had been marking time through the whole Denis debacle. I couldn't move forward with Darren there to pull everything right back to the way he thought things should be, and there was definitely no going back to anything that resembled life before the miscarriages and the job-hopping and the motorcycle and all the arguments and beer. At first, I thought Darren's new job in Pittsburgh would be the way out. I thought he must have wanted out as much as I did. I thought he would get settled, and then things would just fizzle and die without much fanfare. We would sell the practice, and I could start over again wherever, and however, I wanted. I thought it would be perfect, so I tried not to fight or complain. In public, we kept up the façade of a functional marriage. In private, it was strained, but we kept saying words that sounded like we were working together and working things out. I just didn't want any more arguments. I just wanted to give up control and let whatever was coming happen all by itself, one step at a time.

Back in Pittsburgh, the job posting that Darren applied for and took was for an office "Clinic Director" for a chain of chiropractic clinics. When he got there, it turned out to be an entry level associate position in a dingy gym next to a dying retail mall in the suburbs. Nevertheless, he sounded excited about it. He was in awe of his new employers and was introduced to a whole new practice management system run by devout Scientologists.

The move back into his parents' house was supposed to be temporary, as always. We texted and talked on the phone every day while we were apart. Frankly, our phone relationship was good. It was good enough that I almost forgot about what had gone between us before then, and so did Darren. Soon, he found a house to rent. He sent me pictures and wanted my opinion about it. He said that he wanted me to be excited about it before he signed the lease. He said that he loved me and missed me and wanted me to move up there as soon as possible. What I thought was his way of saying goodbye turned into his plan for the two of us together. With the distance between us, the façade had started to feel like the truth.

He had moved the week of Thanksgiving, and his new job started the very next week. I had expected this to be our first Christmas apart. After his first day at work, he started calling and texting almost nonstop. He was like a different person. He sounded like the Darren I married who said loving things and asked me about my day. He said over and over that he missed me and that he was sorry for the way things had been for the last few years. He said that we needed a fresh start and he thought that Christmas vacation was my chance to check everything out and pick out our new house.

…ugh…

Christmas with Charlene. Lovely. The idea of another Christmas with her made me sick to my stomach, but Darren sounded so sincere. He sounded different this time. Believe it or not, I went to Pittsburgh for Christmas as a test. I had invested so many years of my life in this person, to this relationship. I thought that maybe he was right. Maybe we just needed a fresh start, one more do-over. I thought I owed it to myself and to Darren to give it another chance.

...so, I drove myself to Pittsburgh...

I arrived on Christmas Eve. An oddly effervescent Darren met me at the door. He was clearly drunk already. Everyone was there Charlene, Earl, Wall-Cat, Sausage, and both of our dogs. It was a full house. We all made it through Christmas Eve without any open conflict, and I only slept through part of the Christmas Eve service.

I even made it through Christmas Day and the next few days well enough. I spent most of my time in the house with Charlene while Darren was at work. Each night he would come home and drink, and then the next morning he would get up and go to work. When we were alone, he griped about his mother and the women at work. He complained about his new bosses but seemed unusually interested in the Scientology part of their training materials. He thought I should read it and start incorporating it into the practice back in North Carolina while I was still working there. To me, that just seemed like a bad idea.

Being there was difficult, especially when I was alone in the house with Charlene. It was hard not to dwell on the things that had happened there and the things that she had said. I tried to be gone as much as I could, but beyond driving by the house that Darren wanted to rent and wandering through the mall, there wasn't much else to do. It was a bad scene for everybody. Darren was miserable, too, although I wasn't sure why. When I wasn't around, he missed me, and when I was there, he didn't want me around. It was confusing.

Each night when Darren got home, he drank more than the night before. It was clear that he was unraveling over something. Near the end of the week, he was spiraling down into fits of nightly drunken aggression. I asked him if it was because of me. He said that it was not. He swore that he was drinking for fun, and added that I would be more fun if I would drink with him.

Darren drank so much that even his mother started in about it on New Year's Eve. With that, I thought I had found my opening. I had wanted to tell her about his drinking problem for a long time, but I never thought she would be willing to listen. Now, I thought the time was right since she brought it up.

…so, I told her everything…

I told her about the drinking and the drunken driving and the drunken rides on his bike. I told her about his trouble being stable in a job and about his growing rage and aggression. I told her point blank that Darren was out of control and that I needed help. It was one of the hardest conversations I had ever had up to that point in my life. I had no idea how she was going to react. It was a big risk.

To my surprise, Charlene listened to every word. She took it all in. She even agreed that Darren hadn't been himself and confessed that she was worried about him. She even said, "I'm glad you talked to me about this," which was not something I had anticipated at all.

When I was done, I was relieved. I had an unexpected ally. Finally, there was hope. I felt like we were on the verge of a real breakthrough. From here, everything would turn around and every uncomfortable moment would have been worthwhile.

That New Year's Eve was intentionally going to be a quiet one. Darren and Earl had worked all week. Wall-Cat had plans to be somewhere else. Charlene had made dinner, and the four of us were going to ring in the New Year in front of the TV. It wasn't my first choice, but since the dogs were there, it was the only option. They became just as unraveled and destructive at the sound of fireworks as they did at rain and thunder. I couldn't bring myself to put that torture on anyone, not even Charlene and Earl.

Beyond that, I thought it would be good to stay home that night. It wasn't the night for an intervention. It was a night for celebration. Charlene and I had talked. She heard me. She was on my side, and it felt good. With her support, things would be different. Over the next weeks, we could think about what to say to Darren and come up with a plan. For now, I could just relax. Everyone was safe. We weren't throwing money away at a bar downtown on New Year's Eve. Darren wasn't driving home drunk from a party, and I wasn't the awkward designated driver in a crowd of wasted revelers.

After dinner, as we were all sitting around the kitchen discussing plans for the next day, Charlene took her first shot. "Darren," she said loudly as she looked at me across the table.

My eyes widened, and I shook my head at her slightly. *No! No! No... Oh my God! What's happening?!* I screamed in my head. *Not now! Not now! It's not time!* I needed her to stop, but there was nothing I could do. It was happening. This wasn't how I meant for this to go.

"Yeah, ma," Darren said as he pulled another beer out of the refrigerator and popped it open.

"A little bird told me that you've been drinking too much. That true?" Charlene locked her eyes on mine. As she spoke a little sneer spread across her mouth.

"What?" Darren said with a dismissive chuckle, "I'm just having a little fun for the holidays. Why, do you think I am drinking too much?"

"No," she said triumphantly, "I don't." Her eyes never wavered.

My heart sank into my stomach.

"Tell Krystal to keep her opinions to herself," Darren added afterward.

"Oh, it wasn't Krystal. It was your wife." Charlene spoke with devious confidence. Her sneer spread into a wide grin across her face as she stood up and walked toward the door.

"Was it, now?" Darren said more as a statement than a question.

That stupid bitch betrayed me. This was classic Charlene. She would rather hurt me than try to help her own son. "Yes," I said as I stood, "it was. You are out of control, and you need help. I'd hoped to do this later, but I guess we're doing it now. I said something to your mother because I love you. That's all." It was the first time I had said the words "I love you" out loud in a long time. It felt awkward, but I meant it. I had given him thirteen years of my life. I loved him when we met, and I still loved him then. It was a very different kind of love than it had been in the beginning, and it might have been a little more Stockholm Syndrome than I wanted to admit, but it was still technically love.

With that, I retreated to our bedroom. Here I was, once again. I sat down on the ugly green carpeted floor and burst into tears. I cried and cried. It was uncontrollable. My mind was screaming. I wished I had a stupid journal with me so I could get some of the awful thoughts in my head down on paper and out of my brain, but I didn't. I just sat there, hating Charlene, hating that house, hating Darren, and most of all, hating my life.

Several hours later, Darren came into the room. He was inebriated and swaying on his feet again. It was clear that he had chosen to drink a little extra. Maybe he was celebrating the holiday. Or maybe he was trying to prove that he was not, in fact, a drunk. Whatever it was, he was tuned up and had an awful lot to say.

He started with a run-down of all the things that I had done wrong since I got there on Christmas Eve. Apparently, I had ruined the holiday for everyone. He went on to tell me how I had stolen his practice from him and forced him to take a bunch of different jobs working for other people while I ran his practice into the ground. He called me a bitch that night. He said that I was "a fucking bitch" who was "rude and a bitch." I guess he wanted to make sure I understood exactly what he was saying. Honestly, it was hard to follow through all of the slurring. He proceeded to tell me that I was too controlling, and since I could never "just relax," I made him and everyone around me "miserable" ...oh yes, and that was why I "didn't have any friends" and why "everyone hated me." Then he reminded me, again, that I was "a rude fucking bitch."

I didn't have any fight in me, this time. In the past I would have been right there in it, yelling back and defending myself and pointing out all of the heinous things he had contributed to this shit storm. Instead, I just sat on the bed and cried. I figured that he would talk himself out, eventually, and pass out. He didn't. The more he went on about how uptight and frigid I was, the angrier he got until he became so heated that he thrust himself in front of me, his face in mine and his hand on either side of me pressing into the bed. "Are you listening to me? Do you hear what I am saying?" he slurred and spat as he shoved his shoulder into mine.

I wanted this to end. I had to defuse this fast. "I hear what you are saying," I said calmly, "We can talk about it tomorrow." I brought my hand up and pushed against his shoulders thinking that he would back away. He didn't. Instead, he met the force of my hands with the weight of his body and with his feet planted on the floor. I pushed harder, but as strong as I was, it wasn't enough. In one sweep, he swept his hands up under my arm and shoved me back onto the bed pinning me with his hands on my shoulders and straddling my hips and thighs.

"Get off me," I said as I struggled against him. He clamped down harder. The bed was old and rickety underneath me and offered no resistance to use as an advantage.

"I just want you to love me," he said through gritted teeth. "I want you to love me the way you used to."

"NO!" I said as I struggled, "not like this."

"I'm just trying to make you happy. You're always so unhappy," he said puffing his beer breath into my face. "I know what you need…" He dropped his shoulder into my chest and pinned me to the bed as he reached down and pulled his sweatpants down.

"Stop it! Stop it!" I tried to yell, but my breath was spent. I flailed as hard as I could, scratching at his back and kicking with my legs as I gasped for air. I would have bitten his ear off if I could have gotten to it. I wanted him off me. I needed to breathe.

With his shoulder still squarely in my sternum and his penis out of his pants, he pulled the waist of my sweatpants down just enough to get to what he wanted. Then he started thrusting. He was ramming and thrusting as he used his hand to force himself inside me. He grunted and breathed, "yeah, that's it…" like it was a porn.

I could feel the tearing force of his penis and hand as he pushed on. I flailed and flailed with tears streaming down my face and pathetic breathless cries for him to stop until I was spent. I succumbed. I was out of air and out of energy. Fighting was only hurting me more. There was nothing left to do but let go and wait until it was over. The man that I had committed my entire life to was raping me. I knew that no one would ever believe me. I don't even know if I would have believed me if I hadn't been the one pinned to the bed.

As my body gave up to the ridiculous truth of this indignity,

Darren's own body took a turn. In an instant, he went limp—not a little soft, not a little off his game—limp. His penis went completely flaccid. I don't know if it was just the beer or if what was left of his conscience had gotten the better of him. One minute, he was rock hard, and the next, he wasn't. It still hurt like hell, but it was more like he was trying to angrily feed a half-empty sandbag through a keyhole. If he had been sober, the Darren I thought I knew would have been mortified, but this night, this Darren kept shoving away at it like it was all perfectly normal.

This is when I saw my chance. I let my body relax a bit more. As Darren shifted his weight in response, I pulled my knees under him and kick him off. He staggered backward with his mushy dick in his hand. He ricocheted off the wall behind him and went stumbling face first onto the bed where I had been. A moment later, he was out cold.

I stood there staring at him as I gasped. The swelling and the abrasions between my legs throbbed and stung like fire. I could hear the TV playing in the living room. Charlene and Earl had been there through the whole thing. They must have heard the commotion. They must have heard something. They heard it and did nothing. There was no point in asking them for help. They probably would have yelled at me for hurting Darren when all he wanted was a little New Year's fun.

I stayed in that bedroom next to my snoring, drooling abuser because I didn't know what else to do. At midnight the fireworks started. The dogs, who had been in the room for the whole thing, started panicking at the sound of the distant tiny explosions. I struggled with the worst one of the two for over an hour to keep him from hurting or destroying the furniture and bloodying himself. Once that was done, I let myself cry some more out of sheer frustration. That was the moment I decided that I had to leave.

There was no other option. I couldn't sleep in the bed next to the thing that had just raped me. The people on the other side of the door clearly cared nothing about me or the truth. I didn't need to stay and fight when there was nothing left worth keeping. I had to go. Darren had assaulted me. That, alone, was enough. Charlene had betrayed me. Earl had ignored me. There was nothing left to consider.

In the dark, I packed my things. Just before dawn, I left.

I drove from Pittsburgh to Raleigh in a bleary, sleep-deprived fog. Darren called me about an hour into the trip to ask where I was and why I left. He kept saying that he didn't remember what happened. He wanted to know what was wrong, that I shouldn't have left like that, that his mother would be insulted since I didn't say goodbye to her after everything she had done.

All I could do was guffaw into the phone. He was completely bent if he thought I cared about how Charlene felt at all. I told him that he hurt me and that I couldn't stay there. I kept the worst of my rage inside because I couldn't drive and yell like that at the same time. I needed to be home. I needed to be away from him. Chances were good that he remembered most of what he did and was playing dumb, anyway.

While we went back and forth, I went the wrong way at a critical fork in the highway. It took me half an hour to realize my mistake. With no smartphone, no GPS navigator, and no real idea of where I was, I was genuinely lost. Darren insisted on calling over and over again to help me find my way, but I didn't want to talk to him. I didn't want his help. I was in the middle of nowhere, but that was better than where I had been.

It seemed like forever before I found a rest stop with a map. As it turned out, the path back to the right highway wasn't so bad. In fact, it was a beautiful ride through the mountains. It added an extra hour to my trip, the need for extra gas, and an extra ton to the weight of my exhaustion, but I made it, and I made it on my own terms.

Chapter 20

In the days after I got home, Darren and I talked on the phone more than I wanted to. He did most of the talking while I sat silently on the other end of the line. Mostly, he talked himself into corners. I think it was clear to both of us that our marriage had changed beyond recovery.

Back in NC, I threw myself into work. Darren's shitty little office was the only thing I had left. Since he was gone, I was going to have to make it work if I wanted to feed myself and pay all the bills. I decided to treat it like it was already mine. Once again, I started transforming the office into my vision of a chiropractic practice. It was a slow conversion, but it was a good one. The numbers started to turn around in less than a month, and it looked like it would become exactly what I needed it to be—a viable source of sustainable income.

At the same time, Darren called me every day. Every call was the same—a litany of complaints about any and every little thing around him. His mother was unreasonable. He was tired of the weather. The dogs were unhappy. The Scientologists he worked for weren't treating him with the respect he deserved. People drove like assholes. I let him talk and offered little to nothing in response. I should have hung up the phone. I should have been more aggressive about my intentions. I should never have assumed that his intention to leave was equal to my intention for him to stay gone. My plan was to get the office back on its feet, get a little financial stability, and then send him a separation agreement. I didn't want to argue about it. I just wanted to do it. He was under a two-year contract, and he was still talking about leasing a house. I didn't think I had to rush.

I was wrong. I should have rushed.

At some point, he decided not to lease his own place. He claimed it was about saving money. At the same time, he was tracking the office bank accounts online. At the end of the month, he announced that he was quitting his job and was coming back.

The news sent me into a spasm. I tried over and over again to convince him to stay where he was. I reminded him of how bad things had been for us down here, and how much he hated it here, and how much he loved it there, and how unhappy he was and difficult it had been to get reestablished up there this time. I told him outright that he should stay and give it a chance.

I didn't tell him that I wanted a divorce. I had yelled it at him once or twice, but those were only moments of heated frustration. They weren't anything I was prepared to follow through with. I had never said it to him with any certainty. Now that it was what I wanted, I found myself in a quandary. He had once again quit his job. Before things got involved with Denis and his protocol, I never drew a paycheck from the practice. Either there wasn't enough money, or Darren wanted to "put that money back into the business." Up to that point, I was completely dependent on him financially. After Darren started going back and forth with Denis, I finally started paying myself on a W-2. In my mind, it was time to make the office mine. But, by doing the right thing for myself and thanks to my pathological need to follow the rules, I screwed myself over. I had turned myself into the primary breadwinner, and chances were good that I would end up paying him alimony. It was a nightmare. So, I never said the words, *I want a divorce.* All I could do was wait and hope that he would stay where he was.

He didn't.

The next month, he drove back to North Carolina with all of his things and the dogs. He hit the door spouting streams of bullshit about how much he had changed and how much he loved me. He said that he realized what he had lost when I left on New Year's Day and that he couldn't let his mother fill his head with such negativity anymore. She had been bringing him down with all of her hate for everyone and everything.

Two days later, he came back to the office. He took over his old patients that were still around and immediately started retraining my new receptionist with all of the things he had learned from the Scientologists. At the end of the month, when the insurance payments came in for the work I had done the month before, he patted himself on the back and said that the numbers showed that it was good that he came back—it had been our 4th best month ever since he returned. When I pointed out that the payments were for my work from the month before, he said that I was arrogant and selfish and needed to recognize that success is a team effort.

A week later, I spent an entire Saturday in the emergency department of our local hospital. I had been washing dishes that morning when a crushing pain exploded in my chest and upper back, and yes, of course, I was still uninsured. In the end, it turned out to be a panic attack. Actually, it was about a six-thousand-dollar panic attack that added to our debt and made me even more stressed out. I couldn't help but think the whole thing would have been easier if I had just died that day. At least I wouldn't have been the one left fretting over the bill.

Darren's doctorly advice in the aftermath of that horrifically expensive and humiliating experience was that I just needed to relax about things. He promised that he would pick up some of the slack and that things would get easier soon.

That night after we got home, Darren drank by himself while he streamed Pittsburgh Public Radio's blues shows on the computer. Little Water's harmonica ripped through the computer speakers as "Everything's Gonna Be Alright" which resulted in an endless string of repetitious caterwauling from Darren. "Everythang's… gonna be alright…everythang gonna be alright…everythaaannng gonna be alriii-height…ev-er-ry-thaanng's gonna be…all..right…"

It was not exactly as musical as he thought it was, and it certainly wasn't going to be alright. From where I sat, nothing was alright at all. My escape plan had evaporated. I had yet another bill to pay. There was no way I could leave now. I couldn't afford to go. Darren had walked away from the paycheck we so desperately needed and had thrown a wrench into the progress I had made at the office. My job was, again, at the mercy of Darren's whims. He only showed up when he felt like it, and when he did, he wanted to treat all of the patients. Either that or he didn't want to treat any of the patients—not even the ones that had scheduled specifically with him. The rest of the time he stayed home, supposedly working on "marketing," but all I ever found on the internet history was porn. Our livelihood was left up to me. If I faltered, even for a week, we would financially implode. I was up against a wall and had no choice but to stay right where I was.

The panic attacks kept things interesting. In the beginning, they would appear at random at least once a week. As time passed, they came more often and more intensely. Every time I got in the car, my hands and face would go numb, and the horizon would tip to an improbable angle. I had to pull over to the side of the road more than once on the drive to and from the office. The night terrors ramped up too. Each night, when I went to bed, it took a cocktail of herbal downers and Benadryl just to stay asleep for more than twenty minutes at a time without dreaming that I was choking on my own crumbling teeth.

I tried to put my anger aside and smooth things over at work and at home. Despite the horror of my last night in Pittsburgh, I let Darren back into my bed. It was easier than fighting. I was stuck, and things were bad enough. To keep him off my back, I even had sex with him once a week. It was the same as going to work. It had to be done. I just had to grit my teeth and get through it. It wasn't about me or what I wanted. It was about just getting through.

Darren still played Peekaboo Penis from time to time, especially when he was drunk. Fairly regularly, I would walk into the bathroom to find him jacking off in the shower up against the glass shower door. He would get extra excited after I walked in on him. I figured out that if I stood there and pretended to be turned on, it bought a few more days between our requisite sex transactions, so I was a little more willing to play along. It backfired, though. He started masturbating more often whenever he thought I would catch him, and then worse, most nights in bed when I was trying to sleep. I would be there in the dark, on my side, waiting for my sleep cocktail to kick in, when the bed would start to shake. The covers would billow rapidly against my back—a sure sign that he expected my attention. At first, I would turn over and try to help him out. I figured that the faster he was done, the more sleep I would get. This, too, backfired. He just did it more often and then demanded more elaborate help to get him where he was determined to go.

"Talk to me…" he would say as I was just lying there waiting for it to end. Talking had never really been my thing, even when I was into it. I didn't exactly have a deep repertoire of erotic imagery to draw from. But out of hope for a speedy conclusion, I played along.

...and it usually worked...

At the end, he would ejaculate into a dirty sock and then toss it on the pile next to the bed.

In short order, Darren expanded his demand, asking for full physical character development complete with plot lines and surprise endings. (Trust me, the end was never a surprise.) The thing he asked for the most was for me to describe another woman in the room. He wanted explicit details about what she was doing to him or doing to me or doing to him as I was doing something to her or vice versa. It was weird. He had been talking about threesomes for the last few years whenever he talked about sex. At the time, I dealt with it by promising to get him one for my 46th birthday. (As a technical point, I never promised I would be participating in it myself.) I thought that would handle it. I thought he would forget about it eventually. He didn't. He started talking about it all the time, like it was something I should be looking forward to, like it was a present for me rather than a fantasy for him.

As the nights wore on, it took him longer and longer to get where he was going. Eventually, I decided I'd had enough. I really didn't need his constant critiques of my ability to conjure the right images for him or of my storytelling prowess. I stopped participating altogether and started ignoring him. I would pretend to sleep as the bed bounced and the squeaky metal frame squeaked and rattled. Alone on the other side of the bed, Darren would grunt and pant as he worked things out on his own. Honestly, it seemed like it was better for him when I ignored him.

This was our life as a couple for a good long while. I was miserable. Darren was miserable. The practice was crashing at a frighteningly steady rate. Every aspect of my life was either gone, dead, or withering on the desiccated twig that I once thought was a vine.

Time passed slowly and painfully for us both. I worked and stared at the TV. Darren pretended to work, looked at porn, and obsessed about motorcycles and beer. Every night we would walk the dogs and struggle to talk to each other. It was the only time we really tried to work things out together, and it was about as comfortable as having a tooth pulled.

Around the same time, a tattoo shop opened in the same strip mall as the office. Darren was no stranger to tattoos. He had two of them when we met. He got another one around the time that we got married.

I was never a tattoo person myself, but I didn't have anything against them on other people. I just thought they were an awfully big commitment, and I wanted to leave open the possibility that the flaming unicorn with butterflies shooting out of its ass that really spoke to me during some aggressively whimsical phase in my life might not speak to my soul so much in my fifties. I wanted to be able to wear sleeveless dresses and skirts without a trail of drooping swallows marring my shoulder or a ring of blurry hearts around my ankle that might betray the secret fuckups of my youth.

When the shop opened, it just so happened that deep cable channels were making every reality TV show they could think of, including a barrage of shows about tattoo shops, tattoo artists, and tattoo competitions. It was just the inspiration Darren needed to find a new obsession. Tattoos. He spent hours fretting over his next tattoos and watching every show he could find. Eventually, he struck a deal with the owner of the new shop and started adding more ink to himself every other week.

Then he came home one night and announced that he was buying the tattoo shop. He needed $20,000 for the deal, and he would be unable to see patients because he would be apprenticing in the shop for the next six months. He was resolute. This was happening.

I responded to this proclamation with a flat and unemotional, "No." On the inside, of course, I was completely freaking out. Darren could barely draw a stick figure with a dull crayon, let alone successfully tattoo human skin with an electric needle.

I listened to his non-stop sales pitch for all of five days before my head metaphorically flipped open and all of the crazy poured out. That evening we were walking the dogs in the neighborhood. Darren was carrying on about how wonderful and profitable a tattoo shop would be, and how he didn't need to be able to draw to make a good tattoo, he just had to be able to trace and then color inside the lines. He had worked out a different deal to buy it. Now, he just needed $8,000 for the down payment, and then he could earn the rest of it directly from the shop.

That was all it took. I took in a long, deep breath, and then I unleashed. I detailed every problem that I had with the whole stupid idea. Everything I said was true. It was just the way I said it that was crazy. I went on and on and on about what a stupid idea it was and about how much money it would really cost and how much debt we already had and about how the drug deals that happened in the back room of the shop every day were not congruent with his bullshit chiropractic lifestyle. I went on about his bottomless deficit of artistic talent and described in great detail my version of what his first solo tattoo would be like down to the parking lot pummeling he would get from the bubba and his friends who didn't like the horrible monstrosity that he had permanently etched into his skin. I went on to say that he was a doctor and that he still had to pay for his student loans, and if he wanted to buy a "fucking redneck tattoo parlor" that he would have to wait until he had paid off his "fucking six-figure student loan," and if he ever mentioned that "fucking piece of shit redneck tattoo parlor again, I was going to lose my fucking mind..."

I think the entire neighborhood heard my rant. Everyone seemed to freeze in place and turned to look. Our dogs even turned around to stare at me. Everyone in their yards stared at me with their mouths agape. Darren looked at me and started laughing. I inhaled sharply, turned my chin up and threw my shoulders back, and just started walking.

Darren kept laughing as he hurried to catch up with me. "Holy shit," Darren said, "okay…no tattoo shop."

"Really?" I refused to look at him and kept walking.

He laughed nervously, "really. I didn't know you felt that strongly about it."

That was bullshit, but at least he stopped talking about it…for the most part.

◆◆◆◆◆

For the next few months, I worked by day and argued with Darren by night. He tried to stay gone whenever he could be and was drunk most of the time when he was home. He and Travis had gotten even closer, and Darren had worked his way in with more of Travis's military friends and reveled in the reflected glory and respect they would get out in public for their service.

At home, he grew more and more dissatisfied. Our arguments got louder and meaner and usually ended in tears and four-letter words. On his really drunken nights, Darren would shut me down by threatening to go upstairs and shoot himself in the head with the hunting rifle. He had that thing with us since we graduated and never used it other than to threaten suicide when he felt backed in a corner. In the beginning, it freaked me out. It would make me run to him and beg him to settle down and talk to me. I would tell him how much I loved him and that I couldn't imagine my life without him. By the end, I usually ignored the threat and at least once told him to "go ahead and do it." In retrospect, I'm glad he didn't. My guilt over that would never have left me, and if I'm really honest, it would have voided his life insurance policy, and that would have been terrible.

Of course, there was the time we argued in the car on the way back from Pittsburgh after his first meeting with Denis. He didn't like what I was saying about Denis and the whole deal, so he yelled at me and belittled me and disrespected me until I yelled back with a vocal cord wrecking scream that nearly shattered the car windows. He responded by pummeling his fist several times into the steering wheel before stomping on the gas and threatening to drive the car off the bridge and into the river below. I believed him that day. I really thought he was willing to kill us both, but he didn't. In the end, he didn't mean it. He didn't really want to die. That day, just like every other time he threatened to off himself, it was all about control. It was about getting me to shut up. It was about his inability to face the truth, or at the very least, face another opinion other than his own. So, no, I don't think he was ever really going to drive off a bridge or speed the car into a cement barricade or shoot himself in the head with a hunting rifle. He was too cowardly to follow through with anything like that. And anyway, the times that he actually physically hurt me, he didn't threaten to do it, he just did it.

By the end of April, Darren decided that he, once again, needed to recharge. As I had come to understand it, recharging in Darren-speak mostly meant drinking in different bars and riding a motorcycle without a helmet. I suggested that we go away for a weekend to the mountains or to the beach, anywhere that we could have a real vacation without family or motorcycles or dogs.

He wasn't into that idea. If we went anywhere together for more than an afternoon, he insisted that we take the dogs. We had done that a couple of times before, and every time I ended up managing the dogs when they had panic attacks and separation anxiety while Darren complained that I worried too much and got drunk. Deep down, I didn't want to go on a couple's weekend with him, either, but I hadn't been on an actual getaway without dogs or in-laws or a chiropractic seminar since the first miscarriage (in other words, about four years.) I thought maybe it would help.

As I said, he wasn't into it. What Darren wanted was to spend more time away from home with the people that he thought were his friends—that meant Travis and the rest of them. Instead of going anywhere with me, he left me with the dogs and the practice and headed for Myrtle Beach Bike Week.

He had been to bike festivals before. Of course, there was his trip to Sturgis, and he had been to the Outer Banks at least once. I had never been and never wanted to go. I wanted nothing to do with it. I loved the beach, but I hated riding on the back of that stupid bike. I had no interest in sucking up exhaust all weekend long while Darren and his friends drank until they were blind. I didn't want to be surrounded by grimy bikers and their "bitches" in fringe leather bikini tops and cutoff shorts or with their leathery skin and missing teeth or with all of it all at the same time. I didn't want to pretend to have a good time with all of the posers who wanted to act like one-percenters for the weekend. I hated all of it. I had been to the local bike fest in Raleigh a couple of times, and that was more than enough.

I tried to talk him out of it. When it came right down to it, we didn't have the money for any vacation at all, let alone a drunken, leather-clad, frat party on wheels. But no matter how I felt about it, Darren wouldn't be deterred. He went anyway, claiming that he was thinking of me when he decided to go. He was, after all, sharing a room with Travis which meant that the room would cost half as much. He was being frugal. He gave me that instead of wasting money on a gift.

I mean, really, what more could a girl want?

When he got home from the trip, he was full of stories and of himself. He talked about how "cool" everyone was and how "awesome" it was to see all of the bikes. He showed me pictures of the "awesome bar" with body-painted beer girls. Translation—waitresses with airbrushed van art where a shirt should have been. He said that I would have liked the "really cool art" and that the pictures didn't do it justice. He showed me pictures of some woman's bent over, cellulite-dimpled, g-stringed ass and videos of burnout competitions and drag races. That first night, he talked until he wore himself out and wrapped up the evening with a heartfelt, "thanks for being so cool with this. I love you." Then he went to sleep. It was like a kid talking about his first trip to Disney World only without the warm parental satisfaction of a memory well made. I felt more like I had been complicit in some sort of socially sanctioned (yet still debaucherous) crime.

There was a small part of me that was happy that he was happy. The rest of me was just tired and had to get up the next day to run his office. Still, I couldn't shake the feeling that something was off, that something else had happened. Before he left, I was already not sleeping and having at least one low-grade panic attack a day. When he got home, it all ramped up. I didn't know why. I just felt something. That's all it was, just something.

I didn't mention it to Darren, because there was no point in it. He could barely discuss legitimate issues that were happening right in front of his face. How on earth could I expect him to care about something that was just a feeling? He would have told me it was all in my head and that I was too concerned about what other people thought.

Over the next week, as my idiopathic anxiety continued to build, Darren changed. There was no explanation for it; he was just suddenly different. To be specific, he was different with me. He was actually nice about things that would have irritated him just one short week earlier. He started telling me how much he loved me and how grateful he was for me. He would say it two, three, sometimes four or more times a day. By the end of the week, irrational fears melted away, and I was almost ready to become a biker church convert.

After a particularly relaxed and happy weekend afternoon I said with a laugh and a smile, "If this is what Bike Week does to you, I should send you to one every month." I meant it, too. It had been the best week of our marriage in years.

As soon as those words left my mouth, however, everything changed. Darren's demeanor transformed on a dime. In an instant, his smile was gone, and his eyes narrowed. The jokes and the I-Love-You's were gone. One moment things were good, and the next, it was like everything he had just said never happened. I had expected him to say something lame like "hell yeah!" as he pumped his fist in the air. I expected a smiling, "see, I told you I needed to recharge!" That's not at all what happened. He didn't do any of that. He went Manchurian Candidate on me like I had uttered some secret code that unleashed a dark and dormant behavioral directive.

That night, Darren spent an extra hour in the bathroom with the door closed. I had become so numb to Peekaboo Penis that I didn't even think about knocking on the door, let alone trying to open it. When he heard me through the door, he would shout, "Don't come in!" When I would ask him if he was alright or if he needed help all he would say was, "I'm fine," or "Don't worry about it," or just a simple "No."

...it was weird...

As the days wore on, Darren turned even more distant and sullen. Whenever I asked him what was going on, he would hold the line with, "nothing" or with an irritated "don't worry about it."

My annoyance mixed with years of conflict conditioning allowed me to accept his answers. As far as I was concerned, he had toyed with my emotions for a week and then took it all away on purpose, like it was some sort of twisted game for him. He was an ass, and as far as I was concerned, he could suffer alone in the bathroom as long as he wanted.

As the week dragged on, however, it was obvious that whatever was wrong was not getting any better. Eventually, curiosity got the better of me. I had to know what was going on. It took two days of full force inquisition for him to finally spill it. He broke one evening while we were walking the dogs.

"Are you having any...problems?" Darren asked cautiously.

I didn't want to go through the list of everything that I was dealing with in my head again. I was even a little confused that he would ask something like that. He told me long ago that I should just get over everything, and anyway, this was supposed to be about him, not me. "No," I said, "not really. Why?"

"Are you sure?" he asked followed by a long pause.

I was perplexed, "Uh...yeah...what are you getting at?"

Hesitantly, he continued, "Are you itching or anything...in your lady parts?"

"In my lady parts?" I laughed as I said it. "Nope, my lady parts are about the same as they have been since...well you know."

"Oh..." he responded as if he were either gravely disappointed or deep in thought. "Really..."

I let that last word hang there for a while before finally asking intensely, "What's going on?"

Darren seemed to mull this over for an unusual amount of time before speaking. "I think I got an STD from Travis's towel," he eventually said with extreme angst in his voice. He kept looking straight ahead and didn't slow his gait.

"Uh…what did you just say?" This was a bomb I hadn't seen coming. The ramifications went spinning through my head. My legs kept propelling me forward because he was still walking, but I couldn't feel them. It was as if they had spontaneously detached from my body.

"I think I got an STD from Travis's towel," Darren said, still walking.

"Uh…" I was dumbstruck. *That's not how you get an STD! What the fuck?!* I thought to myself.

Darren stopped in front of an empty lot and let the dogs wander. "Travis has some issues…"

"What issues?" I asked firmly. The full weight of what he was saying landed. He had been so insistent that we have sex the day after he got home. He had gone heavy on the romance that day, saying that he wanted us to rekindle our relationship. He had claimed to be sorry for the way he had been and the things he had done. He had said that he loved me and that he wanted us to be the way we used to be. It had been so nice to hear. His words and his demeanor had made recovery seem possible. I gave in to it all.

…but now…

My mind was racing. What the Hell was this? Was it all a lie? Was it guilt? Did he fuck some airbrushed bar wench in a bar bathroom stall or something? Did he take a random chick back to the hotel? Oh my God, did he fuck Travis? Did he fuck some random guy? He was such a homophobe…was that just overcompensation? Oh my God…what the fuck has he given me?! Why would he risk my life like that? What the FUCK?!

"It's not important," Darren said.

"It's important, Darren!" the heat in my voice was intense. "It's really fucking important!"

"There's no reason to get all worked up. This is why I didn't want to say anything to you."

"Seriously?! Are you fucking serious right now?" The possibility of Darren's infidelity was bad enough, but the idea that he could have given me something and worse—he wasn't going to say anything about it—was insane.

The hotter I got, the more controlled his voice became which just pissed me off even more. "I didn't want to tell you because I don't know what it is. I don't know if it's even an STD. It could just be heat rash."

"Oh, my God! Are you fucking kidding me?" I guess without the rash, he would have just let the cheating thing slip right on by. *How many times had he done this before?* I thought to myself. *Fucking son of a bitch!* That designation was now fully literal.

...great...

Darren ignored my question and said as he started to walk on, "I need you to go to the doctor and get tested for STD's."

"Wait...what?" I said refusing to move.

"Let's walk, you are making a scene," he said as he continued walking.

There was no one around that I could see, but I didn't care. "I'll make whatever scene I want!" I said loudly as I hurried to catch up. On a different day I would have stood my ground to make a point, but today, I was thrown. "You go the doctor! You get tested for yourself! Why should I go, first? What the fuck, Darren?!"

"Please go, please," he whined this time. "I don't want anybody to know. What will people think?"

"What will people think?!" I yelled incredulously. "Okay, you're right, Darren, what will people think?"

He stared back at me blankly.

"You cheated on me, and now you want me to go and get tested so you don't have to be humiliated. In what fucking universe is that the way this should work, Darren?"

Darren looked like he was getting angry, but he kept it in check. He dropped his eyes to the ground and refused to look at me. "I don't know…Please, just go. I don't know what to do."

"No!"

"Come on," he insisted.

"No, I will not! You did this. You have to deal with it. I'll go to the doctor after I know what we are dealing with…" We walked the rest of the way home in silence. As we passed by Travis's house, I thought about running in the front door and asking Travis what kind of STD he had and if he told Pam that he fucked my husband over the weekend. I didn't. There was no need to bring them into it until I had proof. This was embarrassing enough as it was. If Travis wasn't in on it, the last thing I needed was Pam's flapping gums telling the neighborhood about the STD-riddled chiropractors around the corner.

That moment things became completely clear for me. I had known that something was up. I sensed it, but I didn't trust myself. Like an idiot, I was lured back into Darren's bullshit by a few nice words and a temporary conflict hiatus. I had been too naive, too quick to consider forgiveness, too willing to ignore twelve years of terrible omens and bad behavior in the hope for a childish fantasy of romance novel resolution.

…I was a fool.

Ultimately, Darren drove two counties away to get tested at a health department where no one would know him. He claimed the doctor he saw said it didn't look like an STD, but they ran tests anyway. He got a letter in the mail stating that his tests were negative. I didn't trust him, so I went to my own doctor, twice to be sure. Thankfully, she found nothing.

I never learned exactly what happened. Darren swore up and down that he didn't have sex with anyone of any kind. He stuck to the STD towel story like it was the truth regardless of the fact that he was a doctor and knew better, and if that wasn't enough, the fact that I was a doctor and I knew better. Looking back on it, it turns out that the whole disgusting incident was a metaphor for our entire relationship. Whatever it was that he did, it was a bad idea borne out of Darren's arrogance and poor decision making. He put me at risk and then expected me to clean up his mess and keep it a secret…and like a fool I did it. What else was there for me to do? Whatever made him look bad, made me look bad. In a small town, whatever made us look bad ultimately hurt the office. Without the office, all was lost.

◆◆◆◆◆

I might have been a fool, but the Bike Week Towel incident was so ridiculous and potentially so dangerous that I was finally ready to make a change. I couldn't stay in our house of tears, in that tiny town, or in that oppressive office any longer. I needed out. But even after that revelation, I still wasn't willing to simply walk away. We were too entwined. Part of the same old excuse mantra still applied—what about the debt? What about the patients? (I dropped the "what if I changed my mind" part of the mantra. That wasn't an issue anymore.)

What I needed was an exit strategy. We were so close to the end when Darren moved to Pittsburgh the last time, but he wrecked the whole thing by quitting and coming home. This time it was up to me. If I left, I wouldn't come back. As soon as I got settled, we could officially separate, take a year to let our putrid marriage die, and then legally divorce. Then I would be free. Of course, it would only be freedom from our legal obligations. It wouldn't undo the vows we made to each other all those years ago. There was no magical unbinding spell or church sanctioned rite that would apologize to God and spiritually make it like it never happened—at least not in any of the churches I had ever visited or Bible passages that I had ever heard. No, our vows would live on as broken cosmic promises that we would have to live with and possibly atone for at some later date. For me, it probably wouldn't be Hell. The odds were pretty good that I had been in Hell since the day we met and our whole marriage had been a twisted long-form demonic torture plot. Reincarnation seemed more likely for me…probably as something objectionable and besmirched like a cockroach or something…

…gross…

So, I started looking for a job. A job in Charlotte, to be specific. I was finally ready to tell my family that our marriage was over. I was finally ready to burn that bridge. I didn't want to go back. Darren and I had nothing left in common other than chiropractic and chiropractic wasn't nearly enough. I couldn't spend another minute in his practice doing all the work for what averaged out to about minimum wage and nothing else in return but ridicule and criticism. I was done…and I figured he was too since he was having sex with "towels."

I made a horrible calculation in my exit strategy, however. I wasn't smart enough to lie. When Darren saw me looking at job postings, I told him the truth about looking for a job. To my surprise, he said that he thought moving was a great idea. He said that he was tired of where we were and he was ready for a change. Of course, the truth I told him didn't include the rest of the plan.

I didn't tell him I was planning to leave him. He had been working hard to mend our relationship since the "towel." I figured we could work all of that out after I found a job. It was cowardly, but I thought it would be easier.

Darren even offered to help me find open positions, which he did. By the end of the next day, he announced that he had applied for a job with one of the most successful chiropractic offices in South Charlotte and he was already set up for an initial phone interview.

When he told me, I was dumbstruck. I had spent all day with patients and paperwork and office business. Instead of helping me, he undermined me for a job—again. My application was pointless, now. We were married. For both of us to apply for the same job looked sketchy, and even if I sent it, my application would probably go right in the trash. For all I knew, Darren mentioned how inept I was in his cover letter.

...son of a bitch...

Needless to say, I was pissed. I unleashed on him, telling him that it was my turn and he needed to handle his office for a while. My anger didn't give Darren even a moment's pause. He said that we couldn't afford for me to leave the practice—that he should be the one to leave and I could stay until the practice sold or I hired someone else to handle it. After that, he went on with the interviews. Being the good initial interviewer that he was, he even got an offer. Of course, the whole thing fell apart in the contract negotiation phase. Darren wasted a whole month with his so-called negotiation process. It ended when the hiring doctor just stopped responding to Darren's calls and emails. To me, this just said that there was never really any negotiation, only the delusions in Darren's beer-addled brain. (The truth is, there is very little contract negotiation in the average chiropractic job. Usually, what's offered is what's offered, and that's it. Most of the time, there are ten other DC's ready and willing to take the deal, no matter what marginally enforceable stupidity might be hidden deep within the contract's pages.)

That was the day I figured out that I couldn't wait any longer for change to happen for me. I had to choose. I had to act. I had to make it happen. Darren wasn't going to make it happen. The Universe wasn't going to magically make it all better or take away all of my problems. I had to do it on my own. There was no one else. That was it.

That was the day after our 13th wedding anniversary. The day after that, I finally told Darren that he could do what he wanted with his practice. I gave my notice and set my mind on finding a place to work. I didn't tell him about the separation part of my plan. I had to take things one step at a time.

Within a week, Darren announced that he had taken yet another job at another office in Raleigh. He announced that our plans to move to Charlotte were done for the time being. He said that he was now in with a regional chain of offices and eventually he might be able to transfer to the Charlotte area, but until then, I had to stay and take care of the patients in his practice. (Actually, he said "your practice" like he had nothing to do with it.)

He really thought I would do it. He thought I would fall in line. He thought I would change my plans because he told me to. He even lashed out when I said no and told him that the future of his practice was up to him. My resistance shocked him that day. After all the years of fighting and arguing, a simple and appropriately applied "no" was all it took to make the change begin.

The next few months were crazy. I gave up on finding a job and decided to open my own office. I found a space and did my best to get it set up from a distance. At the same time, I was still running Darren's practice…our practice…that I had slaved in for so many years. Monday through Thursday I worked for Darren. Friday through Sunday I worked for myself.

Darren's opinion of the whole thing was difficult to pin down. He seemed unhappy and elated all at the same time. It was weird. He decided that he didn't want his practice anymore, and sold the entire patient base to another chiropractor in the area. He gave me most of the equipment for my new practice—he said it was a gift and that I had earned it. He kept dropping hints at things we had never talked about like "when I get to Charlotte," and "at our house in Charlotte."

Like an idiot, I actually thought that things might be different if we were in a different city, Darren had a different job of his own, and I had my own place. However, this time, for the first time, it was going to be on my terms. This time I was strong enough to tell him that I needed some time and that I didn't know what our future was going to look like. I told him that I wasn't ready to end it, but that I needed a little time and a little space to figure it all out. I told him that I thought a little separation would be good for us. He took all of that surprisingly well…so well, in fact, that it was almost a little creepy.

The day after that, I headed to Charlotte for the weekend. While I was gone, Darren and I didn't communicate at all. It was a little strange, but I thought it was probably where we should be headed if I was going to legitimately take some time to figure things out between the two of us.

When I got back after the weekend, I was exhausted. All I wanted to do was take a shower and rest. The next week was going to be hard on me emotionally. All of our patients were to get their office closure and file transition letters over the next few days, which meant the emotional gauntlet would start. I'd be introducing them to their new doctor as I diplomatically explained why I was leaving and that the office was closing.

That isn't at all what happened.

That afternoon, Darren met me at the door with an enthusiasm that I hadn't seen from him in a long time. He grabbed my bags, hurried me in through the door and over to the couch. Next, there was a glass of wine in front of my face as Darren bounced down on the couch beside me with his legs crossed up in front of him like a little boy.

"I understand everything," he told me with wide eyes and nearly breathless excitement, "I couldn't wait for you to get home. I understand everything!"

I took a sip of wine and stared blankly back at him. This was such an odd emotional turn for him. I had been expecting to find him at least six beers down the drain if he was home at all. I couldn't imagine what insanity was coming next. Was it some beer-soaked epiphany about his next big plan? Maybe this time he was going to be a famous rock star, or maybe he needed me to put the equipment for a microbrewery and pub on my credit card or something.

"I know that I love you!" he said triumphantly. He smiled widely as he waited for me to respond.

"Okay…" I said cautiously.

"I had an epiphany. I was sitting here listening to music, and it just hit me. You know how it is when something just hits you and you understand everything after that?"

I let him go on without interruption.

"I know what the lyrics to that song mean!" he blurted out. He said it as if I what he meant was perfectly clear and I should instantly be happy about it. "I know what it means to be 'saved by a woman!'" He closed his eyes and threw his head back as he howled an extremely sharp acapella rendition of the chorus. "I've been saaaaaaaved by a wo-oman…I've been saaaaaaaaved by a wo-oman…" Then he grabbed my hands and looked straight into my eyes. "Baby, you are that woman. You have saved me from my troubles and my worries…over and over again…You are the only person who has ever really cared for me…and I need you…and I love you," after which he inhaled sharply and broke into song, again, "I've been saaaaaaaved by a wo-oman…I've been saaaaaaaaved by a wo-oman…"

"Wow…okay," I said back with a slight smile.

"Come on! This is great! I know that <u>you</u> are where I am supposed to be. I am so happy you are home!" He threw his arms around my neck and squeezed me to him.

My body stiffened at the contact. The last time I was in this spot on the couch and Darren threw his arms around me like this, it didn't end up so well for me.

When I didn't return his enthusiasm, he pulled back and looked at me. "Isn't this great?'

"Um, yeah," I said casting around in my mind for the right words. "That's great…thank you."

"Thank you?" he said laughing. "Come on! This is great!"

"It's really great that you had such a good weekend. I am glad that you worked it all out…" I hesitated for a long time before getting to my point, "…but I still need time."

Darren looked like he had been punched in the gut. "What do you mean you need time?"

"I mean what I said. I'm not sure where I am with this. I just need a little time to heal before I'm in the same place you are. I still love you, but I need a little time."

He sat back at the opposite end of the sofa. "A little time for what?" he asked with full irritation. "What…you need to go out and see other people before you are 'healed' or something?"

"What...no, it's nothing like that, I just need a little time to get my head straightened out. We can still spend the weekends together and maybe go out on dates like we did in the beginning and get to know each other again. I think we both need that."

"I already know you, and I know myself. What else do you need?" He got to his feet and started pacing the floor. "If you don't know me, then that's on you."

My heart was pounding in my chest. I wasn't sure how this was going to go. I inhaled and held my ground, "I just need time," I said trying to remain as calm as possible, "that's all. Can you just give me that? A little time?"

Darren walked out of the room without saying a word.

The rest of that afternoon and evening was an awkward mess. I tried to find something to watch together on TV. He wasn't interested. I tried to start several conversations about anything I could think of—anything, that is, other than Charlotte, my new office, our relationship, or the sentimental song stylings of a difficult-to-categorize balladeer. It was a waste of effort. Every topic degraded into conflict while Darren sucked on a steady stream of beer.

Eventually, I gave up on it. Exhaustion was getting the better of me. I retreated to the kitchen to clean up before bed. Cleaning was almost the last thing I wanted to do at the moment, but starting a bad week with a filthy kitchen would only make me feel worse. Darren followed me into the room without a word. As I collected the trash and washed the dishes, he stood in the doorway sucking on his beer bottle and spitting snuff between sips. I was tired and tired of trying to appease him, so I kept my attention on the dishes and didn't try to speak to him.

The absence of conversation was unnerving. There was only the sound of the water and intermittent sound of his beer bottle swigs and snuff spitting. Then, I heard the beer bottle thunk clumsily on the counter. Then Darren rushed up behind me and pushed himself up against my back, forcing my gut and pelvis into the front of the sink.

I was beyond annoyed, but I was too tired to fight, so I laughed it off. "Not right now," I said quietly, "I have to finish this."

He said nothing as he reached under my arms, grabbed the edge of the sink, and forced himself harder into my back and started thrusting aggressively against me.

"Hey…stop!" I shouted, "Stop it! I don't want to...Ow! That hurts! Stop it" The thrusts ground my abdomen and my pelvic bone into the edge of the counter in front of me. I tried to push away, but I couldn't get any leverage. As I struggled, he pulled my pants down with his thumb and then clamped my arms to my sides locking his hands in front of me. "Stop it!" I screamed. "Stop it! Darren! Stop!" I couldn't break free.

The more I fought, the harder he pushed. Just as it had been that night in Pittsburgh, he couldn't stay hard. When he moved his right hand to force himself inside, I felt my chance. I pushed back as hard as I could and turned around. Darren stumbled back and gawked at me.

"What's wrong with you?" he slurred.

"What's wrong with me? Get away from me!" I yelled and cried.

"There she goes. Crying again," Darren was laughing as he said it. "Always fucking crying."

"Fuck you! Get away from me!" I ran up the stairs and locked myself in our empty guest bedroom. I sat there in the dark listening to the dogs panicking on the other side of the door as Darren stumbled around and slurred at them. This had not been the restful night I had been hoping for. It had been hell. Darren had swung from one crazy extreme to another in a matter of hours. I didn't want to be anywhere near him, but as always, I couldn't just leave. I had too many responsibilities that couldn't be ignored. I decided to stay in that room all night. I found our old air mattress, sheets, and pillows in the closet. They had been in there so long I had almost forgotten about them, but they were a dusty godsend. A night on the floor would have been more than my body could have taken.

Later in the night, I opened the door to calm the animals. That door had only been closed a handful of times, and they weren't handling it well. The dogs pushed their way in and piled on the bed with me for a couple of hours. After that, the cats took their places. They were all stressed and confused which only amplified my guilt. None of this was going to be easy.

The next morning was torture. We moved around each other uncomfortably as we both got ready for work. The house had never seemed so small as it did that morning. I was eating oatmeal in front of the morning news when he said it...

"I can't do this anymore."

...and that was it...

...which brings me right back to where I started.

It was done. It was over. We were finally over. It was a cuttingly painful relief. I was surprised that it hurt me so much when he said it. He didn't even say the D-word, which is probably why it hurt so much. It wasn't just a procedure or a paper to fill out. It was the end of something that I...no, more honestly, we, artificially kept alive long after it had expired. Sometimes it's hard to admit when something is dead and it's even harder to let go of its ghost.

Looking back, I should have been the one to say it. The shredded incorporeal remnants of our relationship had been hanging in the ether around me like ghosts for years. I had said the word divorce plenty of times in fits of anger, but I never admitted that our relationship was over. I always hesitated out of fear and uncertainty—out of misguided loyalty and pathological obligation. Whenever I had invoked the word "divorce," I usually ended up apologizing for it. I would insist that my mouth had been careless when really, they were the only sensible words that either of us had uttered in years.

I should have said it. I was the one who finally put the end in motion. But I had taken the coward's way out. I tried to let it wither and die instead of confronting the truth of what our marriage had become, and ultimately, what we had become. I should have said it, but I didn't.

He didn't even really say it, but he said enough.

I regret that, now. The end was mine to declare. I should have called it. It was mine to say, and I let him take it from me like I had let him take so many things from me over the years.

I didn't realize it in the moment. It took time for me to realize my mistake. Because he said it, Darren thought it gave him power over me. He thought that I was still pining away for him long after we separated. He thought I was still pining away over him even after the divorce was done.

I wasn't.

I think he might have figured that out, eventually.

In the meantime, Darren felt emboldened by his newly acquired power. He moved in with his new girlfriend, whom I believe was a waitress in his favorite biker bar and whom I prefer to call Fuckerella, a month after I left. Fuckerella was knocked up a little over a month later. Darren lied to her and everyone else, telling them that we had been separated since he moved to Pittsburgh. I found out that he had been claiming that for over a year while we were still living together, while I was still running his practice and while he was still wanting sex and tormenting me with daily rounds of Peekaboo Penis. I guess that's how he justified screwing her—if not others and possibly including Travis—long before I actually moved out of the house.

With his deception unchallenged, Darren filed for—and got—our divorce within six months. That's about seven months and a day faster than it should have been in the state of North Carolina. He actually lied to the courts and physically altered our separation agreement. My situation at the time was less than perfect, and he took full advantage of it. I was struggling to start my new practice in a new town from scratch. At the same time, I was broke, injured, and desperately trying to recover from what was either an extreme case of the flu or pneumonia. (It's hard to say what it was. I still didn't have insurance. The doctors at the Urgent Care weren't willing to commit to a diagnosis or run the appropriate tests to find out. As my official treatment plan, the first doctor handed me a sticky note where he had written down the definition of "virus" and the phonetic spelling "Sam-bu-kall" on a sticky note before begrudgingly writing me a prescription for an antibiotic. The antibiotics worked for part of the infection, but it took more than that for me to recover. I was unable to work in my brand new office for about eight weeks.

Darren and I had agreed on an amicable split. Amicable, in his mind, meant that he would keep paying for the mortgage and his small personal credit card and he would give me the practice—his company—the whole enchilada.

On the surface, that seemed great. It looked like he was giving me what was left of his practice. I had worked so hard in it for so many years with little to no compensation for my work, it only seemed fair. What it really meant was that I would take one adjusting table (he took the other) and a nearly obsolete x-ray machine along with my credit card (that had not only opened and funded his practice but had covered its losses for over six years), the full debt of his practice credit card, a monthly installment agreement for account management software, and two monthly equipment lease payments for equipment that I didn't even want to use. He generously "gave" me all of it, and acted like the payout from the sale of his patient base would cover all of it and then some. He acted like it was a gift, and I took it. I was too tired and overwhelmed and distracted to really realize exactly what I was agreeing to.

With that one act, Darren intended to wash his hands of all responsibility. He thought he could walk easily into his new life with his new girlfriend, his new job, his new motorcycle, and his new, fake diamond stud earrings in his newly pierced ears. (Yes, I mean both of them.) He managed to do all of it, too—except for one little thing. He never signed any of the practice over to me—not the company, not accounts…none of it. I dutifully paid his bills for months before I realized what had happened. I was powerless. I had no control over anything. I couldn't even get a payoff amount to consolidate everything without his involvement and approval. He had left everything in his name so that once it was all paid off, he could swoop in and take it all back.

I figured it all out the day before I found his wedding pictures on the internet. That's right, he got married less than a month after our divorce was finalized. He gave me no warning. There was no polite FYI to soften the blow. There were just the pictures of his shotgun biker beach wedding on social media along with the congratulatory posts from all of his asshole friends who knew the truth about the timing of my exodus.

There he was with new full sleeve tattoos, big fake diamond earrings, and a rented tux. There she was with a giant diamond wedding ring set, a new white wedding dress, and a baby bump. There they were, together, kissing and holding hands in the sand.

Darren was smiling like none of the last few years had ever happened. Fuckerella was smiling like she had just landed the big-fish doctor and like all of her Real Housewife fairytale dreams were about to come true.

…and they were, in a way…

I imagine she learned quickly what it was like to be married to Dr. Darren. The day after I found his wedding photos online, I sent all of his debt back to him as a wedding present. I guess he wasn't aware that his forged separation agreement wasn't entered by the court as part of his uncontested divorce and that I still had a notarized copy of the original, unadulterated separation agreement. I guess he wasn't aware that he had already breached our separation agreement when he didn't sign over the company and its accounts. I guess he wasn't aware of a lot of things, including the fact that I was willing to close my new office and let our house go into foreclosure I was willing to wreck what was left of my financial future instead of suffering one more minute to save his lazy, cheating ass. I imagine Fuckerella learned quickly that Darren hates losing more than I do. More than anything, he hates losing to a woman…correction—this woman.

So, what became of us in the aftermath of all that love, hate, and misery?

I followed Darren's progress online for a while. I couldn't help myself, and honestly, it seemed like he wanted me to see it. It took him three years to make all of his accounts private. Even with good privacy settings, it's all there on the internet if you are interested enough to go and look for it.

Darren's marriage to Fuckerella has hung in there as far as I can tell. She is about 10 years younger than Darren and came to their marriage with a divorce and a 6-year-old. I know that Darren changed jobs either right after or right before they had their unsanctified beach wedding that spring. He filed for bankruptcy the next fall. He changed jobs and moved them to Pittsburgh by the end of the next summer. I couldn't be sure, but I think they lived with his parents for a while when they first moved back. I'm sure that was exactly what Fuckerella signed up for when she married "a doctor," and I'm sure that Charlene loved having someone else's kid living in her house—she was always so welcoming to outsiders.

I know that Fuckerella's dad bought them a house. I don't know if it was a present or if Darren offered to pay him back in monthly installments. If so, I hope for her dad's sake that Darren's better at it this time.

Darren finally got into a practice in Downtown Pittsburgh. It looks just like the practice I always wanted, and as far as I know, he's still there. These days, he looks old and tired in his online videos, but it looks like he's actually trying to make this one work, at least.

On the spiritual side of things, I know that Darren converted to Catholicism at around the age of 41. Around the same time, he petitioned the Church to annul our marriage. In the end, he got his annulment, but not until after I fully and completely responded to the Tribunal's questionnaire. I decided that even though it wouldn't be an edict from any god I claimed, I wanted that Catholic annulment, too—maybe even more than he did. I wanted documentable proof that I was absolved of my spiritual responsibility to and for Darren Danky.

I researched the hell out of the annulment process. As it was, I didn't have to participate to get it. Simply not responding at all would have been easier. I didn't have to go through the embarrassment of the Tribunal's written inquisition. My status as an unbaptized heathen would have been enough to get the job done, but I decided to provide detailed answers to their questions, anyway. I felt it was my duty to be thorough. After all, Darren's mortal soul was on the line, and I wanted to help him out with that as much as I could. Truthfully, I wasn't sure that he was competent enough to get the job done on his own.

At last public count, Darren and Fuckerella were on pregnancy number three. That means three babies in about four years. That's a dizzying pace for a tired forty-something, but I think it's what he wanted, so there's a good chance he is happy. Who knows, maybe one day he'll train his kids to make beer for him in the basement, like tiny little brewery elves.

Generally speaking, and quite seriously, I think he is happy—or whatever passes for happiness in his life these days. I imagine Charlene is happily miserable as well. As for Fuckerella, I can't imagine how she feels about her choices in life. If she's lucky, she really loves him and really wanted to be a housewife with a brood of semi-Italian spawn. I genuinely hope for her sake that she did and that she does. No one should ever feel trapped in a life that wasn't meant for them.

As for what happened to me, that's a whole separate book in and of itself…and it's a wonderful story. It's a story that I haven't written about in a single journal. I am too busy living it. It's the life I was meant to have all along. It's the life that all flashing neon signs from the Universe were desperately trying to get me to follow. It's a life full of art, and passion, and magic. There is some chiropractic in there, too, and I actually enjoy it. It's a whole, complete life that had always been there waiting for me. I just had to follow the signs.

It's a story that I would love to tell when I feel that I can do it any justice in writing, but for now, I just don't have words that are right enough. For now, it will have to remain a story for another day.

Epilogue

It's weird to look at the story of my marriage to Darren all at once. To be blunt, it makes me feel stupid. If I had known me and known any single part of what I've written about, I would have told me to walk away and washed my hands of it when I chose to stay. I probably wouldn't have been as nice about it as Laura tried to be, either.

To make matters even worse, this isn't even the whole story. There were more fights, more stupidity, and more flashing neon signs pointing to the emergency exits. There were plenty of happy times, too, especially in the beginning and during the times when we were supposedly working on our relationship. (I guess Darren was right, I do focus on the bad stuff—at least when the bad stuff is so bad that it drowns the rest of it out.)

Now, I don't even miss him. I have no moments of wistful longing for the past. I don't dream about him at all—not even nightmares. His absence is like a weight lifted off my chest. I can breathe. That doesn't mean our final separation and divorce were happy, easy events. That's not how it played out at all.

So, what did I learn from all of this? It's still a little hazy in my mind, even after writing it all down. The best I can say, at the moment, is that it's like making dances. It's all movement—movement toward each other and movement away. Even in moments of stillness, there's movement churning on the inside, a deep and penetrating vibration that never stops. It's the vibration that is life itself. It was that vibration that ultimately propelled me to my next step and the next crescendo.

I lived my life with Darren like I used to choreograph. There were moments of brilliance, offset by extended periods of monotonous running around. Choreographically speaking, monotonous running was always a trap for me. I would get lazy and put it in as a placeholder until I found the next right movement to take the piece from one thought process to the next. Invariably, I would run out of time and end up leaving ten measures of monotonous running in the middle of the whole thing, or worse, I would decide that I liked it and leave it in there on purpose. When the lights went down, the curtain went up, and I watched my own work in the dark with an audience, it usually made me cringe. I could never see the running around for what it was until it was too late to change it.

From the perspective of the end of this marriage, it appears that I lived my life with Darren much the same way—as a series of crescendos and moments of brilliance offset by years of monotony. It seems that I regularly got stuck running around hoping for the perfect next step to appear. Only, in this piece, instead of moving on to a new brilliant movement, I kept returning to the same tired eight count motif that didn't tell the right story and that I had beaten into the ground with a baseball bat.

I'm not saying that our marriage had to always be pretty to be good. I know that life and marriages, like art, aren't always visually appealing. They aren't meant to be beautiful for the sake of beauty. Everything has a purpose, and most of the time, pretty, all by itself, is not enough. Sometimes it takes something dark and ugly and truth-telling to figure out what the word beautiful really means. Not always just for the sake of comparison, but sometimes for the beauty of the dark, ugly truth, itself. No matter how life feels in a given moment, I've found that it's never totally pointless. Even nihilism has its purpose. Personally, I found some pretty profound and beautiful truth within the deepest depths of my nihilism.

Everything is nothing, and *nothing* has meaning…

…until you give it meaning…and then nothing *has* meaning. I discovered that for me, at least, the meaning of all the nothing turned out to be my choice. It's the meaning that I give to my own life that is the point. Once I figured that out, then God and the Universe and all the spirits that have walked with me, made sense. They couldn't do all of the work for me. They could only watch and attempt to herd me in the right direction and try to comfort me when I got tired from all of the running around. They even threw in a few moments of intervention when it looked like I was really going to blow it. (Actually, I think it was more than a few.)

So, what was it that finally put our relationship out of its misery? What was it that, after so much time, was the last straw? The answer is nothing. No single thing finally broke us apart. It was everything—all of it—that snuffed it out.

The bad times were truly bad. There was so much death, both figurative and literal, throughout our entire relationship. There were emotional deaths and physical deaths of family, and friends, and pets. There were dead babies and dead dreams of the future. We died professionally so many times that I started to think that professional success was a mirage, an idea that my brain kept feeding me to make sure I got up in the morning, rather than something that could ever legitimately be attained. Adding to the pile, were the good times. The good times were as much to blame as the bad. Without the good, there would have been nothing to long for, nothing to miss or try to recapture. There would have been no loss of love to fear and eventually mourn. No, our marriage was just over. It had been for a long time.

That doesn't mean that there weren't individual things that contributed to our demise more than others. I know that somewhere along the line Darren stopped being attracted to me. For a long time, he liked me for me. Then one day, it changed. He wanted me to get a boob job. It wasn't because mine were sagging or misshapen. (That was one of the benefits of not having babies. I had the chest of a woman half my age and still do.) He would look at my naked body and tell me that he wished my breasts were bigger—much bigger. He wanted me to color my hair because he said my natural color made me look "harsh and unapproachable." He wanted me to wear cut-offs and a halter top when I rode with him on his bike or went with him to one of his bars and would point out other women as examples as he insisted that he was "attracted to that kind of confidence." (For me, it wasn't about confidence. It was about sunburns, bugs splattering on my skin at 65 miles per hour, and a totally rational fear of road rash if anything went wrong…oh yes, the patients that would see me in town. He didn't get it.) Then, of course, there was the threesome thing. He talked about that until the very end. I contributed, too. I'll admit that near the end, I visualized Darren's death on a fairly regular basis. There were days that he would leave on the bike and I would imagine that he crashed his bike on his way home from the bar. It's sick, I know, but it's honest. I used to worry that I wouldn't cry enough or the right way when the police showed up at my door. Then I would play the scene out in my head and realize that if it actually happened, other people would probably get hurt in the process, or Darren might only be debilitatingly injured instead of dead. I couldn't live with either of those outcomes. I eventually stopped visualizing it due to the slim outside chance that my wishes might actually contribute to a real-life outcome.

It's pretty clear that it was done between us. I didn't really want him to die, and I don't think Darren really wanted me with bleached hair and bigger boobs or in short-shorts and fringed halter tops. What I wanted was liberation. What he wanted was someone else.

It was 15 years, almost to the day, between the day Darren and I met and the day Darren cheated on me. It's possible that it happened before that and I didn't figure it out. In fact, looking back, it's pretty likely that happened more than just that once. But, as far as provable indiscretions go, 15 years, almost to the day, was it. That day, he broke the vow that bound us together—the vow that sealed our union and held us together for so long.

Beyond that vow, it seems that fear was my auxiliary governor. So much fear contributed to my choices—fear of failure, fear of being wrong, fear of confrontation, fear of ridicule and scorn, fear of chaos, fear of change, and maybe a little fear of being alone. Ironically, I was more alone for most of my marriage than I ever was when I was single. I think I might have bought into the fear more than I ever bought into our love. Maybe, I wasn't able to tell the difference.

Sometimes, it's hard to admit that I chose to suffer as long as I did. Yes, Darren was a drunken asshole. His behavior was his responsibility, but the choice to keep suffering was my own. The choice to keep all of it to myself was mine, too.

So, if a martyr suffers herself to death and no one notices, does it make her extra righteous? The answer is unequivocally no. It just makes her miserable and then dead. There's no glory in silent, self-imposed martyrdom. There are no awards for suffering the best or enduring the most. No one cares. They might utter a few platitudes at her funeral, but that's it. They have their own lives to manage and their own suffering to deal with, whether they choose to talk about it or not.

Looking back, I was the girl that I would have called an idiot. Darren did what he did. He was to blame for all of it, but so was I. No matter what he did, I stayed. I let him do what he did over and over again with no real consequences. I could have left way back in the beginning when I first saw the cracks in his shiny perfect visage. I could have left many times after that, too. I had more than enough reasons.

I was hanging onto a fairytale. Deep down, I always knew those pretty stories were lies—and that was before I got married. After all of this, I know it for certain, now. The truth is, love isn't worth fighting for. Love either is, or it isn't. If you have to fight for it, it's probably not love. It's probably something more like lust, or obligation, or adolescent madness.

The idea that fighting for love leads to a happily-ever-after is the very essence of many fairytales. Beyond that, they teach us to do what we're told, to never be arrogant, and to expect to be rescued. (Usually by a prince or some other man who is, of course, better by virtue of his man-ness. Occasionally a woman saves the day, but more often than not, her reward is marriage to the asshole she had to save—and then he usually gets to be king.) We are told these stories as little girls, and we keep telling them to ourselves, over and over as we grow up. They teach us to equate romance with conflict. They teach us that loving someone, means fighting for them and with them. They teach us that the greatness of our love is proportional to the amount we are willing to sacrifice.

After my jacked-up fairytale, here's what I think I know for certain:

1) Romance doesn't equal love. (Love is love. Romance is just decoration.)

2) Not all sacrifice is worthwhile.

3) Fighting for love shouldn't include fighting with each other.

4) Don't be a damsel in distress; be a chick in charge.

5) People don't really change. (Eventually, their true nature will be revealed. So, ask questions. Get to know who they really are before making anything permanent. That perfect demeanor might just be a façade.)

Clearly, when I met Darren, he was living as if he were someone that he wasn't and was headed toward a future that he could never fully achieve. In my fairytale, I believed he was a prince—but when I kissed him, he turned into a frog.

I'm sure the right girl might have the right magic to turn him back into a prince someday. Maybe someday Darren will realize that he'd be better off accepting who and what he his. Maybe he needs to find a nice frog instead of a princess in order to find his happily-ever-after. I honestly don't know, and it's not for me to say. All I know for sure is that I am not that girl, I am definitely not a frog, and my marriage to Darren was not my fairytale.